Dear
Chairman

Dear Chairman

Boardroom Battles and the Rise
of Shareholder Activism

JEFF GRAMM

HARPER
BUSINESS

Letters reprinted by permission:

Graham Letter:
Benjamin Graham Jr.
Estate of Benjamin Graham
Peter Decker
Rockefeller Archive Center

Young Letter:
Robert Young Exum
Barbara Young Kunath
Robert Ralph Young Papers
(MS 1738). Manuscripts and
Archives, Yale
University Library

Buffett Letter:
Warren Buffett

Icahn Letter:
Carl Icahn

Perot Letter:
Ross Perot

Scherer Letter:
Karla Scherer

Loeb Letter:
Third Point LLC

Cannell Letter:
J. Carlo Cannell

Levin Letter:
BKF Capital Group

HarperCollins books may be purchased for educational, business, or sales promotional use. For information, please e-mail the Special Markets Department at SPsales@harpercollins.com.

FIRST EDITION

Designed by Fritz Metsch

Library of Congress Cataloging-in-Publication Data
has been applied for.

ISBN: 978-0-06-236983-3

16 17 18 19 20   OV/RRD   10 9 8 7 6 5 4 3 2 1

For My Parents

Contents

Introduction

IN 1966, WILLIAM SHLENSKY finally snapped. A long-suffering shareholder in a well-known public company, he had endured more than a decade of financial losses and noncompetitive performance. The company was a venerable institution, almost a century old and once the pride of all Chicago. But over the course of the previous thirty years, while its younger competitors harnessed technology to revolutionize the industry, the company hunkered down in its ivy-walled fortress. The president and CEO was one of Chicago's most famous businessmen, but he was also a stubborn traditionalist. "Baseball is a daytime sport," he insisted.[1]

Bill Shlensky's father had given him two shares in the Chicago Cubs when he was fourteen years old. It was a cruel gift that was more than just a lifetime of fruitless sports fandom; it was a bitter lesson in corporate governance. Over the next fourteen years, the Cubs never finished in the top half of the National League standings. In fact, they placed either second to last or last in half of those years, and managed only one winning season. To make matters worse, the Cubs' futility was not confined to the baseball field. The company had not reported an operating profit in years.

By the mid-1960s, about 60% of all Major League Baseball games were played at night. Baseball under the lights had become extremely popular with fans, and most teams scheduled almost all of their nonholiday weekday games in the evening. The Cubs were the only holdout. On the south side of town, Chicago White Sox weeknight games averaged 19,809 fans in 1965. Cubs weekday games, by contrast, attracted a pitiful 4,770 baseball fans. Both teams managed decent crowds on week-ends of around 15,000, but even this turnout paled in comparison to the Sox's weeknight games.[2]

Shlensky believed the Cubs were caught in a vicious cycle: Their re-fusal to light Wrigley Field for night games compromised their ability to hire and develop talent, which in turn ensured losing teams that further depressed attendance. He was going to do something about it.

DEAR CHAIRMAN IS about shareholder activism—the moment when a public company investor is no longer content with being just another bum in the stands. For most people, owning stock in a large corporation is a passive pursuit. They will quickly sell out of an investment if they disagree with how the company is being managed. But some investors decide to actively engage the company to try to enhance the value of their shares. This book focuses on the dramatic moment when a share-holder moves from passive observer to active participant, and picks up a pen to plead his or her case.

Shareholder activism is not a recent phenomenon. As long as corpo-rations have had public stockholders, there have been tensions between investors, boards of directors, and executives. Four hundred years ago, an-gry shareholders in the Dutch East India Company lobbied for expanded rights and accused directors of self-dealing.[3] In nineteenth-century Amer-ica, stockholders kept close watch on public companies that operated bridges, canals, piers, railroads, and banks. The railroads in particular saw many fights for control, including the acrimonious Erie War of the late 1860s. But the last hundred years in America have been the most turbu-lent period for corporate oversight, marked by power struggles between management teams and shareholders that have culminated in an era of unprecedented shareholder power. Today no public company is too big to be confronted. Every CEO and corporate director is a potential target unless they have secured voting control of the company.

How did this happen? Why did shareholders triumph in the struggle for corporate control? Who were the key players that ushered in this pe-riod of so-called shareholder primacy? If we want to understand the rise of the shareholder, I suggest we go to the source—original letters from the greatest investors ever to intervene in the management of public companies. These letters, and the stories behind them, tell the history of shareholder activism through the last century—from Benjamin Graham's battle with Northern Pipeline in the 1920s to Ross Perot's showdown with General Motors in the 1980s to the well-publicized exploits of today's fresh-faced hedge fund rabble-rousers. We'll meet "Proxyteers," conglomerators, and corporate raiders, and we'll see how large public companies dealt with them.

I've chosen eight important interventions from history, featuring original shareholder letters:

BENJAMIN GRAHAM AND NORTHERN PIPELINE

Benjamin Graham letter to John D. Rockefeller Jr.,
June 28, 1927

In one of the first instances of shareholder activism led by a professional fund manager, Benjamin Graham tries to convince Northern Pipeline to distribute its excess capital to shareholders.

ROBERT R. YOUNG AND THE NEW YORK CENTRAL RAILROAD

Robert R. Young letter to New York Central shareholders,
April 8, 1954

Proxyteer Robert R. Young wages war against William White's New York Central in 1954, which *Barron's* calls "the year of battle by proxy."

WARREN BUFFETT AND AMERICAN EXPRESS

Warren Buffett letter to President and CEO Howard Clark,
June 16, 1964

The Great Salad Oil Swindle nearly topples American Express and sparks a minor revolt among its shareholders. Warren Buffett's investment in the company marks a turning point in his career.

CARL ICAHN AND PHILLIPS PETROLEUM

Carl Icahn letter to Chairman and CEO William Douce,
February 4, 1985

After a brief interlude covering Jim Ling, Harold Simmons, and Saul Steinberg, we enter the corporate raider era to watch Carl Icahn's Milken-funded frontal assault on hapless Phillips Petroleum.

ROSS PEROT AND GENERAL MOTORS

Ross Perot letter to Chairman and CEO Roger Smith,
October 23, 1985

Pushed to the brink by poison pills and greenmail, institutional investors finally lose their cool when General Motors pays its largest shareholder, and one of the world's greatest businessmen, to quit the board of directors.

KARLA SCHERER AND R. P. SCHERER

Karla Scherer letter to R. P. Scherer shareholders,
August 4, 1988

The largest shareholder of R. P. Scherer is stonewalled by an entrenched CEO and a captive board of directors. She happens to be the CEO's wife, and the daughter of the company's founder.

DANIEL LOEB AND STAR GAS

Daniel Loeb letter to Chairman and CEO Irik Sevin,
February 14, 2005

Daniel Loeb administers a brutal public hanging of an underperforming CEO. As the hedge fund industry matures, Loeb and his cohorts evolve from pesky gadflies to the kings of the jungle.

J. Carlo Cannell, John A. Levin, and BKF Capital

*J. Carlo Cannell letter to BKF Capital board of directors,
June 1, 2005*

*Chairman and CEO John A. Levin letter to BKF Capital
shareholders, June 16, 2005*

Some sharp, highly paid hedge fund managers target BKF Capital for overpaying its own stable of sharp hedge fund managers. The result is scorched earth and almost total destruction of shareholder value.

TAKEN TOGETHER, THESE cases explain how shareholder activism works, while giving historical context to today's hostilities. Several of these battles were high-profile archetypes of a shareholder movement, such as the hostile raiders or the Proxyteers. Other chapters focus on innovators like Benjamin Graham and Dan Loeb, who refined new techniques for engaging management teams. Then there are men like Warren Buffett and Ross Perot, who had the force of personality to change the markets around them.

By studying shareholder activism through history, we'll see the tremendous influence investors now have over public companies, and what issues this raises for the future. We'll also learn about how boards of directors work, what drives management teams to perform, and why corporate oversight can be so terrible. More than anyone cares to think about, today's corporatized world leaves a lot of responsibility with our business leaders, and the shareholders who hire and fire them. The limited liability corporation transformed the world over the past few centuries. What things will look like in the future will depend on how we manage our large institutions. As Ross Perot said in a speech to his fellow directors at General Motors, "Corporate America has a peculiar process that we must recognize. The managers of mature corporations with no concentration of owners have gotten themselves into the position of effectively selecting the board members who will represent the stockholders."[4]

Not long after giving that speech, Ross Perot walked away from General Motors, leaving his own beloved company, Electronic Data Systems, in its clutches. Perot was not alone in his frustration with public company governance. In *The Snowball*, Alice Schroeder wrote that Warren Buffett believed serving on boards was his worst business mistake.[5] When two of the world's most optimistic and energetic business leaders got a large enough dose of public company boardrooms, they thought, To hell with this! If even Warren Buffett and Ross Perot struggle to have a positive impact in the boardroom, how can the rest of us possibly improve oversight at large public corporations?

Perot's divorce from General Motors seemed like the darkest hour for public company governance, but it proved to be its redemption. When shareholders saw GM spend nearly three-quarters of a billion dollars to rid its board of the most active and engaged member, they snapped out of a decades-long funk and finally began to mind their business.

In many ways, our history of shareholder activism is about the passive investors behind the scenes—the entities that hold most of the votes in corporate America. When Benjamin Graham started his Wall Street career in 1914, a typical public company, if it was not one of the large railroads, was controlled by a small handful of insiders holding large blocks of stock. By the 1950s, public company ownership broadened as many of these blocks of stock were fed piecemeal to a new generation of investors eager to participate in America's growth. The so-called Proxyteers took advantage by trolling the markets for large legacy stakes coming up for sale, and running well-choreographed campaigns to convince shareholders to elect them to boards of directors.

Following the great diffusion of stock ownership that culminated in the Proxyteer movement of the 1950s, there was a long and slow reconcentration of voting power. This time it gathered not in the hands of entrepreneurial capitalists, but in large institutions—professional fiduciaries, such as pension funds and mutual funds, managing money for a broad constituency of underlying investors. In the 1960s these institutional investors ruled the markets, in the '70s they were at its mercy, and in the '80s they were "shorn like sheep" in the battles between corporate raiders and entrenched managers. But in time, institutional investors would begin to exert themselves. Today they are quietly teaming up with hedge fund activists to keep public company management teams on a tighter leash.

Shareholder activists tend to be colorful figures. Many of them started their careers as Wall Street outsiders with something to prove, and found creative ways to make money by targeting public companies. But at their core, Carl Icahn, Robert Young, Harold Simmons, Louis Wolfson, and Daniel Loeb are the same. Behind the "shareholder rights" rhetoric and larger-than-life personas are self-interested economic actors seeking profits. With the notable exception of Warren Buffett, the investors in this book are static characters who undergo little fundamental change. Their tactics differ only because of the dynamic conditions around them, such as access to capital, corporate legal defenses, government regulation, ownership structures, and, most important, the responsiveness of other shareholders.

One of my goals is to help readers assess the wisdom of particular campaigns, and differentiate between good and bad interventions. Each chapter provides a sufficiently deep dive to let us look past slogans and grandstanding so we can rationally evaluate the key players, their intentions, and their incentives. We'll venture into several discussions about public company structure, and entrenchment devices like the poison pill, but this is not a theoretical treatise on corporate oversight. This book is about exercising sound, practical business judgment, not utilizing governance best practices.

As we will learn in this book, shareholder activism can be put to good use and bad. It challenges inefficient corporations that waste valuable assets, but it can also foster destructive and destabilizing short-term strategic decisions. The key issue in an activist campaign often boils down to who will do a better job running the company—a professional management team and board with little accountability, or a financial investor looking out for his or her own interests.

WITH THE EMERGENCE of shareholder populism, embodied by the New York Stock Exchange's promotion of widespread stock ownership as "people's capitalism" in the 1950s, came socially oriented activism led by crusaders such as the Gilbert brothers, Wilma Soss, and Ralph Nader. I have nothing but respect for men like James Peck, who bought one share of Greyhound Bus to push the company to integrate its southern bus lines, but I've largely ignored this brand of shareholder activism. As hard as these activists have pushed public companies to behave responsibly, it's difficult to pressure a management team without appealing to the profit motive of other shareholders. The biggest changes in the corporate governance landscape over the past hundred years have been driven by large shareholders seeking to generate economic profits from their investments. They are the focus of this book.

The conflict between shareholders seeking profits, and stakeholders such as laborers and communities, is also largely outside the scope of this book. For anyone who has fundamental grievances with capitalism, it will be frustrating to read about Carl Icahn demanding that Apple return cash to shareholders, without any discussion of using that money for some higher purpose that benefits society. But I'm not here to debate the merits of capitalism. A key premise of this book is that the purpose of public companies is to generate profits for shareholders within the confines of the law. This might not be the exact legal purpose of a corporation, and it might not be something you philosophically agree with, but it is the practical result of a corporate governance system based on shareholder-elected boards of directors. Thus, when a corporate raider wins control of Pacific Lumber and clear-cuts thousands of acres of old-growth redwoods, I view this as a regrettable result of unchecked capitalism rather than an indictment of corporate raiding or shareholder activism.

Many pundits believe Milton Friedman's 1970 article in the *New York Times Magazine*, "The Social Responsibility of Business Is to Increase Its Profits," ushered in a new era of shareholder primacy. But when you read Friedman's piece today, there is something inevitable about his deconstruction of corporate purpose. In the pages of this book we'll see how and why shareholders have won control of corporate America. Take it from Ralph Nader himself, who in 2014 released a public statement criticizing Liberty Media for "lowballing Sirius XM's shareholder value" in a buyout offer.[6]

In today's world, where even Ralph Nader's activism promotes shareholder value, other public company stakeholders have been marginalized. When Bill Shlensky attacked the Chicago Cubs for refusing to light Wrigley Field, Phil Wrigley argued that night baseball would have a negative effect on the surrounding neighborhood. The courts ruled that the company was justified in using its business judgment to consider the health of Wrigleyville. The stakeholders appeared to win a rare victory over the stockholders, but it wouldn't last. Shlensky failed in his mission to bring night games to Wrigley Field, but no matter what Phil Wrigley did, the economics were too powerful. Those lights were destined to come on. When they finally did, Bill Shlensky was there, sitting in the stands under 110,000 watts of light.

MY EXPERIENCE AS a value investor running a small hedge fund certainly informs my own opinions about shareholder activism. I think it's important to explain this potential source of bias now. My fund has a very concentrated portfolio of long-term investments. We invest in only about fifteen companies, and we are the largest outside shareholder in many of them. This means we sacrifice liquidity in pursuit of higher returns, and we depend on a very long-term-oriented investor base to allow us to execute our strategy. It also means we have limited our ability to "vote with our feet" if we are displeased with a board of directors or management team. When we are forced to sell a position quickly because we have misjudged a company, we suffer sickening losses.

For my fund's investment strategy to work, we need managers to run their businesses well and to allocate cash flows wisely. The quality of management at our holdings is critical, and I spend as much time evaluating CEOs and directors as I do trying to understand and value businesses. I have to admit, the process can be disheartening. In normal market conditions, if I find a good company at a cheap valuation, it tends to have governance problems. If I'm fortunate enough to come across a high-quality, undervalued company that is run well, I lunge for it and try not to let go.

In almost nine years as a fund manager, I've become increasingly cynical about how public companies are run. In the wasteland of small capitalization companies where I often look for investment ideas, corporate governance can be downright abysmal. I've had large investments in several public companies that willfully screwed their shareholders, and I've watched many more such situations from the sidelines. This has given me a greater appreciation for investors like Carl Icahn with a shorter-term, mercenary approach. Icahn draws a lot of ire for his ruthless attacks on companies. But every time I begin to resent him for seeking short-term returns by putting a company in play, I can't help but think, Jesus, he's been investing in public companies for *fifty* years. I'm a cynical bastard after a mere dozen. The longer I've been a professional investor, the more I relate to Carl Icahn's complete lack of faith in public company management teams. Why give them time to screw things up when you can engineer a quick profit for yourself and other shareholders by selling the company?

At the same time, I've been around enough shortsighted investors to feel conflicted about the power accruing to energetic fund managers who often don't understand the nuances of the businesses they've invested in. A few years ago I wrote a "Dear Chairman" letter to a public company whose founder was taking the business private. I argued for a higher valuation on behalf of my fund, which owned a large equity stake. As I was writing the letter, I kept thinking about a meeting I'd attended the previous year with the company's CEO and a few other large shareholders.

The CEO had been on the job for about three months and was faced with the task of revitalizing the company. He actually had a lot to work with. The brand registered higher on consumer surveys than many of its larger and more profitable competitors. It was also a predominantly domestic business in a world that embraces global brands. The CEO knew he had an opportunity to invest in the business to create more value from its brand, but his message fell on deaf ears. As we sat around a table in a faceless hotel ballroom in Manhattan, the shareholders bombarded the CEO with questions about what he planned to do with the company's cash balance. Of course, they wanted him to do anything with the money *except* invest it in the business. When the company announced plans to go private several months later, I couldn't really blame them.

Over time, I've learned that I'm much better suited to finding good investment ideas than managing activist interventions or serving on corporate boards. I've never been the kind of committed activist who promotes change at every company in the portfolio. When I serve on boards, it's usually a defensive measure—I want to protect my investment by helping the company manage its capital spending. Still, because my fund takes large positions in small public companies, it's impossible to avoid the occasional fight. Earlier in my career, I fancied that I was a constructive activist who collaborated with good management teams. It didn't take long to realize this was a delusion. You can be constructive and collaborative 90% of the time, but in the 10% that really matters, management and shareholder interests often diverge. When key decisions are made that affect the future of the company, "constructive" shareholders get walked over.

MY FORMATIVE INVESTING years came during the hedge fund boom of the early 2000s, which happened to be a prolific period for shareholder activists. The best piece of journalism describing that era was a 2004 *New York* magazine cover story by Steve Fishman titled "Get Richest Quickest." It opened with a twentysomething analyst of a now-defunct hedge fund lecturing the fifty-five-year-old CEO of a public company. "Next year we're going to be here, and you won't," the analyst says.[7] I remember passing that article around the office and marveling with my coworkers at how obnoxious that guy was. But, reading it now, I realize that we were no different than him. We were twentysomething analysts at a now-defunct hedge fund with a lot of confidence in our opinions about how companies were undermanaged.

Earlier that same year, I had written my first activist letter, to Denny's, the fine-dining purveyors of Moons Over My Hammy and the Grand Slam. (Choice line: "Mellon HBV finds much comfort in a dependable franchise business whose bread and butter is a reasonably priced plate of eggs and bacon (with bread and butter).")[8] Today the letter still reads well—the stock has appreciated to more than 20 times our first purchase price—but it's ironic how confident it was relative to how little I really knew at the time. Three years before I wrote that letter, I had never even heard of a balance sheet, a statement of cash flows, or Warren Buffett. I didn't know what hedge funds did or what investment banking was. But that didn't matter. We didn't have experience, or a huge pool of capital to lean on, but mixed with our stupid ideas were some really smart and creative ones.

For the young hedge fund set interested in fundamental investing, there were few ways to learn the craft outside of making money-losing mistakes on the job. There are almost no useful books on the subject, and only a handful of business schools taught real securities analysis. To learn how to be better investors, we read Warren Buffett's Berkshire Hathaway annual letters and Joel Greenblatt's *You Can Be a Stock Market Genius*. We also collected activist shareholder letters. Later in the book, we'll learn how fund manager Robert Chapman spawned a rich literary tradition of angry 13D letters. We were its archivists.

To me, the most important feature of this book is the collection of original "Dear Chairman" letters that drives our story. Value investors are journalists at heart who feel compelled to gather their own facts and do their own analysis. I've tried very hard to let the main characters lead the narrative by quoting extensively from their own written and spoken words. The original letter reprinted with each chapter is thus the critical centerpiece of each case. Beyond teaching us about shareholder activism, these letters are filled with valuable lessons about business and investing.

Warren Buffett once said that if he were teaching a course on investing, "there would simply be one valuation study after another."[9] Columbia Business School, which Buffett attended in the 1950s, bases much of its value investing curriculum on this idea. I teach a value investing class there that requires students to research a new company every week. There are no textbooks and no outside reading assignments. Yet my most common request from students is for book recommendations.

Unfortunately for aspiring stockpickers, long-term investing as a discipline is light on theoretical concepts and cannot be easily distilled into a "how to" book. When my students ask me what books they should read, I direct them to original shareholders' letters to boards and management teams of public companies. A good letter from a shareholder to a company's chairman or CEO teaches us how investors interact with directors and managers, how they think about their target companies, and how they plan to profit from them.

It is incredible how much useful information from the business world is becoming lost to history. I can get detailed box scores from decades-ago college football games, but finding a 1975 annual report from a midsize company is surprisingly difficult. This is not really an accident. The truth is, the activities of Wall Street and corporate America have long been dismissed as frivolous, its major characters banished to irrelevance. After a period of excess, the public tunes in just long enough for a morality tale or two (*The Go-Go Years, Liar's Poker, When Genius Failed, Too Big to Fail*), then happily disengages.

Around the corner from my office there is a large, well-funded financial history museum. Its collection contains old stock certificates, bonds, banknotes and currency, as well as stock ticker machines and calculators. But who really cares about that stuff? It's the detritus of our financial system, the discarded tools and tender of the trade. What really matters, of course, are the thoughts and ideas of our business leaders. It's a shame we aren't doing a better job of preserving them.

Public companies are filled with contradiction and conflict of interest. The best place to study these peculiar institutions is at the fault line where shareholders and corporate managers and directors meet. In the pages of this book, we get to walk that line with Ross Perot, Carl Icahn, Warren Buffett, and Benjamin Graham, among others. We won't be able to solve every governance problem at public companies, but we have some of the greatest capitalists who ever lived to guide us.

I've always kept a collection of "Dear Chairman" letters on my desk. To me, each one is a fascinating example of capitalism at work; the critical point at which a shareholder decides to engage management, distilled into a letter. The business world can be a messy place, and I can think of no better way to understand it than to study its many conflicts. These letters teach us how American business really works, through the voices of its most interesting participants.

Dear
Chairman

Benjamin Graham versus Northern Pipeline: The Birth of Modern Shareholder Activism

"The cash capital not needed by these pipe line companies in the normal conduct of their business, or to provide for reasonable contingencies, should be returned to the stockholders, whose property it is, in the form of special dividends and/or reductions of capital."

—BENJAMIN GRAHAM, 1927

HERE WAS I, A stout Cortez-Balboa, discovering a new Pacific with my eagle eye."[1] The year was 1926, and Benjamin Graham was sitting in the Interstate Commerce Commission (ICC) reading room in Washington, D.C., studying Northern Pipeline Company's balance sheet. Nobody on Wall Street—not even the brokerage houses that had followed Northern Pipeline for years—had bothered to look up the company's public ICC report. As the stock languished at $65, the report revealed that Northern Pipeline generated over $6 per share in annual earnings and owned millions of dollars of investment securities worth $90 per share. Benjamin Graham described the feeling years later in his memoir: "I had treasure in my hands."[2] All he had to do now was convince Northern Pipeline's management to share the company's wealth with its stockholders.

At a time when the stock market was little more than a betting pool, Benjamin Graham developed a value investing style based on rigorous analysis of company fundamentals. By focusing on companies' intrinsic values, Graham and his followers were hugely successful at capitalizing on market inefficiencies created by the more speculative investing public. The gradual acceptance of Graham's lessons has led to more efficient markets that trade closer to fair value than they did in his time. But one arbitrage persists to this day. It is caused by the frequent divergence of interests between management and shareholders.

When Benjamin Graham confronted Northern Pipeline's management in 1926, he took a path untrodden. Shareholder interventions at that time usually involved lingering disputes between large minority owners or strategic buyers seeking control. A recent academic study charting shareholder activism from 1900 through 1949 found only seven instances where a financial buyer running an investment vehicle led an offensive activist campaign.[3] And many of those early contests were quite tame. When brokerage firm J. S. Bache sought board representation at Central Leather in 1911, it merely wanted the company to provide quarterly financial updates to shareholders.[4]

Why was shareholder activism so rare in the early twentieth century? First of all, ownership at public companies was concentrated into very few hands—usually founders, family owners, or entrepreneurial financiers. This made it hard for outside shareholders to have any influence.[5] Second, public companies shared very little financial information with shareholders. This limited investors' ability to value companies objectively. Graham saw both of these forces at play at Northern Pipeline. None of the other shareholders knew the company was hoarding so much capital, and the Rockefeller Foundation effectively controlled Northern Pipeline's management through a 23% equity stake.

Beyond these structural constraints there was a subtle societal one: Wall Street was an elite insiders' club that viewed pushy stockholders as extortionists. But all of this was changing. Benjamin Graham himself led a revolution in fundamental analysis that received a tailwind from disclosure requirements in the Securities and Exchange Act of 1934. Ownership in public companies was rapidly diffusing in a way that would drastically alter the nature of corporate oversight. As for etiquette? When real money is at stake, etiquette goes out the window. The large railroads were the first public companies to share detailed financial information with a widespread stockholder base. Before the turn of the twentieth century, many of them were subject to vicious, backstabbing fights for control, such as the Erie Railway proxy battle, and Cornelius Vanderbilt's takeover of the New York Central.[6]

Benjamin Graham is often regarded as a distant intellectual forebear of today's hedge fund managers and shareholder activists. But this view gives him much less credit than he deserves. Graham was a hedge fund pioneer, founding a partnership that shorted securities and collected performance-based fees more than a decade before the launch of A. W. Jones, which is often called the world's first hedge fund.[7] Graham was also one of the first professional investors to regularly employ shareholder activism as part of his investing strategy. Northern Pipeline was his first attempt at actively engaging a company's management. Little did he know how hard it would be to wrest treasure from the hands of Northern Pipeline's executives. Graham's campaign is a classic example of an investor challenging an overcapitalized company to return cash to shareholders, and one of the earliest examples of modern shareholder activism.

A REVOLUTIONARY IDEA

Not long ago I drove to the village of Sleepy Hollow, New York, in search of the letter Benjamin Graham wrote to the Rockefeller Foundation about Northern Pipeline. My trip started in Brooklyn, where more than one hundred years earlier Graham was a star pupil at Boys High School in Bedford-Stuyvesant. The Brooklyn–Battery Tunnel scooted me past Wall Street, where he began his career in 1914 and became, in his words, "something of a smart cookie in my particular field."[8] I took the Henry Hudson Parkway past Columbia University, where students can take securities analysis, based on a textbook written by Graham that remains in print eighty years after it was first published. Then I entered Westchester County, where Graham's student Warren Buffett moved his young family from Omaha, Nebraska, for the opportunity to work at Graham-Newman in 1954. Just off the Saw Mill River Parkway, about ten miles from the Rockefeller estate, I passed Westchester Hills Cemetery, where Benjamin Graham's ashes were buried in 1976.

Almost forty years after his death, Benjamin Graham remains a towering figure in the investment world. While his investment partnership made him famous—Graham-Newman beat the market significantly over its twenty-one years of operation—Graham's writings about investing and the tremendous success of his former students are his legacy.[9] We're all familiar with Warren Buffett, but let's not forget Walter Schloss, a former Graham-Newman analyst who started his own fund in 1955. Through 2000, Schloss's fund compounded at 15.7% annually versus the S&P 500's 11.2% annual gain. If you had invested in Schloss's fund in 1955, you would have made more than 700 times your money, versus about 120 times if you had stuck with the S&P 500.[10] In addition to Buffett and Schloss, Graham taught value investors Bill Ruane and Irving Kahn, whose funds also beat the market handily over long periods.

Benjamin Graham's books have achieved cultlike status among investors and continue to sell today. *Security Analysis* (written with David Dodd) is a dense seven-hundred-page textbook with outdated accounting discussions and mind-numbing railroad bond analyses. But for some value investors, choosing between the 1934, 1940, 1951, and 1962 editions of *Security Analysis* is an act of self-expression in the same way music geeks identify with their favorite Velvet Underground record. I'm partial to Graham's 1949 book for the layperson, *The Intelligent Investor*, which captivated nineteen-year-old Warren Buffett in 1950 and forever changed the course of his life.

Whereas *Security Analysis* focuses on valuing bonds and stocks, and their underlying operating businesses, *The Intelligent Investor* teaches us something just as important—how to think about markets. These are Graham's most enduring lessons because, more than anything else, volatile markets are the downfall of aspiring investors. It's easy to learn how to value companies, but you're in trouble if you don't understand markets and risk.

The Intelligent Investor is most famous for the parable of Mr. Market and the concept of "margin of safety." After Graham describes how market fluctuations put damaging financial and psychological pressure on investors, he introduces Mr. Market, the personification of frenetic stock price movements. Imagine you have paid $1,000 to own a share of a private company. One of your partners, Mr. Market, lets you know every day what he thinks your share is worth. Sometimes he puts a sensible value on your share, but often he gets carried away by greed or fear and offers you a price that is far too high or far too low. Two things are certain: He is always willing to buy your stake or to sell you his at the price he quotes, and he never gets offended if you say, "No thanks!" Mr. Market will be ready with a new quote the next day.

An obliging source of liquidity, Mr. Market should be a valuable business partner. You can sell to him when his price is too high, and buy from him when the price is too low. There's no reason that Mr. Market's prices should influence your own view of what your share is worth. Yet in the real world, investors often buy and sell at the wrong times, because the market's fluctuations affect their judgment. In rising markets, we are easily seduced into speculative buying. In falling markets, we risk losing our conviction to the prevailing pessimism of the moment.[11] Graham wrote, "[P]rice fluctuations have only one significant meaning for the true investor. They provide him with an opportunity to buy wisely when prices fall sharply and to sell wisely when they advance a great deal. At other times he will do better if he forgets about the stock market and pays attention to his dividend returns and to the operating results of his companies."[12]

Benjamin Graham concludes *The Intelligent Investor* by discussing margin of safety as "the central concept of investment." In some ways, Graham had a fairly rigid idea of what margin of safety meant. For railroad bonds, for instance, Graham wanted the company's pretax income to cover its fixed charges five times over. But he also offered a more fundamental description. In the case of an undervalued stock, Graham believed a wide difference between its price and its "appraised value" provided a margin of safety against declining earnings.[13] This notion of a stock having an "intrinsic value" might seem trivial today, but in Benjamin Graham's time it was a revolutionary idea.

WHEN GRAHAM ARRIVED on Wall Street in 1914, markets for corporate bonds and preferred stocks dwarfed trading in common stocks. The total value of outstanding railroad bond issues, for example, exceeded that of railroad common stocks by more than 50%.[14] Railroad stocks, for their part, accounted for over 40% of all publicly issued equity securities.[15] While it would be twenty years until the Securities Exchange Act required companies to file regular financial reports, the Interstate Commerce Commission and various state regulators collected a tremendous amount of information about railroad companies. Cross-holdings were very common, so railroads often owned shares of other railroads. An investor who could find a bargain railroad stock could profit on the issuer as well as other railroads with large holdings of the stock.

With so much publicly available operating data on railroad companies, and such large profits available to anyone who could identify the winners, you would expect Wall Street's finest to diligently pore over ICC reports. Instead, as Graham wrote in his memoirs, "this mass of financial information was largely going to waste in the area of common-stock analysis."[16] What really drove markets were rumors and inside information. A company's stock might shoot up on speculation about an anticipated large customer order. More often, market participants fixated on the intentions of large speculators that could drive a stock up or down with aggressive buying or selling. As Graham explained, "To old Wall Street hands it seemed silly to pore over dry statistics when the determiners of price change were thought to be an entirely different set of factors—all of them very human."[17]

Graham was a clear and rigorous thinker who approached each company by ignoring market rumors and focusing instead on its historical financial data. He would step away from the Wall Street noise to ponder, What do I really know about this company? He worked from there to determine if it had intrinsic value from future earnings or the liquidation value of its assets. Once he had a better understanding of a company's intrinsic value, he valued the shares as fractional ownership interests. Graham later wrote, "I found Wall Street virgin territory for examination by a genuine, penetrating analysis of security values."[18]

Benjamin Graham's nickname, "the Dean of Wall Street," is fitting, given his tutelage of so many future titans of the industry. But it's also a nod to his scholarly manner. Graham's memoirs feature more passages from Roman poets than quotations of the stock market variety. And before he decided to pursue a career in business, he weighed separate offers for teaching posts at Columbia University's departments of philosophy, mathematics, and English. Benjamin Graham was a thoughtful outsider in the investment community, and he used it to his advantage. He was the perfect man to sift through Wall Street's bullshit in search of intrinsic value.[19]

Graham knew that undervalued common stocks could provide a margin of safety while promising greater upside than most bond investments. As with his fixation on hard data and intrinsic value, this view was ahead of its time. In 1914, most investors focused on bonds and dismissed common stocks as purely speculative. Even when Graham retired in the mid-1950s, the stock market was commonly regarded as a wasteland for scams and speculators. And who's to say it wasn't? While most sophisticated investors stuck to bonds, stocks were left to speculators, manipulators, and, of course, Graham and his pupils, who were making a quiet killing. But bond investors were not just overlooking available profits by ignoring stocks. Common stocks allow their holders to vote on the composition of the company's board of directors. This gives large shareholders the opportunity to intervene in the governance of the company. The stock market was the market for corporate control.

AN UNSUSPECTING TARGET

Northern Pipeline was one of eight pipeline companies created in 1911 when the U.S. Supreme Court broke apart John D. Rockefeller Sr.'s Standard Oil monopoly. In 1926, Graham was looking up some railroad data in the Interstate Commerce Commission's annual report when he saw a table of pipeline statistics. Under the table were the words, "taken from their annual report to the Commission."[20] Graham hadn't known that pipeline companies submitted financial information to the ICC, and he assumed none of his peers on Wall Street knew, either. He quickly boarded a train for Washington, D.C.

It turned out that each of the pipeline companies filed a twenty-page annual report to the ICC with very detailed financial statements. The report also contained schedules of employee salaries, capital expenditures, the names and addresses of shareholders, and, of particular interest to Benjamin Graham, investments in securities. The same pipeline companies' financial reports to shareholders, by comparison, were incredibly skimpy—a one-line income statement and a very abbreviated balance sheet. When Graham opened Northern Pipeline's ICC report, he found a detailed breakdown of millions of dollars of U.S. government securities and railroad bonds on the company's list of investments.

After studying Northern Pipeline's operating metrics, Graham believed the company could easily pay $90 per share to shareholders in the form of a special dividend. Even after distributing its investments, Northern Pipeline would remain a profitable, debt-free company. Graham's plan would be a bonanza for shareholders. For each share valued at $65 by the market, holders would immediately receive $90 while retaining the exact same interest in Northern Pipeline's future earnings. All Graham had to do was convince management to pay out the money. He wrote years later, "Naively, I thought this should be rather easy to accomplish."[21]

Graham described his meeting with Northern Pipeline's senior managers in detail in his memoirs. They were horrified at the idea of just giving away their cash hoard to shareholders. After dismissing all of Graham's arguments, they told him, "Running a pipeline is a complex and specialized business, about which you can know very little, but which we have done for a lifetime. You must give us credit for knowing better than you what is best for the company and its stockholders. If you don't approve of our policies, may we suggest that you do what sound investors do under such circumstances, and sell your shares?"[22]

Why should Benjamin Graham take management's suggestion to sell his shares for $65 when he knew the company could immediately distribute $90? The company's pile of cash and securities was arguably worth more than the entire operating business. With no need to invest in its existing operations, and no opportunities to expand by acquisition or development, Northern Pipeline had few sensible options to deploy its capital.

Graham's first foray into shareholder activism was quite modest. He simply wanted to make a statement for the record at Northern Pipeline's annual shareholders' meeting. The company's management was surprised at the idea, but told Graham he would be welcome at the meeting, which was scheduled for January 1927. Northern Pipeline's executive offices were just blocks away from Wall Street, in the Standard Oil Building at 26 Broadway. Seventeen of the twenty-three Northern Pipeline shareholders listed in the ICC report were based in or near New York City. Yet Northern Pipeline held its annual shareholders' meeting in Oil City, Pennsylvania, a small town located ninety miles north of Pittsburgh. Not surprisingly, Benjamin Graham was the only company outsider to attend.

After the meeting's regular business was completed, Graham stood up and asked the chairman if he could read a memorandum about Northern Pipeline's finances. The chairman responded, "Mr. Graham, will you please put your request in the form of a motion?" Graham then made a motion that he be allowed to give his presentation.

The chairman asked the room, "Is there any second to this motion?" Graham had come alone via an overnight train to Pittsburgh and then via an uncomfortable local train to Oil City. Nobody in the room seconded his motion. Graham recounted their reply: "I'm very sorry, but no one seems willing to second your motion. Do I hear a motion to adjourn?" In a few seconds the meeting was over and Graham was sent packing to New York City.[23]

Benjamin Graham returned from his failed trip to Oil City bitter and focused. He began purchasing more Northern Pipeline shares and devising his plan of attack for the next annual meeting. He decided to run a campaign—a proxy fight—for two seats on the board of directors. Over the next year he would personally meet with every stockholder who owned more than 100 shares to discuss Northern Pipeline's finances. If Graham could win the proxies of enough shareholders, he would control two board seats and would have a clear mandate in favor of distributing the company's excess capital. His primary target was the company's largest shareholder, the Rockefeller Foundation.

In June 1927, Graham sent a letter to the Rockefeller Foundation that outlined the "absurd and unfortunate state of affairs" at Northern Pipeline and the other pipeline companies (page 203).[24] After introducing himself as the largest Northern Pipeline shareholder after the foundation, Graham writes that the pipeline companies' investment holdings makes them resemble investment trusts more than industrial

enterprises. The companies' shares had become bizarre hybrid securities representing a large ownership of high-grade bonds coupled with a
stake in a small industrial business. Graham points out how shareholders
like the Rockefeller Foundation are penalized by this structure. Not
only do the pipeline companies pay corporate income tax on their interest earnings, but investors can't sell their shares on the open market
for the full value of the companies' investment holdings. Shareholders
would be much better off if Northern Pipeline and the other pipeline
companies distributed their excess capital.

Benjamin Graham's letter concludes by arguing that shareholders
should decide how a company utilizes surplus capital: "We believe we
may point out without impropriety that the initiative in this direction
should properly come from the shareholders rather than the management. . . . The determination of whether capital not needed in the
business is to remain there or be withdrawn, should be made in the
first instance by the owners of the capital rather than by those administering [it]."

After reading the letter, Bertram Cutler, the financial advisor to the
Rockefeller Foundation, met with Graham in person. Cutler explained
that the foundation never intervened in the operations of its investment
companies. Graham said that he was not trying to interfere with Northern Pipeline's operations, and that this was merely a question of allocating surplus capital. Cutler listened politely to Graham's points but did
not waver.

Without support from the Rockefeller Foundation, Graham needed
votes from the rest of the shareholders. He managed to accomplish this
by winning the proxies of one small shareholder after another. By January 1928, Graham had enough votes to secure two Northern Pipeline
board seats. The night before the annual meeting in Oil City, Graham
and his lawyers met with Northern Pipeline's management to tally their
votes. In proxy fights, shareholders can vote multiple ballots, but only
the most recent one counts. Graham later described the scene: "The
management group was surprised and discomfited to see how many
of their own proxies had been superseded by later-dated ones given
to us. After all this time I still remember old [Northern Pipeline CEO

Douglas] Bushnell's involuntary exclamation of pain when we established our right to one proxy for three hundred shares." Bushnell was shocked that the shareholder changed his vote to support Graham: " 'He's an old friend,' he gasped, 'and I bought him lunch when he gave me his proxy.' "[25]

At the 1928 Northern Pipeline shareholder meeting, Graham and his lawyer won two of the company's five board seats. They were the first outsiders ever elected to the board of a Standard Oil affiliate.[26] Still, they held only a minority position on the board. Despite the strong message from shareholders in support of returning capital, Graham prepared for a hard fight with the other three board members about the company's finances. No such fight materialized. Within weeks of the annual meeting, Northern Pipeline's management presented a plan to distribute cash to shareholders.

JUDGES IN THEIR OWN CAUSE

Modern observers might be surprised by Northern Pipeline management's dubious behavior, but even today it would not be so unusual. Holding the annual shareholders' meeting in a remote location like Oil City, for example, remains a common practice. In 2014, Chevron moved its shareholders' meeting from its company headquarters, near San Francisco, to Midland, Texas, more than four hours from the nearest major airport. And how about Graham's treatment at his first Northern Pipeline annual meeting? While public companies are required by law to address shareholder questions at annual meetings, they sometimes refuse to do so. In 2006, the Home Depot's board of directors skipped the annual meeting altogether. On top of that, the company's embattled CEO, Robert Nardelli, limited shareholders to one question each, with a sixty-second time limit enforced by goons in Home Depot aprons.[27]

The Northern Pipeline CEO's "my way or the highway" speech at the end of his first meeting with Graham is also standard fare. Countless investors since Graham's time have been on the receiving end of the same lecture. Such discussions can even take a perverse turn when insiders actually talk down the performance of the company, in order to dissuade the shareholder from buying more shares. In one of Warren Buffett's early investments, the president of Merchants National Property wrote to Buffett that his valuation of the company's properties was "far too high" and that net income would be substantially lower in the coming year.[28] I've had a public company chairman tell me his business was "worthless" and I was "crazy to buy the stock."[29]

But there is something troubling about the Northern Pipeline saga beyond management dismissing one of its largest shareholders as a nuisance. In the introduction to this book, we discussed how the purpose of a public company is to benefit its shareholders. This means management and the board of directors must harness the company's assets to maximize investor returns. If this is true, why on earth would Northern Pipeline's management hide its large pile of cash and bonds from holders of its stock? The company was not just refusing to share its excess capital with its shareholders; its skimpy disclosure practices obscured the true value of its liquid assets.

Northern Pipeline featured a classic breakdown in the checks and balances of corporate power: a disinterested shareholder base combined with a board of directors dominated by key members of the management team. The company's five-person board consisted of three members of senior management, including the president, plus two directors who were directly affiliated with the Standard Oil system.[30] In the Federalist Papers, James Madison warned, "No man should be allowed to be a judge in his own cause."[31] By controlling the board of directors, Northern Pipeline's senior managers were acting as their own supervisors. The shareholders were left to regulate the directors, but prior to Graham's arrival they were effectively absent.

The Rockefeller Foundation owned a substantial stake in the company but viewed itself as a passive investor. Just a few years before Graham's first trip to Oil City, Rockefeller counsel Thomas M. Debevoise wrote a letter to Wickliffe Rose, one of the original trustees of the Rockefeller Foundation and president of the General Education Board (GEB), in which he discussed the GEB's role as a public company shareholder: "I think it is very important for the Board in these cases to take consistently the position, publicly when necessary, that it is a charitable corporation and as such holds its securities only as an investor; that it is not equipped to direct the activities of a business corporation; . . . and that its only course when it is displeased with the management of a corporation in which its funds are invested is to dispose of its investments. . . ."[32]

Until Benjamin Graham started sniffing around, Northern Pipeline's management was accountable to *nobody.* The company's pile of cash and securities gave its managers a huge cushion that protected their jobs, and the income and status that came with them. Without any pressure to mind the shareholders, management chose not to advertise the company's strong financial position to anyone outside the luxurious confines of the Standard Oil Building. Without accountability, it's easy—even human—for managers to make decisions that benefit them personally more than they benefit their shareholders.

Northern Pipeline was by no means alone in its questionable capital allocation practices. Many other companies—including almost every other public pipeline operator—withheld excess capital from their shareholders. In the decades after Northern Pipeline, Benjamin Graham ran similar activist campaigns against cash-rich companies to pressure them to increase dividends to shareholders. Most of these were sleepy companies like Northern Pipeline, with management teams that generally ignored their investors. During Graham's 1947 proxy fight against New Amsterdam Casualty, for example, the management claimed that their typical shareholders owned so few shares that a higher dividend wouldn't really interest them.

Northern Pipeline's response to Graham was straightforward. A letter to shareholders signed by the board of directors stated, "We believe the whole position may be summed up in one question to stockholders— for the promise of an immediate distribution of cash assets, do you wish to place your Company's management in the hands of those who have had no experience whatever in the management of such a technical business?"[33]

While Northern Pipeline's statement was slightly misleading— Benjamin Graham was not seeking control and he had no intention of interfering with the core business—it does get to the crux of most capital allocation disputes. As an investor, should you trust the management and board of directors to capitalize the business to produce optimal long-term returns for shareholders? Or do you trust an activist shareholder bearing gifts in the form of near-term dividends or share repurchases? Managers will be biased toward self-preservation, while shareholders are easily persuaded by short-term profits. In an ideal world, the board of directors is able to negate these biases, but, in reality, it often just defers to one side. The results can be ugly.

PUBLIC COMPANIES HAVE been responsible for some egregious capital spending, and I can't resist the temptation to list a few examples now. Of course there is General Motors in the 1980s, which we will cover in more detail later. Not only did then-CEO Roger Smith waste tens of billions on questionable acquisitions and capital projects, but he used $700 million to push Ross Perot off the board. In 1989, Occidental Petroleum announced it would spend $50 million building a museum to house the art collection of Armand Hammer, the company's chairman and CEO. The final cost of the project allegedly exceeded $150 million. Hammer also bought art with corporate funds, including a $5 million Leonardo da Vinci notebook, *Leicester Codex*, which he renamed *Codex Hammer*.[34]

Armand Hammer's self-dealings are just the tip of the iceberg when it comes to companies allocating too much capital for the personal benefit of management. In the two years before it imploded in 2002, WorldCom loaned out 20% of its cash balance to CEO Bernard Ebbers so he could repay margin debt in his personal trading account.[35] And of course there is no clearer example of misspent capital than lavish perks, pay, and severance for underperforming executives, as we've seen at companies like Home Depot, Hewlett-Packard, Merrill Lynch, and Pfizer.

A tremendous amount of capital has been wasted on bad strategic acquisitions. Before the 2008 financial crisis, deals for ABN-Amro and Countrywide Financial left their acquirers insolvent in a matter of months.[36] Various mining and coal companies pulled off similar feats of value destruction at the tops of their cycles in 2010 and 2011. And we can't talk about bad deals without mentioning Time Warner giving away 55% of its company to merge with AOL in 2000.

Shareholders are not free from blame in some of these debacles, however, and many cases of terrible capital allocation arise directly from boards of directors trying to appease fickle investors. Just as some cyclical companies buy more assets at the peaks of their cycles, aggressive share repurchases tend to increase when stock prices are rising.[37] Companies from Winn-Dixie to Office Depot have crippled themselves by returning too much cash to shareholders rather than keeping it in their businesses.[38] An extreme example is Circuit City, an electronics retailer that made their stores as dark and cavelike as possible, so the TVs seemed brighter and the stereos louder.[39] Instead of remodeling their stores once Best Buy and Costco offered seizure-free shopping experiences, Circuit City spent a billion dollars repurchasing shares in the mid-2000s, sending the company to bankruptcy and liquidation.

While it's easy with the help of hindsight to poke fun at bad decisions, most capital allocation choices are not black or white, and proxy battles are rarely clean fights between good and evil. Even a straightforward case like Northern Pipeline raises hard questions about how to properly govern companies. We've laid much of the blame on the management team, but bad corporate behavior extends beyond a company's managers. At Northern Pipeline, the shareholder base, dominated by the Rockefeller Foundation, was totally permissive until Graham appeared. The board of directors, which is supposed to oversee management, was a captive entity dominated by the CEO. Both the board and the shareholders deserve blame for Northern Pipeline's "absurd and unfortunate state of affairs."

BENJAMIN GRAHAM'S APPROACH to shareholder activism focused almost exclusively on improving companies' capital spending policies. This made a lot of sense: Even management teams that excel at operating their businesses can be poor stewards of capital. Investors, for their part, are supposed to be expert at valuing companies and allocating capital. If they can understand the economics of a company, they should be good at identifying its best uses of capital. These might include reinvesting cash back into the business, repurchasing the company's stock, paying dividends to shareholders, or making targeted acquisitions and investments. This kind of shareholder intervention is also consistent with how public companies are structured. The board of directors supervises the CEO and holds the company's purse strings. The CEO runs the operations, while the board approves budgets, sets pay for key employees, and answers to the shareholders.

But the shareholder activism movement that Benjamin Graham helped launch would go well beyond targeting companies' capital allocation. Today, any activist campaign that breaches the boardroom can influence more than just the company's spending policies. The CEO's job and control of the entire corporation is in play.

A New World Order

In 1927, Benjamin Graham traveled all the way to Oil City just to make a short speech, yet nobody there viewed him as a real threat. Northern Pipeline's management grossly underestimated Graham's willingness to fight for board representation. Their complacency reminds us just how rare proxy fights were at the time. As Graham explained in his memoirs, shareholders who tried to intervene in company affairs were generally regarded with suspicion and disdain. He wrote, "In the early days, the business of Wall Street was largely a gentlemen's game, played by an elaborate set of rules. One of the basic rules was, 'No poaching on the other man's preserves.'"[40]

True to form, Graham decided not to play by the "basic rules." He believed Wall Street investors treated corporate management teams far too kindly, and he had no qualms about fighting companies on behalf of shareholders. This attitude rubbed off on his followers, many of whom pursued investing careers that, in one way or another, rebelled against the Wall Street establishment. Before Benjamin Graham, common stocks were swapped back and forth by speculators, usually with little impact on the underlying businesses. Graham introduced a new world order. He viewed publicly traded shares as fractional interests in the intrinsic value of a business, and used them as a powerful tool in ensuring the directors and managers of that business were accountable for their actions.

Graham's Northern Pipeline campaign even influenced the elites of Wall Street. He had been surprised at how quickly the other Northern Pipeline directors changed their tune and supported a cash distribution after the 1928 annual meeting. Graham later learned that when the Rockefeller Foundation submitted its proxy in support of management, it also requested that Northern Pipeline distribute its surplus cash to shareholders. Most of the other pipelines followed suit and returned their excess cash. Graham's powerful letter to the foundation apparently found an audience.[41] Despite previous assertions that it would never interfere in the operations of its investment holdings, the Rockefeller Foundation did not stop at the pipeline companies. One year after Graham's campaign, John D. Rockefeller Jr. started a proxy battle of his own, with the support of his foundations, to oust the chairman of Standard Oil of Indiana.

WHILE NORTHERN PIPELINE turned into an excellent investment, Graham ran such a diversified portfolio that its impact on his returns was modest. The account of the investment in his memoirs focuses more on the thrill of the chase than the spoils of victory. I don't want to discount the hard work he did to provide excellent returns to his investors, but this is kind of how Benjamin Graham rolled. After he retired, Graham read Bernard Baruch's memoirs, in which the famous financier describes his decision to quit his job and focus solely on investing his own capital. Graham wrote, "I recall smiling somewhat disdainfully in reading what I considered a lame and egoistical conclusion. How discreditable, I thought, for a highly gifted and enormously wealthy young man to dedicate himself totally to making a lot more money, all for himself."[42]

In Alice Schroeder's *The Snowball*, Warren Buffett recounts the time Graham told him not to fixate on money, "Remember one thing, Warren: Money isn't making that much difference in how you and I live. We're both going down to the cafeteria for lunch and working every day and having a good time."[43] When Buffett began to separate himself from the other analysts as the superstar of the firm, Graham not only bought him dance lessons, he followed up with the studio to make sure he was using them.

Graham retired when he was only sixty-one years old. He offered Warren Buffett the opportunity to take his place as a general partner and portfolio manager of Graham-Newman. Buffett was flattered and tempted, but he tolerated New York only because he was working with his investment hero. With Graham stepping away, Buffett decided to move back to Omaha and set up his own shop. Graham ended up shutting down his firm in 1956 and retiring to California.

Benjamin Graham lived twenty full years after his retirement from the investment business. He traveled the world, testified before Congress on a variety of issues, served on the board of GEICO, and gave lectures about investing. He updated *Security Analysis* once, *The Intelligent Investor* three times, and published a translation of a Uruguayan novel. Graham even invented a slide rule and a clever system for memorizing Morse code. He kept in close touch with Warren Buffett, who helped organize regular retreats for Graham and his former students. In his later years, Graham lived part-time in France, where he died in 1976. About sixty years after he took his first job on Wall Street, and not long before his death, Graham updated *The Intelligent Investor* one last time. It includes the statement, "Ever since 1934 we have argued in our writings for a more intelligent and energetic attitude by stockholders toward their managements."[44]

Even if Graham could have predicted his lasting influence over future generations of investors, he would have surely been astonished at the staggering wealth his pupils would generate in the decades after his death. Buffett's Berkshire Hathaway ended 1976 with $121 million worth of equities. In 1996 that number stood at $28 billion.[45] By 2013, Berkshire owned $128 billion of common stocks plus a host of highly valuable private businesses including GEICO, Burlington Northern Santa Fe, and MidAmerican Energy.[46] Buffett and his cohorts took Benjamin Graham's value investing framework, developed and refined their own investing styles, and then rode America's long economic expansion to mind-boggling wealth.

As America grew vastly richer and the ownership of public companies became increasingly widespread, battles for corporate control erupted everywhere. Graham's proxy battle against Northern Pipeline was tame by today's standards. He wrote, "We did not propose to elect a majority of the board, for that would have given us responsibility for operating the company, and we knew we had no right to assume that."[47] Later generations of activist investors would not be so restrained. Graham's Northern Pipeline campaign was a guerrilla affair that took the company's board by surprise. By the 1950s, many boardrooms doubled as war rooms.

2

Robert Young versus New York Central:
The Proxyteers Storm the Vanderbilt Line

"This sorry state of New York Central affairs, in our opinion, is basically due to the fact that its present Board together owned, according to last year's proxy statement, only 13,750 shares of stock or less than 1/4 of 1%."
—ROBERT YOUNG, 1954

IN 1938, ROBERT R. YOUNG, a hard-charging Texan who often railed against Wall Street's "goddambankers," found himself in a bitter fight for control of the Chesapeake & Ohio Railway. His opponent was Guaranty Trust, a goddambanker who was the trustee of $80 million of debt secured by Young's C&O stock. When Guaranty declared that the value of Young's collateral had fallen below its required level, the bank moved to impound the stock and use its voting power to remove Young from the C&O board. Young had only been in control of the C&O for one year, but in that short period he had alienated the railroad community and its primary lenders. He was convinced that Guaranty Trust was conspiring with another goddambanker, J. P. Morgan, to push him out of the industry.

Several weeks before the C&O stockholders' meeting, a federal court issued an order temporarily restraining both Guaranty Trust and Young from voting the contested shares. When it became clear that the order would remain in effect through the date of the meeting, both sides were forced to campaign for proxies of the C&O's other shareholders. Guaranty and Young had expected a legal fight over voting control of one block of shares. Instead, they had to compete for the loyalties of sixty thousand smaller C&O holders.

Young fought his bankers masterfully in his first-ever proxy fight. His populist charm won over the news media as he appealed to the public's lingering resentment of Wall Street banks. As part of his strategy, Young publicly released a series of vicious letters to Guaranty Trust. These open letters, addressed to Young's opponents but written to influence the C&O's smaller shareholders, became a powerful weapon in the campaign.[1] Young won proxies for 41% of the C&O's common stock. This represented more than 70% of the shares that were not restrained by court order.[2]

The proxy fight for the C&O Railway sent a warning shot through public company boardrooms across the country. The forty-one-year-old Young, whom the *Saturday Evening Post* would later call "The Daring Young Man of Wall Street," bested Guaranty Trust and, allegedly, J. P. Morgan, not with ample supplies of capital, but merely by lobbying public shareholders.[3]

He also caught the attention of a handful of aggressive young men who were beginning to build their own business empires during the Great Depression. Young's campaign for the C&O Railway taught them a winning strategy for seeking control of public companies by proxy vote. When the U.S. economy began to expand after the end of World War II, they worked from Young's playbook to target underperforming public companies, including major railroads and other household names such as Montgomery Ward, Decca Records, Twentieth Century–Fox, and MGM-Loews. This group of feared raiders picked up a name in 1951, when the management of United Cigar–Whelan Stores Corporation labeled Charles Green a "Proxyteer."[4]

The 1950s were bountiful for investors. The decade remains one of the Dow Jones Industrial Average's best ever, with a 240% gain.[5] The '50s also saw significant changes in the ownership structures of public companies. Wall Street vigorously promoted broad share ownership with efforts such as the New York Stock Exchange's "Own Your Share of American Business" campaign. The Proxyteers put this propaganda to the test. They bought large interests in public companies, often from vestigial holders liquidating their stakes, and attacked management teams in the name of shareholders' rights. Managers were incredulous.

Often the CEO's first response was simply a befuddled "Who? I have never heard of this guy." But the Proxyteers were not easily dismissed. As Charlie Green said, "If owning stock doesn't make me a partner, then all that stuff they hand out about how if you own shares you're a partner in American business is a lot of baloney."[6]

The Proxyteer movement marked the birth of corporate raiding as we know it today. Like the merger boom of the late 1890s and the stock market manipulators of the 1920s, the Proxyteers challenged the country's ideas about capitalism and its societal impact. America was wary of these young men in a hurry elbowing their way into the boardroom with a rallying cry that shareholder profits come first. At the time, most people, including many corporate executives, believed companies should prioritize the welfare of their workers and communities over profits. But the country would lose its innocence quickly. *Barron's* proclaimed 1954 "the year of battle by proxy."[7] That same year, Elvis Presley recorded his first single and shocked people with his below-the-belt dance moves. Less than thirty years later, Ozzy Osbourne bit the head off a bat while urinating on the Alamo, and Carl Icahn told a target company's CEO, "I'm only in this for the money."[8]

The biggest proxy battle of 1954—and the defining proxy contest of the era—was waged by Robert Young himself, the founder of the feast. Emboldened by his successes at the C&O, Young targeted the second-largest railroad in the country, the famous New York Central. The fight for control of the Vanderbilt line captivated the nation by showcasing corporate democracy in action. The warring factions spent more than $2 million campaigning for proxies.[9] Young debated his opponent on *Meet the Press* and the daily newspapers were filled with advertisements soliciting votes.

When Commodore Vanderbilt won control of the New York Central in 1867, he did it via cutthroat competition and behind-the-scenes share purchases. Almost ninety years later, when Robert Young began his own assault, he courted the common shareholder. He did so with a flair for the dramatic, turning shareholder communiqués from formal legal documents into entertaining and irreverent missives. One of his most provocative letters to New York Central shareholders ended with this cutting flourish:

WARNING: If any banker, lawyer, shipper, supplier or other person solicits your proxy for the present Board, ask him what his special interests are, or what your Company is paying for his services. Like the bankers now on your Board, he, too, may be hoping to receive special favors from your railroad or from the bankers.[10]

Robert Young was the elder statesman of the Proxyteers, and the New York Central fight was the culmination of his decades-long battle against the Wall Street establishment. He had already made his fortune and built his mansions in Palm Beach, Florida, and Newport, Rhode Island. But the New York Central was the ultimate trophy—his chance to win the Vanderbilts' railroad at the expense of the Morgans and their ilk.

His Own Man

Robert Young started his business career in 1916 as a lowly powder boy at a DuPont gunpowder factory. He was quickly recognized for cutting the most powder on the line and won a promotion when his shift supervisor learned he could read and write. By the end of World War I, Young had climbed all the way to DuPont's treasury department in Wilmington, Delaware, where he worked directly under Treasurer Donaldson Brown.

Young followed Brown to General Motors shortly after Pierre Du Pont assumed control of the company. He later wrote about his seven years at GM, "I received a training in corporate finance I believe I could have equaled in no other job in the country."[11] Young became assistant treasurer in 1927, just as GM headed into its glory years. Brown assured him that he was in line to receive a senior executive role. But Young knew that the very top jobs at General Motors—Alfred Sloan's and Donaldson Brown's—were taken. In the summer of 1929, he took his chances on Wall Street, where fortunes were being made that would be lost to the Great Crash in a matter of months.

Young became treasurer of Equishares, a new investment company formed by Pierre Du Pont and John J. Raskob.[12] There he accumulated a healthy capital base, as well as a good reputation, from his bearishness before the crash and his subsequent stock picks. In 1931, he bought a seat on the New York Stock Exchange and began investing for his own account and a handful of clients, including Brown and Sloan. His results were excellent. From his launch in March 1931 until he terminated the relationship with his outside clients in January 1934, Young's portfolio gained just under 40% while the market fell more than 70%.[13]

But once again, Young's "spring restlessness," as he called it, took hold. He had reluctantly worked with Brown and Sloan on the condition they leave him in complete control of the portfolio and pay large performance-based fees. But it didn't take long before Young regretted the arrangement. When Brown had a tantrum about Young taking an overseas vacation without seeking permission, Young realized that the independence he enjoyed from running his own money was an illusion. Not only did Young have bosses to report to, but they were the very same bosses he had reported to a decade earlier at GM. He wanted his own company to run.

No Idle Threat

In 1935, Alleghany Corporation, a vast railroad empire controlled by the Van Sweringen brothers, collapsed under its massive debt load. The brothers managed to raise enough money to buy the company back in its foreclosure auction, but both men died within fifteen months. In 1937, Robert Young and two partners bought the Van Sweringens' 43% stake in Alleghany for only $6.4 million. The deal gave Young, at forty years old, effective control of 23,000 miles of railroad, and assets with a book value of $3 billion.[14] Of course, the company was heavily indebted and Young quickly learned that he would have to fight his lenders to retain control of Alleghany's railroads. His first battle was the 1938 proxy fight against Guaranty Trust for the C&O Railway. It would take Young until 1942 to secure his ownership of the Alleghany shares and get a clear-cut majority on the C&O's board.

Once he had stabilized Alleghany and the C&O, Young embarked on a series of failed takeover attempts that set the stage for his clash with the New York Central in 1954. His first target was the Pullman Company, which owned and serviced sleeping cars. The business was for sale after the government ordered the breakup of its parent company, Pullman Inc., in 1944. When Young emerged as the highest bidder, a coalition of railroads led by the New York Central submitted its own bid. Young raised his offer, but the consortium proposed a matching bid that the Pullman board accepted. Young cried foul. When he took his case to the ICC and the courts, he decided to take it to the public as well.

The ICC and the Supreme Court upheld the railroad group's Pullman purchase in 1947.[15] But in the court of public opinion, Robert Young had won a clear victory. Shortly after Pullman's board accepted the consortium bid in late 1945, Young began placing ads in newspapers across the country targeting the railroad industry. He believed the railroads' purchase of Pullman would merely perpetuate the lousy customer service that the Pullman monopoly had caused. His most famous advertisement began, "A Hog Can Cross the Country Without Changing Trains—But YOU Can't!" It resonated with customers who were sick of years of bad rail service. Young promoted the C&O as a modern railroad that would put customers first.

In 1947, Young made his first run at the mighty New York Central. The C&O bought more than 6% of the New York Central's stock, and Young demanded board representation. He launched an ad campaign similar to the one he used for Pullman. The ads were framed as memos from the C&O to the New York Central. One of them started, "Memo No. 2 From the C&O to The New York Central—A plea for the long-neglected commuter. Why not give him now the improvements that can be made immediately?"[16]

Fresh off ending Young's pursuit of Pullman, the ICC blocked him from serving on both the C&O and the New York Central boards. The commission ruled that the interlocking directorships would lessen competition between the two railroads. Young was furious at the ICC's "two-faced justice," which permitted various other conflicts, including the railroads' purchase of the Pullman Company. For the moment, the New York Central had won. Though Young walked away in defeat, his efforts won him more points with the public. He even landed on the cover of *Time*. Just before the ICC ruling went against him, Young told a reporter that he could always resign from the C&O chairmanship and "fight it out in the open market." He added, "And they know me well enough to know that I don't make idle threats!"[17]

ON JANUARY 19, 1954, Robert Young announced his resignation from the C&O Railway board of directors. He also disclosed that Alleghany had sold its large stake in the C&O and become a "substantial stockholder in the New York Central Railroad."[18] If anyone was confused about Young's intention, the C&O's press release made it clear: Young was "free to acquire control of another carrier."[19]

Several days earlier, Young had visited Harold S. Vanderbilt in Palm Beach. Vanderbilt, the great-grandson of the Commodore, was famous for inventing contract bridge while his yacht was waiting to cross the Panama Canal. Besides being Young's friend and neighbor in Palm Beach and Newport, he was a member of the New York Central board of directors. Unfortunately for Vanderbilt, Young came to discuss business. He said that he and his partner, Allan Kirby, were buying a lot of New York Central shares, and that he wanted to be chairman and chief executive officer of the company. Vanderbilt told Young that the board would take up the matter at its next meeting, on February 10. When he relayed the news to the New York Central's CEO, William White, Vanderbilt said, "Well, it looks as if we're going to have a proxy fight on our hands at the next annual meeting."[20]

William White had been CEO of the New York Central for less than two years. He was the same age as Young, and his career shared with Young's a dramatic rise to power. But whereas his opponent was trained on explosives, cars, and balance sheets, White was, from the beginning, a railroad man. When he was sixteen, he dropped out of high school to work on the Erie Railroad. After twenty-five years climbing to general manager, he was hired by the Virginian Railway. Three years later, he became president of the Delaware, Lackawanna & Western, where he managed an impressive operating and financial turnaround.

On February 2, the two men met for lunch at the top of the Chrysler Building. After a cordial discussion about the railroad industry, Young suggested a compromise. He proposed that White remain with the company as president and chief operating officer. Young would become chairman and CEO, and would approve a valuable stock options package for White.

William White had no intention of working for Young. Since he had come to the New York Central, he had increased earnings 37% and doubled annual dividends from 50 cents a share to $1. He was one of the country's most respected railroad men, and his outside business experience included board seats at AT&T and National Biscuit (later renamed Nabisco). He rejected Young's offer immediately. A few weeks later, when White was asked how the lunch ended, he said, "Well, I didn't kiss the guy."[21]

On the day of the board meeting, Young announced that he would wage a proxy fight if he and Kirby were not granted board seats. The New York Central board did not blink. It announced, "It would be inimical to the best interests of the company to grant Mr. Young's request. . . . The company contracted some eighteen months ago with William White to be its president and chief executive officer, and the board is not willing that Mr. White relinquish his position."[22] The fight was on. Young responded, "The real issue is whether the owners . . . are to enjoy what every honest business under our American system must have if shareholders and the public are to be served instead of to be damned. That is an ownership board with a strong ownership voice in its chair. The New York Central owners, I am sure, on May 26 will give the right answer."[23]

COURTING AUNT JANE

William White promised shareholders "a bare-fisted fight with no gloves."[24] He allocated his entire advertising budget to the proxy fight and hired New York's top PR firm to work with the company's outside advertising agency. White rounded out his team with other leading specialists including Georgeson & Company, a proxy solicitation firm, and law firms like Cravath, Swaine & Moore, and Cleary, Gottlieb.[25] The team closely analyzed the Central's shareholder base so it could target the right states and media markets. New York led with about 30% of the shareholders, followed by Ohio, Pennsylvania, and Illinois. There were significant numbers of holders in Massachusetts and California—this was to be a national campaign.

The New York Central board was filled with business luminaries, including the country's most powerful banking executives. George Whitney, the chairman of J. P. Morgan, served on the board, as did the presidents of Chase National Bank, Mellon National Bank and Trust, and First National Bank. In addition to these Morgans and Mellons, the board had two Vanderbilts, Harold S. and William H., and a host of other successful businessmen.

White's strategy was simple. He would defend his management record as well as the company's performance since he took charge. He believed that if the shareholders could see through Young's slogans, they would come to their senses and stick with experienced railroad managers. White also felt a responsibility to the American business community to repel the populist threat introduced by Young. He did not want the New York Central to be the first in a line of great companies to fall into the hands of the Proxyteers. In his first campaign meeting, White told his staff, "American business right now has the most widespread ownership that it's ever had in history, and that's a fine, democratic thing. It would be . . . unfortunate if this widespread ownership were allowed to be used as a tool by demagogues."[26]

Robert Young began the contest with a small team. Rather than announce his full slate of board candidates, he chose to introduce them over the course of the campaign to get maximum media attention for each choice. Young did not hire an outside PR firm or advertising agency, as he preferred to write his ads himself. He and Kirby recruited the C&O's head of public relations to join their effort, and they hired a few junior aides to help with administrative functions and the phone bank.

Young planned to address "the public as a whole about railroads in general terms—terms any housewife can understand."[27] One PR executive at the time marveled at Young's ability to write powerful material "using words of only one syllable."[28] But despite the simplicity of his language, Young crafted a sophisticated, multifaceted attack on the New

York Central. His three primary themes were (1) the need for an "ownership board" over the New York Central's banker-dominated board, (2) the New York Central's poor operating performance and dividend record versus the C&O's, and (3) Young's futuristic vision of high-speed commuter rail and nonstop transcontinental service compared to the abysmal commuter experience offered by the railroad establishment.

Young portrayed his campaign as a David-versus-Goliath battle. He argued that the powerful banking interests on the New York Central board were tapping into the company's treasury to fund its Philistine army of proxy solicitors, advertising agencies, and lawyers. Young's team was paying all of its costs itself. If he were to win, Young promised to take only $1 a year in salary as chairman of the board. He explained that his ownership board would have its interests aligned with the small shareholders, the "Aunt Janes," as he called them.

One distinct advantage for Young in refining and then delivering his message to Aunt Jane was time. William White was constrained by having to run a large, underperforming railroad. His campaign team met only twice a week to discuss strategy. Young, on the other hand, was working every day on the proxy fight. He held daily press conferences and even spent hours working the phone bank himself. His barrage of attacks strained White's ability to respond promptly, and when the responses came, Young condemned White for spending time on the proxy fight rather than operating the company. Responding to Young's charge that he was being paid to run a railroad, not a proxy contest, White testily responded that part of his job as CEO was to protect shareholders by winning the proxy fight. He was still actively running the railroad, "from all points along the New York Central's lines." White then added, "But I will never run the railroad from Palm Beach or Newport."[29] Just six days into the campaign, things were getting personal.

ON FEBRUARY 23, William White got news that 800,000 New York Central shares owned by the C&O—about 12% of the company—were about to change hands. When information was not forthcoming from either the buyer or seller, White made his own statement: "There seems to be some conniving going on."[30]

Both White and Young knew that the fate of the C&O's stake in the company, acquired when Young was the C&O's chairman, was important to the outcome of the vote. Financial columnist Joseph A. Livingston wrote about the block, "as it goes, so goes the Central."[31] But because the C&O held the shares in trust to avoid antitrust violations, the management team, led by Young's friend and ally Cyrus Eaton, could not vote the block. The voting trustee was Chase National Bank, whose president, Percy Ebbott, served on the New York Central board. After Young met with Ebbott in January, he felt confident that the bank would remain neutral in a proxy contest. But when Ebbott participated in the unanimous vote to refuse him a board seat, Young concluded that Chase would ultimately vote against him. He needed to get those shares out of the C&O and into friendlier hands.

Young found two prominent Texas oilmen, Sid Richardson and Clint Murchison Sr., to buy the shares. To limit risk for the Texans, and to ensure a price that satisfied the C&O, Young's Alleghany Corporation loaned Richardson and Murchison $7.5 million toward the $20 million purchase. Alleghany also wrote a "put" that allowed the Texans to sell part of the stake at their purchase price even if its value fell. Young's partner, Allan Kirby, loaned the men another $5 million and wrote the other half of the put option. In other words, Alleghany and Kirby were not only loaning the Texans money for more than 60% of the purchase price; they were guaranteeing the investment against any losses.

The New York Central tried to block the sale in any way it could. It refused to transfer the stock certificates to Richardson and Murchison, it petitioned the ICC to investigate, and it filed suit in New York Supreme Court alleging a "sham" transaction. While litigation over the matter would continue through the May 26 annual meeting, Young had accomplished his goal. He had neutralized the shares and taken them out of Chase's voting control. He also added immediate prestige to his slate of directors by including Richardson and Murchison. Both men were perceived as savvy businessmen with valuable political connections. Young's "ownership board" could now claim ownership of almost one million shares. William White was disappointed in the turn of events, but he did get some ammunition for the campaign. He charged that Young, the champion of the small shareholder, had clearly forgotten about the Aunt Janes at his own company, Alleghany. Why should Alleghany's shareholders have to guarantee these rich Texas oilmen against losses on their investment in the New York Central?

PROMISES OF PROFITS

On March 5, Young sent his first letter to the New York Central's shareholders. Written on Alleghany letterhead, it introduces Young, Kirby, Richardson, and Murchison as members of a dissident slate of directors, and notes that they own over 900,000 shares versus 13,750 held by the existing board.[32] It is a short, formal letter written like a legal document. In several instances, Young even refers to himself as "the undersigned." This was typical of shareholder communications before the Proxyteer era. When the Northern Pipeline board defended itself against Benjamin Graham, for example, it opened one letter with a polite acknowledgment of Graham's attack: "Your Directors have noted with interest the letter . . ."[33]

Young soon dispensed with such formalities. Over the following month, as he worked tirelessly on the centerpiece letter of his campaign, he made its language increasingly sharp and engaging. The result, Young's April 8 letter to New York Central shareholders, is a tour de force, reprinted in its entirety on page 208. Its first page is dedicated to just two sentences: "Dear Fellow Shareholder: Put us to work to make your stock more valuable. We have bought stock with a present market value of $25,000,000 in the faith that we can."

Young's April 8 letter lays out his entire case for replacing the New York Central board. He outlines the railroad's poor performance, blames William White and the board of directors, and presents his own record at the C&O. Young also questions the company's capital allocation choices and White's generous compensation and retirement package. The letter ends with the famous "warning" about the intentions of anyone seeking shareholder proxies.

The warning, in particular, struck a nerve. Many of the New York Central's existing directors felt personally insulted at the suggestion of ulterior motives. One director wrote an open letter to Young decrying his use of "threadbare demagogic charges of banker domination and banker wickedness."[34] Young was so surprised by the board's angry response that he decided to run advertisements across the country consisting of only the warning.

They may have been threadbare and demagogic, but Young's charges of banker domination produce the most powerful passage in the April 8 letter. He writes: "Just ask yourself why the four bankers on the present board, together owning only 450 shares of Central, are so determined to hang on to your company. Is it not because of the substantial benefits which have accrued to their four banks?" From the first day of the campaign in February through the May 26 meeting, Young viewed this "simple question" as his most compelling message: "Would you rather have large owners on your board whose interests parallel yours or bankers with nominal ownership, many of whose interests conflict with yours?"[35]

White and the rest of the New York Central board insisted throughout the campaign that Young's contention of banker control was frivolous. "All dictators like to set up straw men," White said. "These are the tactics of little Caesars."[36] White argued that the bankers held only four out of fifteen board seats, and that they dutifully served the interests of shareholders. But Young's innuendo overpowered such responses. In the April 8 letter he writes, "The directors and officers of these four banks interlock with 50 other industrial companies and 14 other railroads having assets of more than $107 billion. How much of the undivided loyalty of these four men do you think your Central enjoys?"

Young uses several sections of the letter to describe the "sorry state" of the New York Central. He contrasts the Central's poor stock performance with the financial returns generated by Alleghany's railroad holdings, including the C&O, under his control. He also highlights a few weak operating metrics for the New York Central and White's previous railroad, the Lackawanna. None of Young's figures are all that compelling. Throughout the campaign, White and the New York Central made similar criticisms of Young and the C&O, aided by their own supply of cherry-picked metrics and time periods. For example, the

Lackawanna's stock gained 157% during White's eleven-year tenure as president. Young's C&O stock declined 7% over the same period.[37]

Young did draw blood, however, by ridiculing White for targeting only a $2 dividend within four or five years. For the rest of the proxy contest, this would be a source of extreme frustration for White. Young repeatedly implied that, in his hands, the New York Central would be able to return much more cash to shareholders. In one debate with White, Young said, "If Central operated at C&O's rate of return on capital, it would earn $11 a share. . . . Given last year's level of traffic, I would be disappointed if we could not bring the Central up to C&O's level of efficiency in five years. It should be conservative by that time to pay out 60% of these earnings in dividends."[38] Money talks, and Young figured that dividends talked especially loud to Aunt Jane.

White saw Young's promise of higher dividends as "the worst kind of blue-sky demagoguery."[39] "That's a lot of hokum," he told the *New York Times*. "I consider it a very unfair thing to do to stockholders to hang before them bait like a big increase in dividends when we know it can't be produced, at least to the amounts that Young talks about, and certainly not in his lifetime or mine."[40] He later ran an advertisement responding to Young, stating, "Ordinarily I prefer to talk about progress *after* it is made and profits *after* they are earned. But these are not ordinary times. . . . New York Central stockholders must decide whether they will continue the progress present new management has made and is making . . . or whether they will throw all that out of the window in favor of some will-of-the-wisp promises."[41]

His Hour upon the Stage

As the two sides bombarded shareholders with letters and placed dozens of newspaper advertisements, Robert Young began to assemble his slate of directors. One of his first additions was R. Walter Graham, a well-regarded Baltimore surgeon who responded to Young's public request for nominees. The men had never met, but the doctor's 41,800 shares were qualification enough for Young to include him.

While most of Young's other selections were business luminaries such as Richardson and Murchison, he threw in a few surprises. Young announced early in the contest that he intended to add a woman to his slate. "We need a woman's touch on the railroads," Young said.[42] He ended up choosing Lila Bell Acheson Wallace, the cofounder and co-editor of *Reader's Digest*. Wilma Soss, a well-known corporate gadfly who founded the Federation of Women Shareholders in American Business, was delighted at the choice. When she asked White if the Central planned to nominate a woman as well, he responded, "there are no vacancies on the board."[43]

Shortly after adding Wallace, Young tabbed William Landers, a retired locomotive engineer for the New York Central. Landers was a forty-two-year veteran of the Central, a member of the locomotive engineers' union, and a shareholder. In the early 1930s, he had purchased 80 shares as part of an employee stock purchase plan. Landers was a genuine workingman, and he would spend much of the campaign touring the New York Central system to line up support for Young.

One of the last men Young added to his list of candidates was William Feeley, who ran Great Lakes Dredge & Dock Company. Feeley was a graduate of Notre Dame, recommended to Young by the school's president, Father Theodore Hesburgh. Feeley was not only an experienced executive, noted Young, but he was also a good Catholic. *New Yorker* writer John Brooks reported that a member of White's staff exclaimed after the announcement, "Gad, the gall of it!"[44]

Shortly after Young finished naming his candidates, he distributed a schedule of stock holdings for nominees from both sides. Young's slate owned 1,089,880 shares versus the incumbent slate's 73,600. Eight of Young's nominees owned over 10,000 shares. By contrast only Harold Vanderbilt on the management slate, with 60,000 shares, owned so much. William White held only 1,000 shares.

AS THE MAY 26 meeting date approached, Young and White intensified their attacks on each other. They appeared on more than a dozen live radio and television broadcasts, and their criticisms became increasingly pointed. "What Manner of Man is Robert R. Young?" screamed a twenty-three-page booklet sent to shareholders by the New York Central.

Young answered with his own twenty-three-pager, titled "Little White Lies—An Answer to the Smear Attack on Robert R. Young." White's response? "Big Black-and-White TRUTHS about Robert R. Young," in which White called it "utterly stupid" to compare the New York Central's operating metrics with the C&O's. To this, Young responded with "Mr. White's SLICK PAPER BOOKLET."

Some of the advertisements were technical and obscure, such as Young's open letter to J. P. Morgan's George Whitney criticizing the Central for losing $247,000 on a bond workout in 1938. Others ads were just plain weird. Harold S. Vanderbilt, the Central board member with a penchant for yachting and bridge, penned an ad stating, "You do not learn railroading relaxing at Palm Beach, Newport and the other resorts at which Mr. Young spends the greater part of his time. I know, because in recent years, I have spent a good deal of my time engaged in more or less similar pursuits. But then, I do not aspire to be chief executive officer of the New York Central."[45]

But some of the advertisements were quite persuasive. The best was a full-page ad signed by Landers, Young's locomotive engineer board candidate. "I put in 42 years as a loyal employee of the New York Central Railroad and have been a stockholder for 23 years," it began. "It doesn't make me happy to point to the dismal dividend record of this once fine property of which I was proud." The ad followed with a table listing the company's dividend payouts since Landers bought stock in 1931. He wrote that he would have been better off leaving his money in a mattress because of the lost principal on his investment. He concludes, "Some people are going to call me disloyal to the Central. They're wrong. One of the things I prize most is my Central Certificate of Service that the railroad gave me when I retired and they put my name on the Honor Roll of the Company. The ones who are really disloyal are the bankers on the present board who are trying to keep the owners of more than 1,000,000 shares out and themselves in. The employees know it and so do the shareholders, whether they own 80 shares like me or 100,000 shares."[46]

VERY LATE IN the campaign, White got an unexpected boost from the May issue of *Fortune*. The magazine led with a brutal editorial titled,

"The Sound and Fury of Robert R. Young." It questioned Young's "business methods and morals" and said his "accession to power would have alarming possibilities."[47] The magazine also contained a story that applauded the company's recent performance, "The Central Rolls Again." White and his team were thrilled with both pieces and tried to figure out how to use them in the campaign. Unfortunately for White, his lawyers vetoed any advertisements that used extensive quotations. Time Inc., which owned *Fortune*, did not want its content used in the campaign, and refused to give the Central permission to reprint the articles. "Damn it all! Don't tell me what I can't do," White yelled at his lawyers. "Tell me something I can do!" One of his PR advisors, a former journalist with a Pulitzer to his name, told White that if he was going to risk infringing copyrights, he might as well do it in style. "There's a man who talks my language," said White.[48] They ended up reproducing both articles word for word, without *Time*'s permission, and sending them to every shareholder. *Time* sued, of course, and the New York Central settled for $7,000. White considered it the best-spent money of the proxy contest.

Two nights before the shareholders' meeting, White hosted a dinner for members of the press who had been covering the proxy battle. He joked about the *Fortune* editorial, "The Sound and Fury of Robert R. Young": "I'm not a literary fellow and I wouldn't have known that quotation. . . . It's from *Macbeth*—'a tale told by an idiot, full of sound and fury, signifying nothing.' Pretty good, eh?"[49]

At the end of the night, with some whiskey in him, White gave a speech and quickly veered off script. "I get messed up when I talk about this thing," he said. White had maintained his confidence and composure throughout the campaign. Whether for his own benefit or to bolster his team, he never got discouraged even in the face of bad news. But that night, White was troubled by something that Robert R. Young and the assembled pressmen before him did not know. The New York Central's financial situation was desperate. The company would have to raise money just to make payroll. He ended his speech by saying, "If we should get licked in this fight—I mean in the unlikely event that we should get licked—I want to see Mr. Young up there on the thirty-second floor meeting our day-to-day problems. I'd just like to see him sit down, by God, and stick it out five years."[50]

ON MAY 26, 1954, the New York Central gave its shareholders a ride on the Shareowners' Special from Grand Central Terminal to Albany. Many of the passengers wore "Young at Heart" or "We Want White" buttons, and they crowded around the two adversaries as they worked the crowds. In Albany, more than 2,200 shareholders and reporters filled the Washington Avenue Armory. Journalists covering the event compared it to a political convention.

The armory is a grand, castlelike building that now hosts the Albany Legends, a minor-league basketball team, and a light schedule of live entertainment including minor-league ultimate fighting, a minor-league version of the Harlem Globetrotters, and why not, MasqueRave, a costume dance party. While the 1954 New York Central shareholders' meeting was a decidedly big-leagues affair, it quickly devolved into something that today's mask-wearing, fight-loving ravers might call a "shit show."

White did his best to keep the meeting on schedule, but rabble-rousers frequently interrupted him. Shareholders roamed the aisles giving impromptu speeches while the PA system occasionally exploded with deafening screeches of feedback from White's microphone. The crowd cheered loudest when Young and his nominees were introduced. After the nominations, the meeting was temporarily peaceful while everyone ate a free chicken box lunch.

The circus resumed after lunch with a chaotic question-and-answer session. Wilma Soss gave a long speech and even climbed onto the stage to scold White before she was forcibly removed by security. When things finally began to settle down, Young interrupted the meeting to announce to shareholders, "I am happy to tell you you have won." White responded through his squealing microphone, "Has Mr. Young the authority to make such an announcement?"[51] He did not. It would take a week for three law professors to tally the votes and another two before the results were official.

Counting the votes was an arduous task because 90% of the stockholders had voted, and they had received seven proxies from each side.

Many people voted several proxies—only the most recent one counted—meaning there were hundreds of thousands of proxies to go through. On June 2 word leaked out that Young had won a complete victory. The official tally was announced on June 14. Young won by 1,067,273 votes. He would have won even if the judges had invalidated the 800,000 shares owned by Richardson and Murchison. Right after the announcement, Robert Young walked from the Chrysler Building to his new office at the New York Central.

Rebels with a Cause

While Robert Young's battle with the New York Central stole all the headlines, "the year of battle by proxy" produced several other fascinating conflicts. Within a few weeks of the Central shareholder meeting in Albany, the much smaller Minneapolis & St. Louis Railway tallied the votes of its own bitter proxy fight. In that situation, an investment group led by brilliant young lawyer Ben Heineman bought 25% of the stock and requested three seats on the eleven-person board. Heineman had made a name for himself three years earlier by demanding, and then winning, a higher dividend from the Chicago Great Western Railroad. But Lucian Sprague, the sixty-nine-year-old chairman and president of the M&StL, did not concern himself with the forty-year-old upstart. He didn't even believe Heineman's claim to be a large shareholder. He said, "If Mr. Heineman can prove he has ten percent of the shares outstanding, he can call a special meeting of stockholders. We rather hope that he will."[52] Heineman stepped up to Sprague's challenge. And rather than seek just three seats, he decided to run a proxy fight for control of the board.

Heineman's battle with the Minneapolis & St. Louis was different than most of the other 1950s proxy fights. The Proxyteers usually targeted struggling companies with disgruntled shareholder bases. But the M&StL was a thriving railroad. The small "Peoria Gateway" made substantial profits by giving shippers an option to sidestep Chicago's congested rails. The company was nearly debt-free and was fully modernized with 100% diesel locomotives. (The New York Central, by contrast, was 75% dieselized.)[53]

Lucian Sprague received most of the credit for the railroad's success. Before he was brought over from the Uintah Railway in 1935, the M&StL had been in receivership for twelve years. Sprague turned the "Maimed & Still Limping" into a hugely profitable line. He was incredulous that a lawyer with no railroad experience was trying to supplant him from the company he'd pulled out of bankruptcy.

Heineman's primary complaint with the Minneapolis & St. Louis was its low dividend payout. The railroad paid a very small percentage of its earnings to shareholders compared to its peers. Sprague responded that investing earnings back into the business was the best way to ensure future revenues. To this, Heineman argued that not only was management inefficient with its capital, but earnings would be much higher without unnecessary corporate expenses, including an obscene number of management perks. "Unfortunately the Minneapolis & St. Louis Railway has been a gravy train for management," wrote Heineman in a letter to shareholders.

Heineman distributed a pamphlet to shareholders called "THIS IS THE STORY OF THE GRAVY TRAIN!" It detailed Sprague's extravagant expenses, which turned out to be multiples of his actual salary. These included international trips for Sprague and his wife, two Cadillacs and a chauffeur on top of a monthly car allowance, and use of a private island in Minnesota. Heineman pointed out that nobody at the company had an incentive to reduce these costs: Sprague and the existing board owned only 2,350 shares versus the Heineman group's 200,000.[54]

The Minneapolis & St. Louis's shareholders ousted Lucian Sprague in May 1954, the same month the Central's shareholders voted in Robert Young. The country's business elites were probably more shocked by Sprague's downfall than by happenings at the floundering Central. Sprague fell to a man whose only operating experience was at the elaborate model railroad in his home.[55] Now everyone knew that even healthy and profitable companies could fall to the Proxyteers.

AT A TIME when Americans found rebels fascinating, if slightly unnerving, the Proxyteers received a lot of attention. In 1955, *Time* published a story titled "Challenge to Management: THE RAIDERS." In the article, one Proxyteer exclaimed, "We are conducting a counterrevolution to the inevitable excesses of the managerial revolution." Another said, "This is a rebellion of the owners."[56] Ben Heineman, always a straight thinker, gave *Fortune* a more grounded perspective on the movement. "What a raid amounts to, when the lines of power are drawn," he said, "is an effort by a group of investors to take executive directorship into their own hands."[57]

Most of Heineman's proxyteering brethren thought of their roles in the markets in more romantic terms. Like Robert Young seeing himself as David to the Central's Goliath, the Proxyteers viewed themselves as brave defenders of shareholders' rights. "I've broken up some clubhouses that were being run on stockholders' money, and I'll break up some more," said Louis Wolfson, the most magnetic of the Proxyteers.[58]

Wolfson was a former college football player with Hollywood good looks who became feared as a ruthless liquidator. In 1949, he bought 51% of the Capital Transit Company of Washington, D.C., for a fraction of its net working capital. He immediately increased dividends to shareholders, and before long his investment had been paid back one and a half times over. At the same time, he demanded fare increases from regulators and refused to arbitrate a pension dispute with the employees' union. In 1955, a strike at Capital Transit idled Washington's buses and streetcars. Wolfson's regulators were furious. He was subpoenaed to Washington, D.C., by a Senate subcommittee to explain his actions. One committee member said on the floor of the Senate that Wolfson "seems to think he is bigger than the Congress."[59] At the hearing, the senator was proven right—Wolfson was defiant. He defended his policies at Capital Transit, explained his philosophy of liberal dividend payments to shareholders, and said that without a fare increase, he would not increase wages for employees. Shareholders came first. And to Wolfson, that idea *was* bigger than Congress. At the time, he was running a highly publicized proxy fight against Montgomery Ward. When a reporter asked him why he was still fighting companies given what a huge fortune he'd already accumulated, Wolfson responded, "I have a responsibility to stockholders, like that little old lady in Washington telling me that her whole income depended on her transit dividends and that she was praying for me to win. What kind of human would I be if that didn't touch me deeply?"[60]

LOUIS WOLFSON WAS the kind of hard-nosed businessman who would protect the dividends of one little old lady by making a bunch of others walk their little old asses home during a transit strike. But as sanctimonious as he seemed, Wolfson was one of the more interesting and genuine figures of the Proxyteer era. He thumbed his nose at Congress and the regulators, and his decision to stand toe-to-toe with the Securities and Exchange Commission cost him dearly. Wolfson's financial career ended in shame and ruin when he was sent to prison for violating SEC registration restrictions on a stock sale.[61] But in the end, Wolfson did something with his own public company, Merritt-Chapman, that few activist investors ever do with their own investment vehicles: Rather than keep his own gravy train running, Wolfson decided it was in the shareholders' best interest to liquidate it.[62]

As for the rest of the Proxyteers, it wasn't too hard to see cracks in the façade of their pro-shareholder populism. As much as these men railed against professional managers, they committed many of the same evils when they got to the head of the board table. Indeed, Robert R. Young used Alleghany's capital to buy the C&O's New York Central stake. All of the potential upside was given to Richardson and Murchison, while Alleghany shareholders got stuck with all the risk. Other Proxyteers were accused at various times of paying themselves too much, and many of their investment vehicles were eventually targeted by other activists.

Even the great Thomas Mellon Evans, who won control of more than eighty companies in his long career, had a habit of shafting minority shareholders when it suited him. Evans was one of the giants of the Proxyteer era, and he built his two primary investment vehicles, Crane Company and H. K. Porter, into massive enterprises. Porter ultimately went private by forcing a deal over the objections of its minority shareholders. Crane neutralized potentially hostile shareholders by installing golden parachutes and a poison pill. As Diana Henriques wrote in her excellent book about Evans and the Proxyteers, *The White Sharks of Wall Street*, Crane said its poison pill would prevent "abusive takeover practices," such as when a raider buys a controlling interest without paying shareholders a sufficient premium. Henriques then pointed out, "That, of course, had been the young Tom Evans's favorite game."[63]

In some ways, Proxyteering was less a populist movement than a killer investment strategy. It seems like every sustained bull market gives birth to a merger boom and a clever way to capitalize on it. In the 1950s, that strategy was takeover by proxy. But we can't ignore the lasting and profound impact the Proxyteers had on markets and public companies. The notions of shareholder rights and shareholder value, which had been forgotten by everyone but a few outsiders like Benjamin Graham, were brought back into the debate about the role of public companies. They would ultimately come to dominate it. And while most of the Proxyteers faded into obscurity, their tactics would be sharpened and used by later generations of conglomerators, corporate raiders, and hedge fund activists.

A Constant Downward Slope

Robert Young's first year as chairman of the New York Central lived up to his hype. He brought in Alfred Perlman from the Denver & Rio Grande Western Railroad and the two men set to work improving the Central's weak financial condition while modernizing its decaying assets. The company's earnings and stock price shot up in 1955, and for a brief moment Young's investment had more than doubled. Then, in 1957, the entire railroad industry stumbled on a steep decline in freight traffic. As the economy slid toward the recession of 1958, the New York Central's earnings fell 78%.[64]

In late 1957, rumors began to spread that Young was having financial problems. By that point, the exercise price on Richardson and Murchison's put option was double the price of their Central stock, and they had sold all of their 800,000 shares back to Alleghany and Allan Kirby. The value of Young's shares in Alleghany and the New York Central took a tremendous beating.

When the New York Central board of directors met in January to discuss the company's finances, it voted to cancel the quarterly dividend.

During the meeting, several directors sensed that something was wrong with Young, who seemed quiet and distant. They had heard rumors about his financial condition and offered assistance. Young thanked them and replied that his finances were in good shape. Later that week he killed himself with a shotgun in his Palm Beach mansion. Word spread that Young died penniless, bankrupted by his holdings in Alleghany and the New York Central.

In fact, Robert Young left behind a vast fortune including cash, securities, artwork, and property.[65] He had succumbed to the depression he struggled with for most of his life. Twenty years earlier, shortly after Guaranty Trust declared him in default, Young suffered a major breakdown that left him hospitalized. In a Newport rest home, just before he summoned the strength to wage the proxy battle with Guaranty Trust that launched the Proxyteer movement, Young wrote a poem with the lines, "Until today it seemed my path led upward, / But now I find myself upon a constant downward slope / Which gains in pitch until I see / Dim, distantly, a void. . . ."[66]

AFTER YOUNG'S DEATH, Alleghany's large shareholders battled for control of the company. Allan Kirby briefly replaced Young as chairman and president, before being ousted in 1961 by Clint Murchison's sons, Clint Jr. and John. As Kirby sat on the outside looking in, he tried to figure out the best way to regain control of Alleghany. By this point in time, public companies were much more sophisticated at defending themselves from war by proxy. Gone were the days when an overconfident executive like Lucian Sprague would underestimate his opponents and leave himself vulnerable.

In the late 1950s, the cottage industries that had formed around proxy fights—public relations, proxy solicitation, and legal defense—became big business. The influx of money and talent was most noticeable at law firms, where a new generation of brilliant lawyers emerged to specialize in takeover battles. The 1959 proxy battle for United Industrial Corporation was a training ground for two men who would help shape the takeover industry in the coming decades, Joe Flom and Martin Lipton.[67] Flom would turn Skadden Arps into one of the largest firms in the world by cultivating its takeover business. Lipton would become the most prominent corporate defender and would invent the poison pill.

With the help of these high-powered brain trusts, corporations developed clever tactics to repel hostile shareholders. When Ben Heineman went after B. F. Goodrich, the company entered into a $250 million loan agreement that would instantly default in the case of a takeover.[68] Often, companies would deter raiders by making acquisitions that depleted excess cash or created antitrust problems for the acquirer's vehicle. Some companies even played defense by waging a counterattack. While Leopold Silberstein was running a proxy fight against Fairbanks Morse, the company's president, Robert Morse Jr., backed Art Landa in a successful attack on Silberstein's vehicle, Penn-Texas.[69]

At Alleghany, Allan Kirby did not want to run an expensive and uncertain proxy battle against the savvy Murchison brothers. Instead, he quickly and aggressively bought enough shares to guarantee control. This was his best offensive tactic, and it would turn into the favored takeover weapon of the 1960s. The most effective way to accomplish huge open-market share purchases was the hostile tender offer. When the proxy fight gave way to the hostile tender, the Proxyteer was replaced by the corporate raider.

Warren Buffett and American Express: The Great Salad Oil Swindle

"Let me assure you that the great majority of stockholders (although perhaps not the most vocal ones) think you have done an outstanding job of keeping the ship on an even keel and moving full steam ahead while being buffetted by a typhoon which largely falls in the 'Act of God' category."
—WARREN BUFFETT, 1964

ARREN BUFFETT MAKES INVESTING sound easy. Part of his investment philosophy comes directly from Benjamin Graham: He views shares of stock as fractional ownerships of a business, and he buys them with a margin of safety. But unlike Graham, when Buffett finds a security trading at a large discount to its intrinsic value, he eschews diversification and buys a large position. To Warren Buffett, with his superhuman gift for rational thinking, this value investing strategy *is* easy. For the rest of us mere mortals, it is a minefield littered with the corpses of its practitioners. It is very hard to avoid career-imploding mistakes with a hyperconcentrated value investing strategy. Warren Buffett is the exception that proves the rule.

Every year, I make a pilgrimage to Omaha to hear Buffett and his partner, Charlie Munger, take questions for six hours at the Berkshire Hathaway shareholders' meeting. I never tire of hearing them talk about business and industry. I don't even mind listening to them discuss politics and macroeconomics. When they philosophize about value investing, however, it makes me a little uneasy.

To be clear, Buffett and Munger don't say anything about value investing that isn't true. They are right that you don't need a superhigh

IQ to be a successful investor. They are right that it is relatively easy to evaluate the competitive dynamics of an industry and value companies. They are right that, if you are patient enough, the market will give you some fat pitches to swing at. And they are right that concentrating your portfolio into your very best ideas will give you the best outcome if you do good work.

Every tenet of Warren Buffett's value investing strategy holds true, but there's a cruel irony to contend with: Buffett-style investing is tailor-made to magnify irrational thinking. Nothing is going to coax out the inherent irrationality of a portfolio manager—his or her weakness to the forces of greed and fear—like supersize positions. Munger once said he would be comfortable putting more than 100% of his net worth into one investment. Most of the earnest business school students attending the Berkshire Hathaway meeting wouldn't stand a chance if they started investing like that. Investors need ice water in their veins to make concentrated value investing work.

Warren Buffett's biography, *The Snowball*, is not the story of an everyman from America's heartland succeeding on just hard work and determination. Buffett is a singularity, and even his worst mistakes tell an interesting story. Berkshire Hathaway, for instance, was a bad investment. The company featured a lethal combination of high capital intensity and low returns on invested capital. In other words, you had to put a lot of money back into the business for little, if any, return. Yet Buffett somehow parlayed Berkshire into one of the most valuable companies in the world, with more than 340,000 employees.

Berkshire Hathaway is itself an anomaly, just like the man who built it. It is a huge, decentralized, global conglomerate that somehow retains a corporate culture of excellence. Berkshire's business model is simple—find good businesses run by capable managers, let them do their jobs, and then harvest the cash flows. Like Buffett's value investing strategy, it is intuitive, it generates incredible results, and nobody else does it nearly as well.

It's hard to believe there was ever a time when Warren Buffett's aptitude for business was anything but superhuman. We think of him as a fully formed portfolio manager from the moment he launched his first investment partnership in 1956, when he was only twenty-five years old. He compounded wealth for himself and his investors at an astounding rate over the next twelve years and never suffered a losing year. Despite this stellar track record, the Buffett Partnerships were very much a work in progress. Buffett was constantly refining his investment style, even toying with short selling and pair trades at one point. As he told the *New York Times* in 1990, "I evolved. I didn't go from ape to human or human to ape in a nice, even manner."[1] Buffett learned lessons from his mistakes as well as his victories. His biggest triumph was American Express. It proved to be a major turning point in his career.

The Great Salad Oil Swindle was an audacious fraud that nearly toppled American Express in the 1960s. It is a complicated story filled with valuable lessons about the fallibility of businessmen, and their capacity to ignore reality at critical junctures. While the saga exposes terrible behavior and a true villain, it features many more honest and capable people who unwittingly developed deadly blind spots. The fallout from the fraud also pitted Warren Buffett against a handful of shareholders who wanted American Express to maximize its short-term profits by ignoring salad oil claimants.

When Warren Buffett intervened at American Express as a large shareholder, he didn't demand board representation or ask probing questions about the company's operating performance. He didn't call for a higher dividend or question the company's capital spending. Instead, he wanted American Express to use its capital liberally to recompense parties who were defrauded in the swindle. Buffett had done enough research on American Express to understand that it was a phenomenal business. He would later refer to companies like this as "compounding machines," because they generate huge returns on capital that can be reinvested at the same rate of return. Buffett knew that walking away from the salad oil claims would damage American Express's reputation and its substantial long-term value. He wanted to prevent short-term-oriented shareholders from jamming the compounding machine's gears just to save a few dollars. This was a new position for Buffett to be in. Before he bought American Express stock,

Buffett was the kind of penny-pinching investor who sought to extract value from his stock holdings as quickly as possible.

WILTING WINDMILLS

At around the same time that Robert Young's New York Central began to collapse in 1957, a young Warren Buffett fired off a letter to a board member of a company he'd invested in. "I am writing this to you as you are apparently an 'outside' director of Merchants National Property," he wrote. Maybe my sensibilities, almost sixty years removed, are different than Buffett's, but I read that line as dripping with sarcasm. His next four words won't surprise you: "I am disturbed by . . ."[2]

Though he wasn't rattling a saber or testifying before Congress like the Proxyteers, Buffett was quietly employing a similar investment strategy for his partnerships in Omaha. He bought undervalued, often underperforming companies, and pushed for board representation or even control. One classic Buffett Partnerships investment was in Dempster Mill Manufacturing Company, a Nebraska windmill and farm equipment maker founded in the nineteenth century. Buffett framed it this way: "The qualitative situation was on the negative side . . . but the figures were extremely attractive."[3]

Dempster was a manufacturing business operating in a tough industry. It produced only nominal profits but traded at a very steep discount to its book value. Buffett was buying the company for less than half the value of its cash, inventory, and accounts receivable minus all liabilities. He first bought Dempster stock in 1956, joined the board in 1958, and then crossed 50% ownership to get control in 1961.[4]

Buffett pushed management to improve profit margins, but nothing worked. After years with no progress, he found an able manager, Harry Bottle, and installed him at Dempster to clean house. Bottle cut expenses, sold unprofitable facilities, and liquidated inventories. He turned Dempster's stagnant assets into ready cash, which Buffett promptly invested in stocks. By 1963, those stocks were worth more than Buffett had paid for the entire company. As he wrote that year:

B.P.L. [Buffett Partnership Ltd.] owns 71.7% of Dempster acquired at a cost of $1,262,577.27. On June 30, 1963, Dempster had a small safe deposit box at the Omaha National Bank containing securities worth $2,028,415.25. Our 71.7% share of $2,028,415.25 amounts to $1,454,373.70. Thus, everything above ground (and part of it underground) is profit.[5]

Buffett's investment in Sanborn Map, which he describes in the partnerships' 1960 annual letter, is also worth examining. Sanborn was a better business than Dempster. It sold detailed city maps to fire insurance companies, and was highly profitable for decades until the 1950s, when a new method of underwriting cut into revenues. By the time Buffett started buying Sanborn stock, it traded at $45 per share but had $65 per share of securities on its balance sheet.[6] There was also some potential in the existing operations. Profits were shrinking, but Buffett felt Sanborn's board of directors, populated by insurance executives, was neglecting the business.

Buffett bought enough shares to land a board seat, and then proceeded to wage war with the other directors to distribute the securities and revive the map business. When they rejected his idea of returning excess capital to shareholders, Buffett threatened to call a special stockholders' meeting to replace the board.[7] He complained to *The Snowball* author, Alice Schroeder, about his experience with Sanborn, "I remember cigars getting passed around. I was paying for thirty percent of every one of those cigars. I was the only guy not smoking cigars."[8] Buffett eventually prevailed and the company used its excess securities to repurchase 72% of its stock.

In the early years of his investment partnerships, Warren Buffett bought a lot of asset-rich companies at large discounts. These situations were messy, time-consuming, and often demanded conflict. In tiny Beatrice, Nebraska, where Dempster Mill owned the only factory in town, Buffett was vilified in the local press for laying off one hundred workers. He never wanted to go through that experience again, and he wouldn't have to. An improbable series of events was about to drop American Express, one of the best businesses in the country, into the lap of a bargain hunter.

LENDER OF LAST RESORT

In June 1960, an anonymous tipster called American Express to expose a massive fraud at Allied Crude Vegetable Oil Refining Corporation. At the time, Allied was the largest customer of American Express's field warehousing subsidiary, which was in the unenviable position of having guaranteed millions of dollars' worth of Allied's soybean oil inventory. The tipster, whom American Express employees called "the Voice," said he worked the night shift at Allied's facility in Bayonne, New Jersey. He challenged American Express employees to inspect Tank No. 6006, one of the largest tanks on the property. He explained that there was a narrow metal chamber filled with oil positioned directly under the measuring hatch. Everything else in the tank was seawater.[9]

Now, I'm guessing that you don't run a field warehousing company. But if you did, no phone call would scare the hell out of you like one that goes, "Psst! That warehouse you think is full is actually empty!" A field warehousing company's only job is to oversee and verify its customers' inventory in storage. American Express had issued warehouse receipts certifying Allied's ownership of millions of pounds of soybean oil. Allied was using these receipts, stamped with the American Express guarantee, as collateral for millions of dollars of loans. Norman C. Miller, who won a Pulitzer Prize for his reporting on the Salad Oil Swindle for the *Wall Street Journal*, quoted one of Allied's lenders: "We figured with American Express issuing the receipts, we couldn't go wrong."[10] American Express was risking its capital and reputation on the contents of a bunch of rusty storage tanks in Bayonne. How hard could it be to figure out what was inside them?

After talking with the Voice, Donald Miller, president of American Express Field Warehousing, ordered a surprise inspection.[11] American Express's inspectors checked empty tanks for hidden chambers, finding none. They took samples from the operational tanks, including No. 6006. The inspectors reported to Miller that about 15% of the tanks had more water in the sample than could be explained by condensation. They also could not rule out a hidden chamber in No. 6006, because all the openings except the measuring hatch were welded shut. Despite these warning signs, the inspectors concluded that the tanks contained enough oil to cover all outstanding warehouse receipts.[12]

When the Voice first talked to Donald Miller, he wanted $5,000 before providing more details about the fraud.[13] By the end of the summer, he was so frustrated with American Express's milquetoast response that he wanted to prove he was right, reward or no reward. Exasperated with Miller, the Voice called higher up in the organization all the way to President and CEO Howard Clark's office. Rather than offer mysterious leads, the Voice suggested a detailed six-point plan to expose the fraud.[14] The most important step involved hiring independent engineers "who cannot be compromised" to examine the tanks in Bayonne.[15] Clark's executive assistant immediately found the Voice credible and ordered an American Express investigator to take a closer look at Allied.

WITHOUT HAVING TO do an awful lot of digging, the American Express investigator, R. T. Roche, learned some alarming facts about Allied's owner, Anthony "Tino" De Angelis. Roche's internal memo, dated November 18, 1960, noted that De Angelis had been indicted by the Justice Department seven years earlier, and that IRS officials seriously considered criminal prosecution for tax evasion. Tino had more than a million dollars of tax liens against him and was suspected of bribing a government inspector. Roche implied that Tino was tied to organized crime and recommended that American Express plant an undercover man at the company.[16]

De Angelis's previous business dealings were especially troubling. Tino was a butcher who launched his own meatpacking business in 1938. He made a fortune in the 1940s, allegedly through black-market meat sales during World War II, and shady export deals after it.[17] In 1949, Tino bought control of Adolf Gobel Company, a large meatpacker listed on the American Stock Exchange. In 1952, the company lost a lucrative government contract by delivering substandard meat to a federal school lunch program and then overbilling the U.S. Department of Agriculture.[18] A year later, the Securities and Exchange Commission began investigating the company for overstating earnings and, you guessed it, *inflating inventory*. Within five years of buying control, Tino drove Gobel into bankruptcy.

The SEC contended that De Angelis booked phony orders on Gobel's income statement and borrowed money against inventory that did not exist. The Justice Department indicted him in 1953 for pressuring an employee to make false statements about the value of Gobel's inventory during the SEC investigation. This is worth repeating: When Allied became American Express's largest field warehousing customer in 1957, Tino was under indictment for forcing an employee at his previous (bankrupt) company to lie about inventory values. American Express was guaranteeing millions of dollars of inventory for someone the SEC was accusing of borrowing against phantom inventory.[19]

Allied's recent actions also dispelled any hope that De Angelis had changed his ways since Gobel. In 1958, the Agriculture Department investigated Tino for falsifying shipping papers to defraud the U.S. government out of $1.2 million. The government filed a civil fraud suit against De Angelis and Allied in 1960, the same year the Voice called American Express to warn about Allied's inventory scam.[20]

None of Roche's information about Tino's shady past was very hard to find. The *Wall Street Journal* reported on the Gobel scandal and the civil fraud suit against Allied. Any credit report on Allied would detail Tino's tax troubles as well as Gobel's bankruptcy and legal scrapes. This is why Allied needed American Express in the first place. The banks would never lend money to Tino De Angelis without independently verified collateral. By guaranteeing Allied's inventory, American Express, one of the most respected financial companies in the country, was the lender of last resort to a con man who repeatedly defrauded the U.S. government and fed substandard meat to America's schoolchildren.

THE SIEGE OF BAYONNE

American Express in 1960 was not all that different from American Express today. It was a venerated company with a valuable brand, operating in a profitable line of business. Most people didn't know American Express even had a field warehousing business until the Salad Oil Swindle brought the company to its knees. American Express's dominant travelers checks business exceeded $1 billion in volume per year, and its fledgling credit card unit was growing 25% a year. The field warehousing business, by contrast, had lost money in about half of the previous sixteen years and had never made a meaningful profit. Not counting the Allied business, which of course turned out to be fraudulent, the warehousing subsidiary was losing money.[21]

Even if the subsidiary had reached Howard Clark's goal of $500,000 of annual net income, field warehousing was a lousy business that American Express should have avoided. Warehousing customers are so capital-intensive that they must borrow against their inventory, and they have such weak credit that lenders require verified collateral. Because field warehousing companies compete for customers by promising to limit disruption, they compromise their ability to safeguard the inventory. The so-called independent field warehouse is really the customer's own warehouse with a new sign on it. The "independent employees" are existing workers who have been temporarily moved to the field warehousing company's payroll. These situations are rife with conflicts of interest and competing agendas, and the years leading up to the Allied fraud saw several large field warehousing scams.[22]

The *Wall Street Journal*'s reporting on the salad oil scandal revealed that Tino was still paying Allied employees even after they had been moved over to American Express's payroll. Almost all of these workers received more money from De Angelis than they got from American Express, so their loyalty to Allied was never in doubt. Only these men knew how the tanks really worked. Only they understood the labyrinth of drainage pipes that connected the tanks, and they were the ones responsible for taking inventory readings for American Express.

THE VOICE FIRST explained Allied's fraud to executives at American Express in the summer of 1960. At that point, American Express could have extracted itself from Tino's swindle with very minor damage—it had warehouse receipts outstanding for 65 million pounds of soybean oil, worth $6.5 million. Incredibly, the swindle was not exposed until *three years later*. By then the fraud had increased tenfold—to the point where American Express was guaranteeing more salad oil in Bayonne than existed in the entire United States.[23] The warning signs were everywhere. The weekly inventory increases were so large that it was physically impossible to receive that much oil in so short a time, yet American Express officials watched without blinking an eye.[24] Even some of the bankers making loans against Tino's warehouse receipts called with questions along the lines of, "Are you sure you guys are on top of this thing?"[25] But American Express never uncovered the fraud on its own. Was it really possible to overlook such obvious warning signs without some kind of devious intent?

American Express field warehousing executives were more delusional than they were dishonest. Tino never bribed any of them, nor did he even pressure them to bend rules. He didn't need to. The closest American Express came to discovering the swindle was the surprise inspection after the anonymous phone calls. Tino coolly responded by terminating the field warehousing contract with American Express.[26] The best defense was a good offense, and American Express quickly rushed to soothe Tino's anger at the disruption.

While they were appeasing Tino, American Express officials were feebly processing the warning signs. The inspection report concluded there was enough oil in the tanks to cover outstanding warehouse receipts, but it also stated, "There is still no explanation for the mysterious telephone calls. There is definite information that water was in the tanks. There is the probability that there may have been kiting of warehouse receipts which represented the greatest possible loss to American Express Field Warehousing Corporation."[27] So why would American Express Field Warehousing move forward with the Allied contract with only minor upgrades in staff and oversight? The conclusion to the inspection report is telling: "Since Allied is the largest revenue-producing account on our books and our company would be operating at a loss without the account, I believe that an attempt should be made to salvage the account."[28]

At American Express, the field warehousing subsidiary needed large customers to make the business viable. The pursuit of short-term profit and professional success blinded the field warehousing executives to the risks of taking on a client such as Allied. By 1963, American Express's field warehousing executives had convinced themselves of Tino's honesty and integrity. Several of them, including division head Donald Miller, invested personal money in one of Tino's other ventures.

In a relatively short time period, a handful of complacent and delusional employees at American Express put the whole institution at risk. CEO Howard Clark toyed with the idea of closing the warehousing business for years, but he kept letting his underlings talk him out of it. Clark even personally visited Allied's facility on one occasion. The only storage tank he climbed turned out to be rusted through on top, but he did not voice concern.[29] When he finally decided to get rid of the Allied business, a few weeks before the scandal broke, it was way too late.

THE GREAT SALAD OIL SWINDLE blew up in spectacular fashion in 1963, when Allied's creditors descended on Bayonne after Tino quietly filed the company for bankruptcy. Confusion gave way to panic as lenders and exporters holding American Express warehouse receipts for 1.3 *billion* pounds of soybean oil—receipts for 395 million pounds turned out to be forgeries—learned that most of the tanks contained water or unidentified sludge.[30] When Allied's bankruptcy trustees drained Tank No. 6006, they found seawater and a narrow metal chamber with soybean oil. More than fifty companies were affected, including Bank of America, Bankers Trust, Brown Brothers Harriman, Chase Manhattan, Continental Grain, Morgan Guaranty, and Procter & Gamble.[31]

Tino had taken his swindle to Wall Street, wreaking havoc on markets and collapsing his empire in the process. He used warehouse receipts to open margin trading accounts in a reckless attempt to corner the market in soybean oil. When the trade inevitably turned against Tino, the Produce Exchange had to shut down for an entire day so it could unwind his position. A well-respected brokerage firm with 20,000 clients holding half a billion dollars' worth of stocks took huge losses by letting Tino trade on margin. It was suspended by the New York Stock Exchange—only the second occurrence in 171 years—and was liquidated.[32]

The situation at American Express was grim. The company had roughly $80 million of insurance, but it wouldn't cover loss by fraud. Publicly, Howard Clark alluded to American Express's insurance policies and was optimistic about the company's future growth and prosperity. In private, he huddled with lawyers to figure out if the company would have enough capital to meet claims against its warehousing subsidiary. Shortly after the scandal broke, Clark released a formal statement: "If our subsidiary should be held legally liable for amounts in excess of its insurance coverage and other assets, American Express feels morally bound to do everything it can, consistent with its overall responsibilities, to see that such excess liabilities are satisfied."[33] As accusations and lawsuits piled, the company's stock collapsed, attracting the attention of thirty-three-year-old Warren Buffett in Omaha, Nebraska.

UNLIMITED VIABILITY

American Express stock fell by more than 50% in the months following Allied's collapse. Investors' concerns about the company's exposure to Tino's swindle were exacerbated because shareholders did not have limited liability. American Express was the last major public company to be organized as a joint-stock company, meaning anyone who owned shares could be liable for the company's debts and obligations. Warren Buffett explained this dynamic to *The Snowball* author, Alice Schroeder:

> So every trust department in the United States panicked. I remember the Continental Bank held over five percent of the company, and all of a sudden not only do they see that the trust accounts were going to have stock worth zero, but they could get assessed. The stock just poured out, of course, and the market got slightly inefficient for a short period of time.[34]

Buffett bought an enormous position in American Express. At one point the stock accounted for almost one-third of his portfolio.[35] But he never wrote about the investment in any of his partnership letters. Buffett only mentioned control positions and obscurities by name. In early

1964, when he was buying American Express as quickly as he could, the only new stock to appear in the investor letter was Texas National Petroleum, a tiny buyout deal that netted just over $100,000 in profits. But despite its low profile in Buffett's partnership letters, American Express's effect on his investing philosophy was profound.

Buffett divided his portfolio into three categories: "control positions," like Dempster Mill or Berkshire Hathaway; "work-outs," which were special situations like Texas National Petroleum; and "generals," where American Express would fit. His description of "generals" in early 1963 focused mostly on bargain prices and margin of safety. He wrote, "Many times generals represent a form of 'coattail riding' where we feel the dominating stockholder group has plans for the conversion of unprofitable or under-utilized assets to a better use."[36] In other words, many of these stocks were low-return businesses trading at a discount to book value just like Dempster Mill and Berkshire Hathaway.

A year later, after Buffett had begun purchasing American Express, he updated his description of generals: "[W]hile the quantitative comes first and is essential, the qualitative is important. We like good management—we like a decent industry—we like a certain amount of 'ferment' in a previously dormant management or stockholder group."[37] By 1967, after he had made a killing on American Express stock, Buffett wrote:

> Interestingly enough, although I consider myself to be primarily in the quantitative school (and as I write this no one has come back from recess—I may be the only one left in the class), the really sensational ideas I have had over the years have been heavily weighted toward the qualitative side where I have had a "high-probability insight." . . . So the really big money tends to be made by investors who are right on qualitative decisions but, at least in my opinion, the more sure money tends to be made on the obvious quantitative decisions.[38]

Buffett was attracted to American Express stock's steep fall, and the company's joint-stock structure, with unlimited liability, neatly explained the market's overreaction. But he did not buy into American

Express just to take a quick profit when the market stabilized. After surveying the performance of the company's products, he knew he'd found a great business—the kind that rarely crossed his desk before 1963.

Buffett had focused much of his career on buying asset-rich businesses for cheap. But American Express had basically no plants or equipment. Its value rested in its name, and Buffett surveyed banks, hotels, restaurants, and customers to determine that the scandal had not affected the brand.[39] His research helped him recognize the immense power of an asset-light business model. Whereas asset-rich companies like Berkshire Hathaway required a lot of investment to operate efficiently, American Express's travelers checks business actually created excess capital, a large float, between the time customers bought checks and used them. Because of the enduring power of the American Express brand, he likened the settlement with salad oil claimants to losing one dividend check in the mail—an annoyance, but by no means a catastrophe.[40] What was Buffett's "high-probability insight" on American Express? As he told *Forbes* in 1969, "Look, the name American Express is one of the greatest franchises in the world."[41]

The Typhoon Will Pass

American Express lost $125 million in market value after the swindle became public. It eventually reached an agreement with salad oil claimants that would cost only $32 million net of taxes.[42] But a funny thing happened on the way to resolution: American Express's settlement was delayed by an unlikely group—the company's own shareholders. A small group of shareholders filed suit to block any settlement, on the grounds that American Express had no legal obligation to pay the warehousing subsidiary's liabilities. Howard Clark may have felt he had a moral obligation to creditors, but shareholders argued that American Express legally owed nothing. They believed paying a cash settlement was a "gift" and a negligent use of assets that would damage shareholder value. They were especially frustrated that holders of forged receipts would receive any cash at all.

When public company shareholders don't have opinions, or hold them tighter than they hold their stocks, the few who choose to speak up are afforded a tall soapbox. But if an empowered few assume the voice of all shareholders, how can we be sure they are looking out for committed, long-term owners? The outsize influence of active shareholders probably weighed on Warren Buffett's mind when American Express holders began agitating for the company to ignore the salad oil claims. Buffett knew the odds of this happening were slim, but why risk letting a handful of shareholders dominate the debate?

In Buffett's early years, he occasionally clashed with management teams and boards of directors of underperforming, asset-rich companies. When he was forced to go active, it often meant seizing control and dismantling assets. At Dempster Mill, for example, he generated shareholder value by taking money out of the business as quickly as possible. American Express was a different situation altogether. Management was making the right moves to protect the franchise, yet other shareholders were agitating to block them. The swindle generated national news coverage and many of the claimants were large financial institutions that sold American Express travelers checks. Buffett worried that shareholders' shortsighted attempt to avoid a settlement could permanently impair American Express's valuable brand. With a quality business at stake, Buffett wanted to intervene to protect the company's competitive advantage.

In some ways, Buffett's June 16, 1964, letter to Howard Clark (page 218) reads like a pep talk. He praises management, and then encourages them to keep up the good work. Behind the outward positivity, Buffett seems to be saying, "Come on, we have a great business here and we almost have this mess behind us, let's not screw it up now." The most astounding part of the letter is Buffett's suggestion that the Allied scandal would ultimately *improve* American Express's reputation for integrity. He writes, "While I am certain that management must feel at times like it is in the midst of a bottomless pit regarding the field warehousing activities, it is our feeling that three or four years from now this problem may well have added to the stature of the company in establishing standards for financial integrity and responsibility which are far beyond those of the normal commercial enterprise."

The idea that American Express could emerge from this debacle with heightened stature seems like a fantasy, or perhaps an attempt by Buffett to ingratiate himself to Clark. But as Peter Grossman explained in his 1987 book about American Express, the worst crisis in the history of the company had the perverse effect of strengthening the business and management team. Grossman wrote, "In fact, so much was gained that someone asked Howard Clark if a Soybean [scandal] was not a good idea every few years. But he replied, 'I don't think I have enough years of my life to give away for another scandal.'"[43] As it turned out, Buffett was completely right. Thus was born the Oracle of Omaha.

As Warren Buffett tallied huge profits from his American Express investment, the market around him devolved into a feeding frenzy for conglomerates and flashy mutual funds. But Buffett quietly continued on his own evolutionary pathway. His American Express investment pushed him further away from Benjamin Graham's investment style. He explained years later, "I became very interested in buying a wonderful business at a moderate price."[44] In 1969 he announced his plan to close his investment partnership. He had made enough "sure money" on quantitative decisions and was ready to move on to larger prey. Over time, Buffett became interested in buying whole companies. In light of American Express, this made perfect sense. Owning a great business is easier, and much more fun, than buying fractional interests in wasting assets. Buffett would use the value investing style he'd refined like golden soybean oil to raise Berkshire Hathaway, a doomed New England textile company, to the commanding heights of industry.

WALL STREET WIZARDRY

While Buffett added tremendous value to Berkshire Hathaway in the late 1960s by buying an insurance company and a bank, many of his contemporaries took sound businesses and desecrated them with senseless acquisitions. The "go-go" stock market of the 1960s launched what is known as America's third major merger wave (after the 1890s and 1920s). It was in large part a pointless bastardization. Whereas the previous merger booms focused on horizontal and then vertical integration, public companies in the '60s binged on acquisitions merely for the sake of growth, which was richly rewarded by Wall Street no matter how it was obtained. The go-go era collapsed quickly, but a new generation of corporate raiders emerged from the ruins. Jim Ling's 1978 battle with Harold Simmons highlights the hostile raider's ascendance.

"Jimmy Ling the Merger King," who ran Ling-Temco-Vought (LTV), is a prime example of a conglomerator who built a fortune on Wall Street's willingness to pay up for growing companies. In 1955, he took his small Dallas-based electrical contracting business public. It was a challenge to find buyers for his stock—he even got a booth at the Texas State Fair to distribute copies of his prospectus—but Ling managed to raise about a million dollars.[45] From this start, he made a slew of acquisitions that put his company in the Fortune 500. Ling perpetually raised money from Wall Street and pursued baffling restructurings that facilitated future fund-raising. He sold various hybrid securities, such as preferred stocks convertible into common stock, and frequently made confusing offers to swap new securities for old ones. By 1969, after successful hostile tender offers for Chance Vought, Wilson & Company, and Jones & Laughlin, LTV was number fourteen on the Fortune 500. Ling's $425 million hostile tender for Jones & Laughlin was, at the time, the largest ever cash tender offer.[46]

As LTV grew, Ling was widely praised for his "financial wizardry." The description was unintentionally apt: LTV's rise was a ruse facilitated by Ling's powers of obfuscation and Wall Street's emphasis on earnings growth and price/earnings ratios. Because Ling's company received a high valuation on public markets, he could raise enough capital to buy more earnings growth through acquisition. But this would not go on forever. There was a dirty secret behind LTV: Ling's acquisition record was spotty. Wilson may have been a success, but Chance Vought and Jones & Laughlin were both disasters. Before long, investors wised up to the conglomerators' game, and LTV's stock collapsed. Because Ling had borrowed heavily against his LTV holdings, his personal wealth was decimated.

From Omega to Omega

In the mid-1960s, at the height of the Merger King's fame, Harold Simmons, a thirty-three-year-old pharmacy owner, wrote to Ling seeking a meeting. Simmons had followed Ling's career from afar and was impressed by his ability to snatch up companies. When he was not managing his drugstore, Simmons was reading annual reports and dabbling in the stock market. He thought he had found a particularly undervalued company, Bath Iron Works in Maine, and he wanted to hear what Ling thought of the idea. Simmons was thrilled when Ling agreed to meet with him. He was even more excited when Ling praised Simmons's investment analysis.

When the two men met again in 1976, Jim Ling was in dire straits. His newest venture, Omega-Alpha, should have been called Omega-Omega, because it quickly fell into bankruptcy. It was another in a succession of low moments for Ling, who had been the toast of Dallas less than a decade earlier. Simmons, for his part, was riding high. He had sold his drugstore empire for $50 million and was on his way to building a billion-dollar fortune raiding public companies. Simmons mimicked Ling's creative use of tender offers to win control of companies, but where Ling's goal was to grow LTV at all costs, Simmons focused on buying undervalued businesses. One of Harold Simmons's best talents was finding companies with hidden assets that the rest of the market overlooked.

In 1975, the same year Ling's Omega-Alpha filed for bankruptcy, Simmons found an obscure company called Valhi that traded at only $5 per share despite owning $50 per share in properties. Simmons figured out Valhi owned this hidden treasure by following the actions of D. Doyle Mize, former CEO of Zapata Corporation. Mize resigned as CEO of Zapata to become CEO of its small landholding subsidiary, Southdown. When Zapata spun off Southdown to its shareholders, Mize concentrated his ownership and made a fortune. He then tried to repeat the feat with Valhi. Mize pooled Southdown's best assets into Valhi, resigned as Southdown's CEO to become Valhi's CEO, and then spun Valhi off to shareholders including himself. Simmons surprised Mize by tendering for Valhi's shares at $15 per share. Mize topped Simmons with a $17.50 offer, but Simmons ultimately won control with a $22.50 tender offer.[47]

Shortly after Simmons's Valhi triumph, Jim Ling stopped by for a visit. Simmons did not form a partnership with Ling, as the former Merger King suggested, but he did take pity on his former investment hero. Simmons offered Ling a two-year contract as an advisor to Contran, Simmons's main investment vehicle. Ling immediately pitched several investment ideas—and Contran would go on to make good money buying Omega-Alpha bonds on Ling's recommendation—but there were flaws in his analyses. While Ling was smart, Simmons realized that he was also a consummate bullshitter. He spoke quickly and used a lot of confusing jargon when he explained his ideas, yet he was often blind to critical and obvious details. Still, the humiliating collapse of LTV and his personal finances had not dampened Ling's self-confidence. A week after his two-year contract with Contran expired, Jim Ling informed Harold Simmons that he planned to make a hostile tender offer for Contran shares.

"This is typical Ling," Harold Simmons told his lawyer: "overlook the details that'll kill you."[48] After two years inside the company, Ling knew that Contran was deeply undervalued by the market. He saw how much value was hidden in Contran's constituent parts like Valhi. He also knew that if he could win control, he could liquidate the company for a massive profit. But he was neglecting one critical detail: Harold Simmons already controlled 42% of the stock. For Ling to prevail, he would have to purchase almost 90% of the remaining stock outstanding. That is a tall order.

With Contran stock trading at $20 per share on the open market, Ling offered $35 to buy out several large shareholders. He later publicly tendered for shares at $50, getting control of 41% of the company. At that point, Simmons had boosted his stake to 44%. If Ling could just get over 50%, he'd be on his way back to the LTV glory days. If he failed, however, he would own a huge, illiquid, debt-funded block in a company controlled by his enemy.

Jim Ling wasn't able to secure 50% of Harold Simmons's Contran. To make matters worse for him, Contran stock, which hovered around

$50 per share in the last days of the battle, was sure to plummet in value. Ling wanted Simmons to repurchase his block at $50. Simmons replied, "You can just keep that stock forever, because I'm not interested."[49] Contran ultimately bought the stake for a combination of cash and securities worth under $30 per share. Jimmy Ling the Merger King was back in the dumps, banished to a desert planet of irrelevance. The circle was now complete. When they first met, Harold Simmons was but the learner; now he was the master. When he was asked later about Ling's attempted coup, Simmons showed no anger. It was just business, he insisted.[50] The age of the cold-blooded hostile raider had arrived.

Jimmy's (Woodlawn Tap) and Harold's (Chicken Shack)

Jimmy Ling and Harold Simmons both made careers out of exploiting the market's ability to grossly misvalue public companies. Ling thrived in an era that saw superstar fund managers crowd into speculative companies promising growth. He used his own overvalued stock to raise money to purchase other businesses. Simmons prospered in the '70s, when the economy stagnated, markets tanked, and "go-go" was a gritty form of underground funk music in Washington, D.C. He scoured the wreckage in the markets for valuable companies that he could buy for a bargain price. One man capitalized on irrational optimism, the other on irrational pessimism. It's hard to believe, but over the same period a revolution was brewing in academia based on the curious notion that financial markets are near perfect. It altered the debate on hostile takeovers and helped bring corporate raiders out of the shadows and into the boardrooms of America's largest companies.

The efficient market hypothesis came out of the University of Chicago in the 1960s. It states that stock market prices fully reflect all publicly available information about a firm and represent the best possible estimates of its value. Even if some investors are irrational and respond to news poorly, they are random, normally distributed, and balance each other out. With efficient market theory, we can use fancy math formulas like this to compute a stock's expected return:

$$E\left(\tilde{r}_{j,t+1}|\Phi_t\right) = r_{f,t+1} + \left[\frac{E(\tilde{r}_{m,t+1}|\Phi_t) - r_{f,t+1}}{\sigma\left(\tilde{r}_{m,t+1}|\Phi_t\right)}\right] \frac{\text{cov}\left(\tilde{r}_{j,t+1}, \tilde{r}_{m,t+1}|\Phi_t\right)}{\sigma\left(\tilde{r}_{m,t+1}|\Phi_t\right)}$$

Now, I'll admit to having a soft spot for academic economics and finance. There is a beauty to a scientific proposition, and a good one helps us think clearly about a question at hand. Nobel laureate Merton Miller, who like many of his Chicago colleagues is a joy to read, described the utility of one of his finance theories in an interview: "[the] proposition is the beginning of wisdom; it's not the end of it."[51] He explained that when the theory fails in the real world, we become wiser by understanding which assumptions failed and why.

But when early proponents of the efficient market theory focused on empirical research, it was more like the end of wisdom than the beginning. Economists love to process data, and this led to critical biases. Their own love of information made them view investing in the stock market as a game of information gathering. They worried more about their assumption that market participants have equal access to information than they worried about collective lapses in judgment. Because it is easier to do research on discrete events like earnings announcements, dilutive stock offerings, stock splits, and mergers, many of them focused their empirical work on pockets of the market that were more likely to be efficient. But it's easy for investors to get out their calculators and price stock splits quickly and accurately. It is much harder to research investors' collective judgment of a company's long-term prospects. For several decades, academic economists took for granted the rational expectations of market participants.

In an efficient market, divergent opinions balance each other out and guide stock prices to an optimal level. In the real world, misjudgments are much more likely to be biased in one direction, and mass hysteria is not uncommon. Even in periods when the stock market is stable, investors are capable of dramatically misvaluing a company. Joel Greenblatt, who taught me securities analysis at Columbia, likes to open the *Wall Street Journal* on the first day of class and point out the large difference between the fifty-two-week high and fifty-two-week low stock prices of stable companies like Coca-Cola and Wal-Mart. Fund manager Howard Marks cites Yahoo!, which saw its year-end market value between 1997 and 2001 go from $3 billion to $29 billion to $115 billion to $16 billion to $9 billion.

Why does this matter to us? If markets are not efficient, participants have the opportunity to exploit dislocations for their own benefit. Companies can take advantage of shareholders, and shareholders can take advantage of companies. Here's a good example of this phenomenon: If you believe in rational markets, a company buyout at a premium to its market price is a profit-maximizing event for all shareholders. In the real world, buyouts are opportunistic, and people can, and do, get screwed.

We also shouldn't ignore the role markets play in influencing management teams. Every CEO interested in protecting his or her job must worry about stock price performance. As Carl Icahn once said, "You better get that price up or someone else will do it for you."[52] But what happens when the investor base misvalues the company? All of a sudden the incentives can get twisted, leading to poor management decisions.

I saw Eddie Lampert, a hedge fund manager who is chairman of Sears Holdings, make some interesting points at a New York Public Library event in 2006. When he was discussing the challenges of managing a public company, he raised a question few people in the room had considered. How do you run a company well when the stock is *over*valued? What happens when management can't meet investors' unrealistic expectations without taking more risk? And what happens to employee morale if everyone does a good job but the stock declines? Lampert, of course, knew what he was talking about. Sears closed that day at $175 per share versus today's price of around $35. In an efficient market, it's easy to develop tidy theories about optimal corporate governance. Once you realize stock prices can be totally crazy, the dogma needs to go out the window.

SAUL BELLOWS

As the efficient market hypothesis became more widely accepted in the 1970s, it had an important effect on the country's tolerance of takeovers.

In the 1960s, men like Jim Ling used hostile raids to fold small and medium-size companies into their conglomerates. Wall Street and its regulators tolerated the strong going after the weak, as well as medium-size companies gobbling up each other. But when blue-chip companies found themselves behind crosshairs, everyone freaked out. Saul Steinberg's brief dance with the mighty Chemical Bank in 1969 was proof.

Chemical was a 150-year-old bank with $9 billion in assets. Steinberg was a twenty-nine-year-old go-getter who launched his first business in 1961, Leasco, which leased IBM computers to customers at cheaper rates than IBM offered. He took Leasco public in 1965, received a nice valuation for his stock after a couple of years of strong growth, and then had the good sense to diversify into businesses that IBM couldn't squash without a moment's notice.

In 1968, Steinberg announced a tender offer for Reliance Insurance Company, an overcapitalized property and casualty insurer ten times larger than Leasco. The tender was successful and transformed Leasco from a niche equipment rental company to a Fortune 500 business with $27 million in annual earnings. Over the five-year period ending in 1968, Leasco stock had increased 5,410%. John Brooks called it "the undisputed king of all go-go stocks."[53]

The following year, Steinberg turned his attention to the banking industry, which he thought was as sleepy and conservative as the insurers. He began to buy shares in Chemical Bank and make early preparations for a tender offer. When Chemical's management got wind of Leasco's stock purchases, it waged a preemptive war. To force Steinberg's hand, the bank tipped off reporters that it was a target. It then used its power with regulators to stymie Steinberg's chances of launching a successful offer. The Department of Justice sent Leasco a letter raising antitrust concerns about a merger. The state of New York introduced and then passed an anti-bank-takeover law. Even the chairman of the U.S. Senate Committee on Banking introduced an anti-takeover law that would have blocked the takeover.[54]

"We'd touched some kind of nerve center," Saul Steinberg later told John Brooks. "All through those two weeks, bankers and businessmen I'd never met kept calling up out of the blue and attacking us for merely thinking about taking over a big bank," he said. "I always knew there was an Establishment—I just used to think I was a part of it."[55]

Steinberg's willingness to target giants was years ahead of its time, but luckily for him he was not yet thirty years old. It wasn't long until Steinberg and his fellow corporate raiders would have their day. With help from the efficient market hypothesis and the free market movement of the 1970s, raiders were viewed less as a scourge and threat to industry and more as a disciplinary force. In the '80s, the hostile raiders rode strong economic growth and Michael Milken's blank checkbook to fame and riches.

4

Carl Icahn versus Phillips Petroleum: The Rise and Fall of the Corporate Raiders

"However, what I strenuously oppose is the Board not allowing the shareholders to receive a fair price for all *their shares."*
—CARL ICAHN, 1985

ON FEBRUARY 4, 1985, Carl Icahn sent a letter to William Douce, chairman and CEO of Phillips Petroleum, offering to buy the company. He wrote that if Phillips did not accept his bid, he would launch a hostile tender offer for control. Phillips was Icahn's fifteenth target in his seven-year career as a raider, and his note to Douce was a classic corporate raider's "bear hug letter"—an offer to purchase the company, followed by threats should he be ignored. While Icahn had used the same playbook for his earlier battles, this showdown was markedly different: Phillips was one of the largest corporations in the world, many times bigger than any company he had ever pursued.

Icahn once said of his early corporate raids that he was merely "playing poker."[1] He borrowed heavily to fund his stock purchases, and his threats to tender for controlling stakes were often bluffs. He explained, "I didn't have the money to fight for the long haul—to pay the interest on the shares I held."[2] When Icahn threatened an $8.1 *billion* tender offer to take control of Phillips, few people took him seriously. Phillips's investment banker, Joe Fogg, told him, "That's preposterous. What the hell do you know about the oil business?"[3] Phillips, which had just endured an intense fight with raider T. Boone Pickens, ran full-page newspaper ads asking, "Is Icahn for Real?" This time, he was. "Cash! We have cash," he responded to Fogg. "We'll hire people who know about the oil business."[4]

Attached to Icahn's bear hug was a letter from Drexel Burnham Lambert's Leon Black. He wrote that the investment bank was "highly confident" it could raise $4 billion to fund the entire cash portion of Icahn's tender offer. If called to action, Drexel would raise the money for Icahn by selling a mixture of junk bonds and preferred stock to its network of high-yield investors. This would give Carl Icahn enough cash to buy out Phillips without borrowing a penny from any of the traditional, money-center banks. When Phillips questioned the value of Drexel's "highly confident" letter and said it proved Icahn had no real funding for his offer, Icahn gave Drexel the green light to obtain firm commitments for the first $1.5 billion. Michael Milken, the man behind Drexel's money machine, lined up the money in just forty-eight hours. Icahn ran his own newspaper ads stating, "MY TENDER OFFER IS FOR REAL."[5]

THE SECRET OF MY SUCCESS

America's fourth great merger wave proved to be much more substantial than its conglomerator-driven predecessor. The 22,000 mergers and acquisitions of the 1980s "deal decade" included leveraged buyouts by private equity firms, strategic acquisitions by corporations taking advantage of lax antitrust enforcement, and expansion into the U.S. market by international companies.[6] But it was the hostile takeovers, though they made up only a small percentage of the decade's deals, that defined Wall Street in the '80s.[7]

That the public was so taken by battles between such unsympathetic figures says something about the high stakes and drama of hostile takeovers in the 1980s. A few people may have looked on with disgust as vulture raiders pecked at fat cat CEOs, but for everyone else, these clashes at the top of our largest companies were Hollywood material.

Thirty years earlier, nobody really knew what to make of fledgling corporate raiders picking fights with company CEOs. By the 1980s, such men were known as "masters of the universe." In many ways, the corporate raiders of the '80s were not so different from the '50s Proxyteers. Both groups featured aggressive and motivated young businessmen operating on the fringes of Wall Street. But while the

Proxyteers struck fear into the hearts of CEOs with their ability to harness the discontent of public shareholders, the corporate raiders had something much more powerful at their disposal: ready cash. It came from Michael Milken and the vast market he created for new-issue junk bonds. Milken used his network of high-yield buyers to create a liquidity boom for young takeover artists. Financier Nelson Peltz got a $100 million "blind pool" in 1984. Fellow raider Ron Perelman got $750 million the following year. The next year, Sanford Sigoloff, the so-called Skillful Scalpel, got $1.2 billion.[8] The blind pools were raised without specific acquisitions in mind—they merely served to build war chests for future raids.

In her excellent book about the rise of Michael Milken and Drexel Burnham, *The Predators' Ball*, Connie Bruck called Icahn's battle with Phillips Petroleum "Drexel's gala coming-out." As for Carl Icahn, "it was a giant—almost magical—step up."[9] But within a year of the book's publication, Milken was indicted by a grand jury and the Drexel money machine ground to a halt. Icahn's assault on Phillips may have trumpeted the arrival of Drexel and the hostile raiders, but it also turned out to be the beginning of the end.

Since Milken's downfall, the giant pool of money scouring the globe for yield has grown immensely. The original-issue junk bond market he largely created has increased ten times over.[10] But even in the mid-2000s, when the entire world binged on cheap capital, nobody lined up to buy bonds from unproven corporate raiders angling for a buying spree.[11] That's quite a testament to Milken's immense power in the 1980s.

Whether Milken's machine at Drexel Burnham was made possible by abuses and securities violations, or whether it was a legitimate franchise created by a visionary genius, the fact remains that it was an aberration. When Milken was incarcerated and permanently barred from the industry, the raider movement of the 1980s faded away. But after Milken collapsed in flames, many of the men presumed to be his puppets—and ridiculed in some circles for being small-timers but for the good graces of Drexel Burnham—compounded their success. *The Predators' Ball* was particularly dismissive of Nelson Peltz, but over the next twenty years, he became a superstar, one of the elder statesmen of activist investors.

And of course there is Carl Icahn, brash and bold, gunning for bigger prey with every new investment. One of his latest targets is Apple, the largest company in the history of the world.

Behind the glamour and the glitz of the 1980s—and this was true in finance as well as in music, film, and literature—was an era of improbable substance. Flock of Seagulls might have had ridiculous hair, but "Space Age Love Song" is a pretty darn good song. When the stock market crashed in 1987, pundits called it the end of an age of debt-fueled excess. They were wrong. The corporate raiders were not dancing on a house of cards. Economic growth in the '80s was real, the stock market recovered its losses quickly, and the next decade would see further expansion and bigger deals.

More than any of the other raiders', Carl Icahn's career in the 1980s exemplified the decade. He had an unlikely ascent followed by a crash that almost left him ruined. Yet today he is the best known of the corporate raiders. And, to use the metric that probably matters most to him, he is also the richest. Early in his career, Icahn was dismissed as a simple "greenmailer," someone who would agitate at a company only to win a preferential buyout of his shares. But his tussle with Phillips showed him at his instinctive and gunslinging best. As a former Drexel managing director described it, "Carl Icahn became *the* Carl Icahn."[12] The deal also showcased the awesome power of Milken and Drexel, and by doing so, numbered the days for both. It was a landmark in the history of M&A, with a very early version of Martin Lipton's poison pill and the first "highly confident" letter. The drama began when Boone Pickens, a corporate raider who started his career at Phillips Petroleum, made a run at his former employer in late 1984.

Survival of the Unfittest

One of Carl Icahn's famous spiels is his "anti-Darwinian" theory of management. He explains that corporate America rewards politically minded people who don't rock the boat. Like Gilbert and Sullivan's Ruler of the Queen's Navy, who stayed close to his desk and never went to sea, these men climb to the top by being likable and nonthreatening. Because the

CEO then secures his position by making sure his second in command is even dumber than he is, the corporate governing class evolves into a vast idiocracy. Of course, Icahn is being somewhat facetious—he's quick to point out that he's worked with many excellent CEOs—but he's also onto something. The best and brightest candidates often don't make it to the top of the corporate ladder. Boone Pickens's experience at Phillips Petroleum brings Icahn's yarn to life.

Pickens joined Phillips as a junior geologist when he graduated from college in 1951. He had been born and raised in Oklahoma, and his father had worked for Phillips years earlier in Amarillo, Texas. But moving to Bartlesville, Oklahoma, where Phillips was headquartered, did not feel like a homecoming. His father hadn't much liked being a company man, and Boone would find it didn't suit him so well, either. His superiors at Phillips were bored and distrustful. He even got in trouble for staying at work late: He was to leave the office by five fifteen, with no exceptions.[13]

When Pickens was a well-site geologist in Corpus Christi, Texas, he saw firsthand how Phillips made noneconomic decisions. One time he determined that a new well was not going to produce enough oil to pay for its cost of completion. His boss agreed that they should plug the well, but headquarters in Bartlesville ordered them to complete it, at a cost of $300,000. As Pickens and his boss expected, it did not produce nearly enough oil to justify the cost. But senior management saved itself from having to report a "dry well." They were happy to waste real money if it made their batting average look better on paper.

After three years, Pickens had developed a good reputation at Phillips. But when a senior executive from Bartlesville told him, "If you're ever going to make it big with this company, you've got to learn to keep your mouth shut," Pickens decided making it big at Phillips wasn't worth it. He wrote in his memoirs, "I wasn't going to stay around for twenty years and then find myself bitter because I had pissed away my productive years."[14]

Thirty years later, Pickens came back to Phillips Petroleum as the largest stockholder, brandishing a hostile tender offer to buy an additional 15% of the company at $60 per share. Bartlesville was even less welcoming to Pickens the second time around. The town became a symbol of the threat corporate raiders held for small-town America. It was abuzz with residents in "Boone Buster" T-shirts at twenty-four-hour prayer vigils, who believed Pickens would gut the company, and thus the town, if he won control.

As the fight got messier—Phillips was suing Pickens in multiple jurisdictions to delay his tender offer—and as oil prices began to fall and put a dent in his investment thesis, Boone decided to focus his resources on another target, Unocal. Bartlesville cheered when Phillips negotiated a deal with Pickens to buy back his stock. But when the former Phillips geologist, who had been raised a couple of hours away, in Holdenville, Oklahoma, exited stage left, a streetwise poker player from Far Rockaway, Queens, was waiting in the wings.

ON AN EQUAL BASIS

When T. Boone Pickens first moved on Phillips Petroleum in December 1984, he vowed to not take greenmail during the fight. He told reporters he would not sell shares back to Phillips, "except on an equal basis with all other shareholders."[15] Greenmail had become a hot topic for debate earlier that year, when Texaco spent $1.3 billion buying out the Bass brothers at a huge premium to market.[16] Carl Icahn was also notorious as a greenmailer. In his fourteen deals leading up to Phillips, Icahn had taken greenmail in more than half of them. Public company shareholders were rightfully indignant at the wave of greenmail buyouts in the early 1980s. They were proof that all the talk from CEOs, as well as corporate raiders, about working on behalf of shareholders was mere posturing. Self-interest reigns supreme, and CEOs jumped at the opportunity to use company funds to free themselves from hostile attack. For their part, the raiders usually took the money, even though it weakened the company and further entrenched management.[17]

In his memoirs, Pickens wrote that Phillips used Joe Flom as an intermediary to propose a greenmail buyout worth as much as $70 per share—$300 million in profits for Boone at the expense of shareholders.[18] But Pickens not only had his reputation on the line for publicly stating he would reject greenmail; he also prided himself on being a champion of shareholders' rights. He proposed that the two sides work together to buy out Phillips. But management was not interested in teaming up with Pickens, despite his promises to keep the company basically unchanged.

Phillips proposed a complicated recapitalization plan that would pay Pickens $53 in cash per share. As part of the recap, Phillips's employee stock ownership plan would effectively purchase 30% of the company's remaining shares with debentures worth $60 per share. Phillips would also commit to asset sales to reduce debt, a dividend increase, and an additional $1 billion in share repurchases over the following year. Because Phillips's investment bankers valued the package at $53 per share for remaining shareholders, the company hoped it would satisfy Pickens as equal treatment.

Pickens wrote, "I thought $53 was too low, but we were in the mood to make a deal."[19] He said he would accept the plan if the debenture exchange for remaining shareholders was raised from 30% of the shares outstanding to 50%. The two sides ultimately agreed on 38%. Pickens signed a standstill agreement preventing him from raiding the company in the future. Phillips agreed to pay Pickens $25 million for his expenses, and both sides dropped their lawsuits. On his flight home, Pickens told his daughter, "I'm so glad to get loose from Phillips I don't know what to do. I felt the same way in 1954, when I quit."[20]

PHILLIPS'S RECAPITALIZATION PLAN was about as popular with shareholders as New Coke. The company's long-term investors didn't know what to make of the complicated stew of debentures they would receive in exchange for stock. The arbitrageurs, who had piled into Phillips with hopes of a near-term buyout, couldn't care less about the company's commitment to buy $1 billion in shares on the open market. Jesse "Big Daddy" Unruh, the colorful state treasurer of California, who sat on the boards of the California Public Employees' Retirement System (CalPERS) and the California State Teachers' Retirement System (CalSTRS), said he didn't "know what the hell [the deal] means" and worried it was just "camouflaged greenmail."[21] Arbitrageur Ivan Boesky, who had bought a huge stake in anticipation of a buyout, was despondent that Pickens sold out. He said, "It's Christmas. I was looking forward to a feast."[22] What everyone *did* understand was that Phillips stock had crashed 18% into the low $40s, and Pickens was walking away with $53 per share in cash plus $25 million to cover his expenses. Everybody thought it looked like greenmail.

Within a few days, several Wall Street analysts valued the recap at around $45 for shareholders. Influential energy analyst Kurt Wulff, from Donaldson, Lufkin & Jenrette, said it was worth only $42, although he thought Phillips might have a breakup value of $75 a share.[23] This caught Icahn's attention. As Icahn saw it, Boone Pickens, a smart guy who understood energy companies, was willing to bid $60 per share for Phillips. The company rejected his $60 offer, and then angered shareholders by offering them a package worth $45. To make matters worse, the deal would secure voting control for management by parking more than 30% of the company's stock in the employee stock plan. Icahn thought to himself, "Well, they have got to pay more."[24]

THE ARBITRAGE

Carl Icahn was born in Brooklyn in 1936 and grew up in Bayswater, Queens, which abuts Far Rockaway. Like many of the key figures in the history of corporate raiding, he was the very gifted child of a middle-class Jewish family. His mother was a fifth-grade teacher and his father was a frustrated lawyer who was cantor at a synagogue in Cedarhurst. According to his biographer, Mark Stevens, Icahn's parents were repelled by ostentatious wealth. Icahn said of his father, "Wealthy people outraged him. The social juxtaposition of a tiny group of people living in great splendor and many more living in abject poverty was anathema to him."[25] When one of the leaders at the synagogue recognized that the cantor's son was exceptionally smart, he arranged for him to get a scholarship to a private school. Icahn's parents visited the school but decided against exposing Carl to the values of entitled private school children. They kept him in public school.

Icahn was an excellent student at Far Rockaway High, which produced three Nobel Prize winners, including Richard Feynman, and MC Serch from 3rd Bass. When Icahn decided he wanted to go to Princeton, his advisor scoffed at the idea and said they wouldn't even read his application. He applied anyway—"I already put the stamp on it and don't want to waste it," he told her—and got in.[26]

At Princeton, Icahn didn't take his meals at the Ivy Club and transform himself into a future titan of Wall Street. He played a lot of chess, majored in philosophy, and won an award for his senior thesis, an epistemology paper on the empiricist criterion of meaning. After college, Icahn went to medical school at the insistence of his mother. When he realized he didn't much like being around sick people, he quit and joined the army. He figured at least the army would provide refuge from his mother's nagging. Carl didn't like the army, either, but he did make a lot of money playing poker against his commanding officers. When he got back to New York he took a job on Wall Street.

While Icahn was training to be a broker at Dreyfus, he made a killing using his poker winnings to speculate in the stock market. He accumulated almost $100,000 by the time the market cracked in 1962. When stocks declined, he lost everything. Icahn was in his mid-twenties, broke, and his mother wouldn't let him live at home unless he went back to medical school.[27] He wanted to continue working on Wall Street, and he'd learned a valuable lesson. He needed to put his brain to good use and develop some expertise—he needed a specialty.

WHEN CARL ICAHN searched for a niche in the market where he could develop some expertise, he found options trading. The options market was illiquid, with no central exchanges, and significantly less broking competition than equity markets. Icahn built a business model around transparent pricing and gained a large following for his weekly newsletter, which reported recent transactions and prices.[28] He infuriated his competitors, who thrived on an opaque market with wide spreads, but he built such a big book of business that nobody could afford to ignore him.

In the late 1960s, Icahn started his own firm, Icahn & Company. He hired Alfred Kingsley, a bright young analyst who would work with him for more than twenty-five years. The two men looked for other profitable niches in the markets and found arbitrage, which involved buying and selling securities from the same issuer. For example, they searched the mess of convertible LTV securities that Jim Ling dumped on the market for arbitrages—securities that were trading out of line with each other. The real profits in convertible arbitrage, however, come from tweaking your hedges to make directional bets on underlying stocks. Icahn and Kingsley made a lot of money using their expertise in options to enhance their arbitrage plays.

The two men began discussing "undervalued opportunities" in the mid-1970s. In 1977, Icahn bought 20% of Baird & Warner, a real estate investment trust, and asked for a board seat. When his request was ignored, Icahn ran a proxy fight to replace the board. He attacked the company's mediocre performance and promised to take no salary or fees should his slate win. When Icahn prevailed, he became chairman of the board and changed the company's name to Bayswater Realty. He immediately began liquidating assets and building the company's cash reserves. He would later invest Bayswater's cash in his takeover attempts.

ICAHN'S CAREER AS a corporate raider was off and running. He viewed his new investment strategy as "a kind of arbitrage."[29] In 1980, he wrote a memo for prospective investors outlining the opportunity. Icahn explained that asset values were increasing rapidly in the United States, but that market valuations of asset-rich public companies were not keeping pace. Because corporate management teams owned very little stock, they had little interest in selling their companies to achieve fair value for shareholders. There were plenty of interested buyers for these companies, but few of them would ever launch a hostile takeover attempt. Icahn continued, "However, whenever a fight for control is initiated, it generally leads to windfall profits for the shareholders."[30] Icahn had discovered an arbitrage between assets trapped in a public company and those sitting on the auction block. He wrote, "It is our contention that sizeable profits can be earned by taking large positions in 'undervalued' stocks and then attempting to control the destinies of the companies in question by: a) trying to convince management to liquidate or sell the company to a 'white knight'; b) waging a proxy contest; c) making a tender offer and/or; d) selling back our position to the company."[31]

As Icahn parlayed his winnings into larger and larger deals, his reputation began to precede him. When it did, he was often greeted with greenmail. Kingsley said, "For a while there, all we had to do was call up and they would pay. Some even called us first . . . it was like taking candy from a baby."[32] Icahn received large greenmail payments from Saxon Industries, American Can, Owens Illinois, Anchor Hocking, and Dan River.

As Icahn's fortune grew, he began to develop a philosophy of corporate governance. He frequently talked about the lack of accountability at public companies as a threat to American prosperity. But despite some of his populist rhetoric, Icahn never saw himself as a shareholder advocate as Boone Pickens did. In 2006, just before he turned seventy years old, Icahn summed it up for the *New Yorker* writer Ken Auletta, "I'm not going to sugarcoat this, I enjoy winning and making money. I've always been an obsessive character. I don't see a psychiatrist, but, if you really analyzed it, people like me are out to win, and winning is money."[33]

When Icahn came across Phillips Petroleum in late 1984, it looked ripe for the taking. Management had its back against the wall and had already tried to greenmail Pickens. Icahn felt certain that, if pressured, Phillips would sweeten the recapitalization for shareholders. To him, the situation cried out for a hostile raid. But Icahn had a problem. His strategy worked best when he could wield a big stick in the form of a tender offer for control. Phillips was number sixteen on the Fortune 500, with almost $17 billion of total assets. Icahn's stick just wasn't big enough. To be a legitimate threat to buy the entire company, he needed much more money. He needed thirty-eight-year-old wunderkind Michael Milken.

High Confidence

In less than a decade, Drexel Burnham transformed itself from a mid-tier investment bank with only a handful of clients to the envy of Wall Street. During that period, Michael Milken's domination of the rapidly growing market for junk bonds drove a twenty-five-fold increase in the bank's revenues.[34] In 1985, the year Carl Icahn took on Phillips, Milken focused on a promising new niche in the market—hostile raids financed by junk bonds. At the company's annual high-yield conference—the so-called Predators' Ball—Drexel CEO Fred Joseph said, "For the first time in history, we've leveled the playing field. The small can go after the big."[35] Within a few weeks of the conference, Pickens went after Unocal, Steve Wynn bid for Hilton Hotels, Sir James Goldsmith targeted Crown Zellerbach, and Lorimar bid for Multimedia.[36] All of these deals saw smaller players funded by Milken's bonds trying to gobble up billion-dollar companies. But none of them seemed as topsy-turvy as Carl Icahn's bid for Phillips Petroleum.

Icahn first worked with Drexel to recapitalize ACF, a railcar manufacturer he'd purchased in early 1984. Milken raised $380 million for ACF, which included about $150 million of overfunding for the company's war chest. Unlike most of Drexel's other clients, Icahn haggled over fees and refused to give up equity in ACF as part of the deal. Milken would have tripled the amount of overfunding if Icahn had been more generous. Icahn told Connie Bruck, "I don't like giving up equity. I've learned over the years, a dollar bill is a better partner than a partner."[37]

When Icahn met with Drexel to discuss Phillips, the haggling continued. Drexel was anxious to raise the $4 billion Icahn needed, but Icahn rejected the 1% commitment fee, which Drexel would charge even if the funds were not used. When Saul Steinberg's Disney raid ended in greenmail, for example, Milken's customers, who signed written commitments to buy bonds, received 1% without having to produce any money. Icahn told Drexel that a $40 million fee for the Phillips deal was out of the question.

On top of the steep costs, the entire process of soliciting commitments from a large universe of bond purchasers was problematic. It was impossible to prevent valuable information—in this case, that Icahn was preparing a hostile tender offer—from leaking out. Before Phillips, Drexel had lined up capital for two hostile raids: Pickens versus Gulf, and Steinberg versus Disney. Pickens was thwarted because the stock ran up so much *before* his announcement that he couldn't price an attractive tender offer. As for Drexel's handling of the Disney raid, the bank sent out sealed envelopes to prospective bond purchasers with a note warning that material inside information was enclosed.[38] For any

Drexel clients with a taste for illegal insider trading, this was practically an invitation to "front-run" the deal.

Icahn asked if Drexel could provide its own commitment letter, just as large commercial banks do when they finance acquisitions. Drexel's Leon Black balked at the suggestion but proposed a letter saying the bank was "highly confident" it could raise the money. As Black told Connie Bruck, Icahn considered the idea, then turned to his lawyer and asked, "What do you think?" The lawyer replied, "Leon's full of shit. It's not legally binding, what good is it?"[39] If Drexel's high confidence turned out to be misplaced, Icahn would be the one looking like an idiot.

After sleeping on it, Icahn called up Leon Black and said they should give it a try. Thus, out of Carl Icahn's reluctance to pay a high commitment fee, and the inability of Milken's high-yield buyers to keep a lid on inside information, the "highly confident letter" was born. It was quickly accepted by the financial community and would serve as credible evidence that a buyer could finance an acquisition. It didn't take investment bankers long to figure out they could charge real money for this particular lack of a real commitment. When Pickens went after Unocal, just two months after Icahn's attack on Phillips, Drexel charged $3.5 million for it.[40]

CARL ICAHN FIRED his opening shot on war-weary Phillips Petroleum on the evening of February 4, 1985 (page 220). He sent a package to the company's investment bankers containing his letter to Chairman and CEO William Douce, along with Drexel's "highly confident letter." Icahn begins his letter by announcing that he owns 7.5 million shares of Phillips, "which makes me one of the company's largest shareholders." He writes that he has examined the recapitalization plan and finds it "grossly inadequate." His alternative? Icahn offers to buy the company for $55 per share, composed of $27.50 in cash and another $27.50 in subordinated notes. He explains that Drexel Burnham is "highly confident" it can raise the necessary cash by February 21.

Icahn then offers Douce a way to free Phillips from his bear hug: "If you raise your offer so that you acquire *all* the outstanding Phillips shares for a package worth $55 per share, I will gladly step aside." Icahn warns that if Phillips rejects his buyout offer and refuses to offer share-holders $55 per share, he will run a proxy fight to defeat the recapital-ization and make a hostile tender offer for 51% of the shares. He gave management two days to accept or reject his buyout offer.

On February 6, the day of the deadline, Phillips sued Icahn in the U.S. district court in Tulsa for violating proxy solicitation and antimanipula-tion rules. The company also made two slight changes that sweetened its recapitalization for shareholders. It added a new preferred stock divi-dend, and replaced the share repurchase with an immediate cash tender offer. Phillips said these changes increased the value of the recap by $3 per share. But into this little bag of goodies, Phillips slipped an unwel-come morsel—a "rights plan" to preserve long-term value. Boone Pick-ens, whose buyout deal forced him to support management, described the rights differently: "Bullshit! This was a poison pill."[41]

Now I've Got the Pill

Martin Lipton created the first poison pill in 1982, to defend El Paso Nat-ural Gas against a hostile takeover attempt by Burlington Northern. Lipton saw the pill as a way to slow "two tier and bust up takeovers" that were sprung on companies with no notice. The poison pill does not prevent hostile takeovers, but it blocks raiders from buying effective control on the open market, or stampeding shareholders into a front-loaded tender offer.[42] Icahn saw the poison pill as "legal trickery." As he told his biographer, Mark Stevens, "What it amounts to is a law firm trying to rewrite the law."[43]

In a typical poison pill, a company gives its shareholders special rights that are triggered when a buyer crosses a certain ownership threshold. The trick is, once the threshold is crossed, the rights are exercisable for everyone *except* the buyer. When shareholders exercise the rights—usually for preferred or common shares—they dilute the buyer's own-ership stake.

The "rights plan" Lipton designed for Phillips was unique. Had a buyer crossed 30% ownership, the other stockholders could convert each share into $62 worth of senior debt in Phillips paying 15% interest.

The buyer would be left owning a dangerously overleveraged company with $7 billion of short-term debt. On the surface, the purpose of the pill was to pay shareholders "fair value"—which management pegged at $62 per share—if any shareholder crossed 30%. In reality, it served as a shark repellant. Douce thought nobody in their right mind would trigger the pill and bury the company under a mountain of debt.

The following day, Icahn sent a letter to Douce that took everyone by surprise. He wrote, "In order to activate the rights for Phillips stock-holders, I intend to initiate a tender offer for approximately 25% of Phillips' common stock."[44] With Icahn's 5% ownership, his tender for 25% would intentionally trigger Lipton's poison pill. Douce couldn't believe it. He wasn't sure if Icahn was really threatening to use Phillips's own poison pill as a way to purchase the company, or if he had simply mis-understood the rights.[45] Douce sent an emotional reply asking Icahn to reconsider the sweetened recap: "We believe that its value is so close to the values you seem to find, that you would not really wish to attempt to force the bust-up and liquidation of Phillips, and the resultant hard-ship to the thousands of employees who would be thrown out of work, all for the purpose of your making a few dollars more per share profit on the stock you bought during the past few weeks. Phillips is acting re-sponsibly and responsively to the interests of its shareholders. We hope that you too will act responsibly."[46]

Poison pills were a rarity at the time, and Phillips's particular "rights plan" had a peculiar structure. Icahn was quoted in the *New York Times* saying, "I responded by offering, in effect, to swallow the poison pill."[47] But when the company clarified the pill's structure, Icahn issued a statement complaining that Phillips had not previously disclosed its "discriminatory provisions." Douce needled Icahn in a public letter for misunderstanding the pill: "We suggest that you might want to review the supplementary proxy material prior to making further proposals to take over or bust up Phillips."[48] But, in fact, the brouhaha benefited Icahn by bringing extra media attention to Phillips's poison pill. The compa-ny's institutional shareholders were already frustrated about the recapi-talization. They viewed the pill as a punch in the gut.

On February 13, Icahn commenced a tender offer for control of Phillips

Petroleum at $60 per share. It was the largest tender offer ever made without committed capital.[49] The offer was contingent on shareholders voting down the recapitalization at the February 22 shareholders' meeting, and, of course, Drexel's ability to raise the money. To sidestep the poison pill, Icahn ran an alternative slate of directors and conditioned his tender on their election and on the repeal of the "rights plan." If the tender offer was unsuccessful, Icahn wrote, he would run another proxy fight at the next shareholders' meeting. He vowed to liquidate the company if he won that proxy fight. The message was clear: Carl Icahn is not going away.

ABOUT 4,500 PEOPLE packed into a gymnasium in Bartlesville for the shareholders' meeting. Outside the building, a marching band played while a group of schoolchildren protested Icahn.[50] Inside, an emotional and partisan crowd rallied to the company's defense. One shareholder drew loud cheers when he said, "people who've bought stock in Phillips in the last few months are not your real stockholders. . . . They want that extra dollar or quarter. I hate to use this word, but we call them prostitutes."[51] Another shareholder voiced his displeasure at the recapitalization and the Pickens buyout before adding, "But I'm going to vote for it. It's the personal equation. I fear for the people who live in Bartlesville, and for the retired people who stay on here for the rest of their lives."[52] A Lutheran pastor echoed that sentiment, saying, "There came into Egypt a pharaoh who did not know Joseph. That's what Bartlesville is afraid of—a pharaoh who does not know Joseph. We are afraid their ownership will change to people who do not care. Without care, there is no community."[53]

Alfred Kingsley was greeted with groans when he got up to speak on behalf of Icahn. In response to the concern from townspeople, he offered, "We also love Bartlesville. We love all the employees and Phillips. What we're against is the recapitalization." The comment elicited snickers from the crowd.[54] But despite the anger at Icahn and the concern over the fate of the town, the real issue at hand was the recapitalization. A lawyer for CalSTERS quieted the room with his statement, "We are long-term investors. We have owned Phillips stock for many years—we're in it for the long haul. And there are certain aspects of the recap plan we don't approve . . . the poison pill—if it's not a poison pill then a difficult vitamin to swallow. We're opposed to greenmail, and we think the payment to T. Boone Pickens was greenmail. We are voting in opposition to the recapitalization."[55]

About ninety minutes into the meeting, Douce surprised shareholders by announcing a recess. He said the meeting would reconvene the next day, a Saturday, and that the polls would remain open. The following afternoon, Phillips postponed the meeting again, this time until Tuesday. The company used the delay to try to convince some of the larger holders to switch their votes. It didn't work. On March 3, Phillips announced that the recapitalization had lost by a whopping 9 million votes. It was the first time a company as large as Phillips Petroleum had ever lost a proxy fight.[56]

In the end, Phillips sweetened its recapitalization one more time and eliminated the plan to park shares in the employees' stock trust. This time the market agreed that the recap was really worth around $55 per share. After an all-night negotiating session that saw Icahn storm out of the room twice, Phillips agreed to pay $25 million for his expenses. Icahn walked away with an estimated $50 million in profits in just ten weeks.[57] In an ironic twist, Carl Icahn, the reputed greenmailer, won a richer payout for Phillips shareholders, while Boone Pickens, defender of shareholders' rights, accepted a deal most people thought was greenmail. Icahn didn't let it get to his head, though. "I'm happy the shareholders benefited," he said. "But I'm no Robin Hood. I enjoy making the money."[58]

Passing Fads

Very few onlookers thought Icahn might actually buy Phillips. Even some large Phillips shareholders who supported Icahn's proxy fight said they didn't believe his bid was serious.[59] They thought he was in the stock just to squeeze a few more dollars out of the recapitalization. But not long after Phillips, Icahn proved he was willing to acquire even his most unwieldy targets.

In the spring of 1985, Icahn purchased a large stake in TWA and got in a bidding war to take over the company with Texas Air's Frank Lorenzo, who had purchased Continental in 1981. Lorenzo had long coveted TWA, but he felt Icahn was merely angling for a good price for his equity stake. In what turned out to be the early stages of the face-off, Lorenzo had a chance to win TWA if he also agreed to pay $9 million in fees to Icahn. He balked. "Carl will never take over the airline," he said.[60] Lorenzo was wrong.

TWA turned out to be a near catastrophe for Icahn. He had a few successes on the cost side—mostly because he used his credibility as a potential liquidator to bludgeon the labor unions into major concessions—but Icahn was never willing to make the large capital investments necessary to make TWA competitive. This was probably a wise move, but not wise enough to make up for the mistake of buying the airline in the first place.

In 1988, Icahn raised $660 million for TWA through Drexel junk bonds and paid himself a large dividend. From there, he sold off whatever decent assets TWA had left. As the airline slid toward bankruptcy, the labor unions worried that Icahn might leave the company with no ability to fund its enormous pension obligations. In 1991, the U.S. Congress passed legislation designed to ensure that Icahn's personal assets could be seized to help fund a pension shortfall.[61] When TWA filed for bankruptcy two months after the bill passed, the federal government's Pension Benefit Guaranty Corporation said it would pursue Icahn for the entire $1.1 billion shortfall.

BY THE END of the 1980s, the golden age of corporate raiding was fading away. A few high-profile blowups, including the bankruptcy of Robert Campeau's overleveraged department store empire, rattled the junk bond market. Beneath the headline failures, junk default rates were creeping up and would blow open in the 1990–91 recession. Corporate raiders were having a harder time finding compelling bargains, it was more difficult to raise capital to pursue them, and, when they did, the target company's defenses were likely to be much stronger.

After the Phillips Petroleum proxy fight, *American Lawyer* magazine's Steven Brill quoted a well-regarded takeover lawyer who dismissed

Martin Lipton's poison pill as a "passing fad." Brill agreed, writing, "soon we'll all find out that in *The Roaring Eighties* fads like the pill pass quickly indeed."[62] But just a few months later, the Delaware Supreme Court upheld the pill's legality in its *Moran v. Household* decision. By the end of the decade, more than one thousand companies had implemented a poison pill, including 60% of the Fortune 500.[63]

In addition to growing acceptance of the poison pill, the regulatory environment got tougher for raiders. In 1988, Delaware enacted an antitakeover statute, Section 203, which prevented shareholders from pursuing takeovers within three years of crossing 15% ownership. The U.S. Congress also considered various takeover bills. Boone Pickens believes a proposal in the House of Representatives to tax mergers and acquisitions was a major contributor to the 1987 crash.[64]

Still, none of these factors was especially unique to the 1980s. Previous merger booms ended because of higher lending standards, fewer good targets, sophisticated corporate defenses, regulatory pressure, and slowing economic growth. What was different in the '80s—what ushered in the era of superstar corporate raiders and then made it disappear forever—were the rise and fall of Michael Milken, and the hard-knocks education of large institutional investors.

CORNERS CUT

Right before Judge Kimba Wood sentenced Michael Milken to ten years in prison, she spoke about the public's intense interest in Milken's fate. She'd received many letters demanding a harsh sentence because of the economic damage wrought by the abuses of the '80s. It was late 1990 and the country was halfway through a recession, as well as a financial crisis that saw a third of all savings and loan associations fail.[65] "These writers ask for a verdict on a decade of greed," Judge Wood said.[66]

Even Wall Street's finest were shocked when federal prosecutors revealed that Drexel Burnham paid Michael Milken $550 million in 1987. Billionaire David Rockefeller, former chairman of Chase Manhattan Bank and the grandson of John D. Sr., worried that the financial system was "unbalanced."[67] And to deepen the suffering of his envious investment banking peers, Milken augmented his Drexel income via hundreds of investment partnerships he managed from his trading desk. Some of the partnerships even bought and sold junk bonds directly from Drexel.[68] According to the General Accounting Office, Milken's twenty-five largest partnerships distributed $2 billion from 1981 to 1988, with $1 billion going directly to Milken. In *Den of Thieves*, James Stewart estimated that Milken and his family were worth at least $3 billion by the end of 1986.[69]

Milken's defenders say that he was persecuted for his immense wealth, as well as his role in helping raiders like Carl Icahn attack the corporate establishment. His crimes, they argue, were trivial. On this issue, they have a point. Much like Louis Wolfson going down in 1967 for selling unregistered stock, Milken got a ten-year sentence for offenses that, for a lesser investment banker, would never be prosecuted criminally. The only reason he pleaded guilty to any counts at all was that the government offered a deal to drop the charges against his younger brother.[70]

But even if the government's charges seem flimsy, something about the Milken legend doesn't sit right with me. Making gobs of money is not a crime, but no bond salesman before or after has made anything close to half a billion 1987 dollars in a year. Milken was not the first bond salesman to dominate a profitable niche in the market and win large profits as it grew. But ultimately, this is a competitive business. Why was Milken so successful at defending his lucrative franchise as junk bonds went mainstream?

Milken pleaded guilty to charges involving tax avoidance schemes and "stock parking" deals that helped clients avoid SEC filing requirements. Four of the six counts involved arrangements with arbitrageur Ivan Boesky, several of which saw Milken promise to cover any of Boesky's losses. This was a running theme in Drexel's shadier deals. In one example, Wickes, a retailer controlled by raider Sanford Sigoloff, was trying to rid itself of a pesky convertible preferred issue that cost the company $15 million in yearly dividends. The company was permitted to retire the preferreds if the common stock closed at 6⅛ or better for 20 days out of any 30-day stretch. On day 29 of a stretch that saw Wickes meet the target

19 days, Drexel convinced Boesky's firm to aggressively buy at the close to ensure a 6⅛ closing price.[71] This might have been a "minor" offense, but it was clear market manipulation.

Even more troubling was the way Milken created captive customers and then enriched their managers with gifts or participation in his partnerships. Milken first raised capital for Kinder-Care, which ran day-care centers, in 1978. As the company grew, it began to buy loads of junk bonds from Drexel. This was common for Milken's issuers: He often overfunded them and then sold them other junk bond issues. Kinder-Care later increased its junk bond capacity by purchasing an insurer and two S&Ls. At one point, the company held about $650 million of Drexel junk bonds.[72]

Presumably as a reward for being such good customers, Milken funneled valuable securities to Kinder-Care's executives. Kinder-Care's high-yield portfolio manager later testified that Milken gave warrants in a company called Storer Broadcasting to him and Kinder-Care's CEO. Buyout shop KKR had given Storer warrants to Milken as an equity kicker for investors in Drexel's offering. Little did they know that Milken kept most of the warrants for his partnerships and distributed the rest to cronies. Kinder-Care's shareholders deserved the warrants for the company's participation in the Storer deal. Milken instead gave them directly to the company's managers. They allegedly made more than a million dollars on warrants they received from Drexel.[73]

Tom Spiegel, CEO of Columbia Savings & Loan, fared even better on Storer. Milken gave warrants to a partnership controlled by the Spiegel family that made $7 million of profit in about a year.[74] Columbia was one of Milken's best customers: Between 1982, when the Garn–St. Germain Depository Institutions Act allowed federally insured S&Ls to buy junk bonds, and 1989, Columbia bought $10 billion of Drexel issues. Milken even cut the Spiegels in on one of his lucrative partnerships, which made bonanza investment returns.

Milken's top customers became almost indiscriminate buyers of Drexel's bonds. Investigators were surprised to learn that many of Drexel's bond issues were taken up by only a handful of purchasers. One insurance company, First Executive, participated in about 90% of

Drexel's new issues, and bought $40 billion worth of junk bonds from 1982 to 1987.[75] First Executive, as you probably guessed, also had a very tight relationship with Milken. The company frequently won insurance business from Drexel-funded buyout targets. When Ron Perelman acquired Revlon, for instance, he moved the company's pension plan over to First Executive.

THE VERDICT

At Milken's sentencing, Judge Wood said she did not know how much of Drexel Burnham's junk bond business was legitimate. She could not make that judgment, she said, but maybe someday a historian could. That was twenty-five years ago. Within a year of Milken's sentencing, the U.S. economy sprang back to life. As it turned out, the 1990–91 recession was a mild affair that stood between the deal decade and the longest expansion in American history—1991 until the bursting of the Internet bubble. The S&L crisis, which spanned a decade, lasted until 1995. At the end it was clear that the industry's collapse into widespread fraud was not caused by the handful of doomed S&Ls loaded up with Milken's bonds.[76] And rather than disappear with Milken, the junk bond market thrived. In the late 1990s, U.S. junk bond issuance skyrocketed to levels many times higher than the peak years of the 1980s.

Today, Michael Milken's reputation is in repair. A 2010 article in the *Economist* about Drexel's legacy called Milken's "democratization of credit" a "boon to the American economy."[77] His legal troubles were barely discussed. Milken's name adorns George Washington University's school of public health. An institute for business law at the University of California, Los Angeles is named for his brother. Milken's think tank, the Milken Institute, hosts an annual global conference with even more star power than the original Predators' Ball.

For a young business school student in the early 2000s, the story of Michael Milken was no longer a cautionary tale about greed and corruption. It went a little like this: Mike Milken was a visionary genius whose innovations revolutionized Wall Street and the broader economy. Unlike his investment banking peers, he was studious and professorial. He had an encyclopedic knowledge of junk bonds, and figured out that a broad portfolio of them would outperform higher-rated bonds. Junk bonds had higher default rates, true, but interest payments and capital appreciation from surviving companies more than compensated for the failures. Of course, Milken's brand of genius, alien to most men of business, comes with a dark side. It caused him to cut corners he did not need to cut, drawing the ire of regulators who already resented him. Though none of his transgressions had any material impact on his success, they ended Milken's career.

I was one of those young students who believed that Milken was more Icarus than Autolycus (the prince of thieves). My first job out of business school was at a distressed-debt hedge fund, where we channeled one of Milken's best insights: Being smart about risk doesn't mean buying the best assets and ignoring the bad ones. We spent our time looking at the dirtiest scraps in the junkyard, and we made a lot of money buying really terrible companies at great prices. Our business model was indebted to Milken—both the intellectual property and the raw materials, the bonds themselves. Of course, I like to think I've gotten a little wiser over time. I now spend much more of my time tracking really good businesses and waiting for the market to sell them to me for cheap. And when I look back to my days of buying subordinated debt of crappy industrial companies in default, I can't help but think I got the legend of Michael Milken wrong.

Michael Milken occupied an obscure niche in the market that enjoyed strong tailwinds from falling interest rates and economic growth. As Milken achieved greater scale, he directed an impressive amount of capital through large, captive customers like First Executive and Columbia, loyal and indebted clients like Ivan Boesky, and his own investment partnerships, which he controlled alongside Drexel's funds. Milken was in a perfect position to manipulate the market in order to greatly expand his selling power. Along with his bonds, Milken's customers bought the idea that he was a visionary, ideological genius who cared about "democratizing capital" more than making money for himself. In truth, he was a master salesman, a likable fraternity president with a gift for evaluating people as well as bonds. Like any good bond salesman, when the party was ending, he stuffed his most gullible clients with crappy paper while there was still money to be made. Columbia, First Executive, and Kinder-Care would all go bust.

Drexel's money machine was not the invention of a visionary genius. Instead, Milken greased its wheels to create artificial, indiscriminate demand for his junk bond issues. For men like Carl Icahn, Ron Perelman, and Nelson Peltz, Milken created a once-in-a-lifetime opportunity to raid America's largest corporations. They wisely took advantage of it and never looked back.

We're Not Gonna Take It

Corporate raiders in the 1980s were not only blessed with Michael Milken bearing wads of money; they were aided by passive institutional investors who struggled with their responsibilities as large public company shareholders. The investors sat idly by as Carl Icahn and his cohorts took candy from their babies in the form of greenmail. By the mid-'80s, their frustration was building at both greenmailing raiders and self-interested management teams. But they had a hard time keeping tabs on fast-moving corporate defense teams and hostile raiders.

Not long after the Phillips vote, Carl Icahn told Steven Brill that he attributed his victory to the poison pill. "That turned everybody off," he said.[78] Martin Lipton didn't argue. "Carl's right," he told Brill. "We just completely misread this. We didn't appreciate how these institutional voters just cared about keeping the company in play."[79] When Brill polled Phillips's institutional shareholders himself, he agreed with Lipton and found "by and large a surprisingly uninformed and just plain dumb group of voters." One pension fund manager who didn't understand the details of the recap, the poison pill, or Icahn's tender offer bristled at a question about the long-term interests of shareholders: "I'll define the long term," the man said. "That's my job. And I define it as jumping to the best opportunities I find every day."[80]

But the institutional holders who weren't just plain dumb were just plain angry. A California money manager told Brill, "We believe shareholders ought to have the right to vote on all offers. And we also saw the part of the recap plan that would put the company in control of the employees' trust as a total management entrenchment device. You know, we're not going to take that stuff anymore, and those investment bankers and lawyers who get millions of dollars to come up with this garbage ought to be thrown out on their asses."[81]

After suffering several years of egregious greenmails and costly entrenchment tactics, institutional investors were teetering on the edge of rebellion. General Motors' buyout of Ross Perot the next year drove them into the abyss at 55 miles per hour. By the end of the decade, many large institutional investors were doing their homework. They ran proxy fights, questioned management teams as well as hostile raiders, and formed opinions on sophisticated corporate governance issues. With Milken's fund-raising machine shut down and historically passive institutional investors finally using their brains, the last great hostile raider era was over.

BECAUSE THE PHILLIPS raid made Icahn a public figure, TWA's highly publicized collapse left him an easy target. He was overdue for a humbling. Before TWA imploded, Icahn was asked at a congressional hearing why he chose the airline as a target. He responded, "Do you ask Willie Mays why he jumped a certain way for a ball?"[82] But despite the blame and ridicule, Icahn emerged from TWA's wreckage like Chuck Yeager in *The Right Stuff*. Rather than being forced to fund the company's massive pension shortfall in 1992, he got away with loaning the airline $200 million and agreeing to sponsor its pension plans for eight years.

Today, Carl Icahn continues to produce stellar investment returns by capitalizing on the arbitrage between public and private market valuations that he wrote about in his 1980 memo. But he's never matched the hot streak that culminated in his 1985 bear hug of Phillips Petroleum. He had fifteen successful campaigns in a row, most of them more audacious than their predecessor. Early in the streak, he profited when companies abused their passive institutional shareholders by employing greenmail. At Phillips, Icahn channeled shareholders' anger over greenmail—with the critical help of Michael Milken's money machine—to win concessions from management. Carl Icahn was economic self-interest personified, and he was willing to wear whatever hat it took to generate profits. But there was one company Icahn didn't want to go after. When Alfred Kingsley pitched General Motors as the perfect target, Icahn rejected the idea. "They'll hang us," he said.[83] In the mid-1980s, there was really only one man with enough political goodwill to wage war with the mighty General Motors: Ross Perot. Let's reconvene in the Motor City, where business management as a scientific discipline was born . . . and where it died.

Ross Perot versus General Motors:
The Unmaking of the Modern Corporation

*"An increasing number of GM people are asking me
to tell you something that—*

—they feel you need to know;
—are concerned that you won't want to hear;
—that they are afraid to tell you.

*I will tell you anything that can build and strengthen GM,
whether you want to hear it or not."*

—ROSS PEROT, 1985

NO CHALLENGE WAS TOO great for Ross Perot. When the
Iranian government imprisoned two of his senior employees
over a contract dispute in 1979, Perot boarded a plane to Teh-
ran, entered the country on his own passport, and assembled a team led
by an ex–Green Beret to break his men out of prison.[1] Iran was on the
verge of revolution, and U.S. diplomatic efforts were stalling, so he took
matters into his own hands.

Ten years earlier, Perot tried to deliver a Braniff jet full of gifts and
food to American POWs in Vietnam without the permission of North
Vietnamese diplomats.[2] In 1983, he led a commission to reform public education in Texas that recommended deemphasizing high school
football. And of course, Ross Perot ran for U.S. president in 1992 on a
pro-choice, pro-gun, protectionist, antidrug, pro-environment, budget-
hawk platform that won 19% of the popular vote, the most by a third-
party candidate since Teddy Roosevelt in 1912.

Because of his presidential run—and folk-hero exploits including
his record-breaking ascent to Eagle Scout—some may forget that Ross

Perot is also one of America's greatest businessmen. In the late 1950s, Perot started his career at IBM, where he quickly became the company's best-ever salesman. In 1962, he reached his annual sales quota on January 19.[3] Later that year he formed his own company, Electronic Data Systems, which became one of the highest-flying stocks in the go-go stock market of the 1960s.

While Ross Perot was making a name for himself, another American icon, General Motors, was faltering. GM was the largest carmaker in the world, but it was losing market share to foreign competitors like Toyota and Honda. In 1980, GM lost money for the first time since 1921.[4] Even Ford and Chrysler, GM's much smaller domestic competitors, would surpass the company in efficiency.[5] Superstar engineer John DeLorean, who quit GM in 1973, explained the decline: "What was happening was a predictable result . . . when the control of a consumer goods company moves into the hands of purely financial managers."[6] GM's management had been taken over by a succession of accountants who valued short-term profits over quality products. One of these bean counters was Roger Smith, who summed up his management style: "I look at the bottom line—it tells me what to do."[7]

When Roger Smith became chairman and CEO of General Motors in 1981, he embarked on a massive acquisition and investment binge to modernize operations. In 1984 he set his sights on EDS and bought the company in a deal that made Ross Perot GM's largest shareholder and added him to the board of directors. GM's investors were enthusiastic about the legendary Ross Perot bringing energy to the boardroom. Smith explained, "Perot's style fits right in with what we're trying to do at General Motors."[8]

Ross Perot did not fit in at GM for very long. The more he learned about the car business, the more he thought Smith's fascination with new technology was missing the point. While General Motors spent billions of dollars on robotics and automated manufacturing, Japanese automakers were winning market share by building better cars on old equipment. GM was not tapping the potential of its employees, and the company's huge bureaucracy couldn't get out of its own way. Perot later told *Fortune* magazine, "I come from an environment where if you see a snake, you kill it. At GM, if you see a snake, the first thing you do is go hire a consultant on snakes. Then you get a committee on snakes, and then you discuss it for a couple of years. The most likely course of action is—nothing. You figure, the snake hasn't bitten anybody yet, so you just let him crawl around on the factory floor. We need to build an environment where the first guy who sees the snake kills it."[9]

On October 23, 1985, Perot penned a scathing five-page letter to Roger Smith, challenging his autocratic management style. He wrote:

In the interest of GM, you are going to have to stop treating me as a problem and accept me as—

—A large stockholder
—An active board member
—An experienced businessman

You need to recognize that I am one of the few people who can and will disagree with you. . . .

I do not believe that GM can become world class and cost competitive by throwing technology and money at its problems.

—The Japanese are not beating us with technology or money. They use old equipment, and build better, less expensive cars by better management, both in Japan and with UAW workers in the US.
—We are not closing the quality and price gaps in spite of huge expenditures on automating plants. The fact that we have not set a date to have competitive prices indicates the prevalent attitudes about our will to win.

The foundations for a future relationship are honesty, openness and candor—or simply put, mutual trust and respect. From this point forward, actions count—words do not. We must focus all our energies on helping GM win.

Ross Perot's reason for tackling General Motors was simple: "It was the opportunity to save millions of American jobs. It was too exciting to pass up."[10] This is a man who has engaged in many difficult battles over his lifetime and fought to their end. But perhaps none of these was harder than making positive changes at a poorly run public corporation. Perot's letter turned out to be the breaking point in his relationship with Roger Smith. From that moment forward, Smith focused his energy on getting Ross Perot off the board of directors.

General Motors ended up spending $80 billion on new plants and equipment through the course of Smith's nine-year tenure as chairman, plus another $10 billion for acquisitions of high-tech companies like Hughes Aircraft, whose purchase was approved over Perot's lone dissenting vote. Much of this money was wasted, as was more than $700 million used to buy out Ross Perot in 1986 to make him walk away from GM. One of the world's greatest industrial companies—once a model of good management and governance—was on a path to insolvency.

When the buyout was made public, Perot, who was as astounded as anyone that GM's board of directors would approve such a large payment just to get rid of him, challenged shareholders to do something about it. He said, "I've alerted the stockholders that if they accept this, then they deserve what they get."[11] Perot's battle with General Motors became a turning point in shareholder activism and public company governance in the United States. Large pension funds that had held GM stock for years without making a peep were aghast that a company would spend $700 million to *weaken* its board of directors. Institutional investors were finally discovering their voice. Ross Perot ultimately left General Motors without accomplishing any of his lofty goals for the company, but on his way out he stoked a fire under the country's largest institutional shareholders that remains burning today.

Alfred Sloan's Triumph

Roger Smith receives a lot of blame for the demise of General Motors, but the company's woes were decades in the making—the legacy of a long line of ineffective CEOs. Before we can properly examine Smith's last-ditch gambit on technology, Ross Perot's failure to sway a single

GM director to his cause, or the sleeping institutional giants that constituted GM's shareholder base, we need to understand how General Motors evolved into such an unwieldy beast. How does one of the world's greatest corporations become one of the worst companies ever to exist?

General Motors was founded by William Durant, a leading carriage manufacturer who refused to let technological progress sink his fortune. He was dubious of "horseless carriages," which were loud, unreliable, and dangerous in the hands of most drivers. But unlike most of his competitors, Durant embraced the future.[12] He became general manager of Buick, and then formed General Motors in 1908 to acquire other automakers.

While Henry Ford centralized his operations around the Model T, Durant believed in diversification. General Motors owned dozens of companies that made cars, car parts, and accessories. Each one was effectively autonomous, and Durant kept only loose financial control over the whole operation. Durant believed that automobiles would soon gain mass acceptance and sell over a million units a year—an extreme view at the time—but he wasn't sure which approaches to automotive engineering and design would win out. To be safe, Durant had his fingers in a lot of pies.

Durant's lack of fiscal discipline kept General Motors permanently on the brink of default. This was a bad place to be in the boom-and-bust auto business, and Durant lost control of GM several times in its early history. In 1915, he found a financial backer in Pierre Du Pont, whose DuPont Company made numerous cash infusions into GM. Every time Durant needed more capital for an acquisition, or merely to stay afloat, DuPont put in more money. By the end of 1919, DuPont owned almost 30% of General Motors.

When the depression of 1920–21 struck, Durant lost control of his company for good. He racked up more than $30 million of margin debt trying to prop up GM's stock price as the market fell. DuPont was forced to bail out Durant, who resigned as president in November 1920. The Fabulous Billy Durant never again matched the success he achieved at General Motors. At the end of his life, he was managing a bowling alley in Flint, Michigan. When Durant died in 1947, he was reported to have lived out his last years in poverty. In fact, he and his wife received a generous pension arranged by Alfred P. Sloan Jr., the man who would take General Motors' random assortment of car companies and turn them into the greatest industrial enterprise on earth.[13]

AFTER DURANT'S EXIT in 1920, Pierre Du Pont faced the challenge of how to manage General Motors and its disparate divisions. Du Pont had no operating experience in the industry and knew he could not rely on his intuition as Durant did. He decided to restructure General Motors based on an organization study drafted by Alfred Sloan. Du Pont promoted Sloan to run GM's operations, and then made him president in 1923.

Alfred Sloan started his career at a New Jersey roller bearings company that serviced the automotive industry. He rose to general manager before selling the business to Durant in 1916. Durant must have seen something special in Sloan, because he immediately put him in charge of his entire car parts division. It was there that Sloan developed the principles behind his groundbreaking organization study.

The car accessories division looked a lot like the rest of GM. It was a diverse collection of companies scattered across the country. Sloan wanted to run the division in the decentralized spirit of General Motors, because he knew he was not fit to intervene in businesses that made ignitions, radiators, or horns. But he saw that the utter lack of financial controls wreaked havoc on his performance. This issue plagued the rest of General Motors as well. There was no logic to the company's capital spending choices because nobody could evaluate the best uses of capital. Division heads supported each other's expenditure plans in order to ensure that their own budgets were approved. Sloan wrote, "This was decentralization with a vengeance."[14]

While Sloan was not an accountant, he developed a system to track the performance of his companies. His primary focus was not the profit of each business, but its return on investment. By learning where the highest returns on invested capital could be obtained, Sloan knew which businesses warranted additional funding and which ones needed improvement. As he later wrote, "no other financial principle with which

I am acquainted serves better than rate of return as an objective aid to business judgment."[15]

Alfred Sloan based his vision for GM's future on the wisdom he acquired improving the performance of his own division. He believed foremost in rational financial controls based on the return on invested capital of each operating division. With these established, he focused on preserving the "spirit and substance of decentralization" while maintaining sensible centralized functions to provide proper oversight and cure needless inefficiencies. Sloan understood the delicate balance between decentralization and proper controls, and he knew the principles were inherently contradictory. As he wrote in his classic book, *My Years with General Motors*, "its very contradiction is the crux of the matter."[16]

Alfred Sloan believed in decentralization as a way to channel the independence and competitive spirit in each of the divisions, but he could never develop a foolproof system of operational controls. Indeed, several of his greatest contributions to the company were decidedly centralist. One of his first actions after Durant left GM was to overhaul the product strategy, focusing each brand on a segment of the market delineated by price. He later wrote, "there is no hard and fast rule for sorting out the various responsibilities and the best way to assign them."[17] Instead Sloan relied on his management and leadership skills. He was fanatical about fostering dissent and having open discussions. He built consensus rather than administer top-down orders, and he delegated responsibility as low as it would go in the organization. Sloan established a large number of committees and policy groups to improve the institution's decision making, and he served on all of them himself to make sure they stayed on task.

Under Sloan's leadership, General Motors came to dominate the global automobile business. This was a remarkable feat in an industry with few barriers to entry and a formidable competitor in Ford. When Sloan finally retired from GM's board in 1956, the company controlled half of the domestic auto market. GM's economies of scale made it the low-cost producer, its brands were household names, and its large and wealthy dealer network gave it a clear advantage in marketing its cars. Alfred Sloan's triumph seemed complete.

Running Against the Wind

In 1943, a thirty-three-year-old professor of political science named Peter Drucker began an intensive two-year study of General Motors. GM vice chairman Donaldson Brown invited him in with hopes he would analyze GM's procedures for the benefit of its future managers. Drucker had become fascinated by the rise of large corporations in the United States, and he jumped at the opportunity to examine one from the inside.

Drucker's *Concept of the Corporation* helped launch the study of business management after its 1946 publication. The book is also disturbingly prescient about General Motors. Drucker was amazed at the ability of one enterprise to successfully produce such a diversity of products. His research coincided with GM's mobilization to support the war effort, and Drucker credited the company, and Alfred Sloan in particular, with playing a large and underrated role in winning World War II.[18] But despite GM's achievements, Drucker wondered if the company was organized in a way that could perpetuate its good fortune.

Peter Drucker marveled at GM's informality, and the responsibility it delegated to its employees, but he worried about the lack of clear divisions of power.[19] He wrote, "This raises the question of how General Motors avoids the dangers which according to age-old experience threaten . . . every committee form of government: the danger of a deadlock between coordinated organs, the danger of a break-up of the organization into factionalism, intrigues and fights for power."[20] Drucker argued that the freedoms enjoyed by GM's managers would eventually be lost without a "clearly defined order with a strict division of authority and responsibility." Of course, no "clearly defined order" existed. Sloan was never able to determine a systematic way to divide responsibilities between the divisions and the corporate headquarters.

Alfred Sloan built General Motors so that it harnessed his leadership skills in the best possible way. He was an exceptional manager with a gift for rational, open-minded thinking, but as hard as he tried, GM could not institutionalize his decision-making process or his fanatical hiring practices. The system worked incredibly well with Sloan in charge, but it did not suit a GM without him. When Drucker addressed whether

GM worked solely because of Sloan's management style, he wrote, "If it were true that the General Motors system rested on individual good will, it could hardly survive the life span of one man."[21] In fact, by the time of Sloan's death in 1966, General Motors was already in decline.

IF ALFRED SLOAN'S *My Years with General Motors* is the definitive inside account of GM's rise, then *On a Clear Day You Can See General Motors*, by John Z. DeLorean (as told to journalist J. Patrick Wright), is the definitive account of its fall.[22] DeLorean was one of the brightest stars ever to shoot through the General Motors system. The son of immigrant parents who both worked in Detroit factories, he became the youngest man to run a GM division in 1965, when he was put in charge of Pontiac. DeLorean's book describes his rapid ascent to the executive fourteenth floor, and his decision in 1973 to do something few senior GM executives had ever done—quit the company.

DeLorean placed most of the blame for GM's troubles on Frederic Donner, who became chairman in 1958. Donner was a career accountant who significantly weakened the role of president, a position Sloan earmarked for experienced operators. This placed control of GM in the hands of its finance executives. DeLorean described how Donner carefully preserved the form of Sloan's organization study while eliminating its substance—the company's commitment to decentralization. Under Donner, GM's committees began to dictate day-to-day operations while ignoring popular trends sweeping the industry. DeLorean wrote, "I felt that the emphasis at General Motors had switched . . . to one taking the last nickel out of every part to improve profits in the short term."[23]

DeLorean's biggest success at Pontiac was the GTO, which launched the muscle car craze in the mid-1960s. The story of its development is an example of the factionalism that developed at GM under Donner. To create the GTO, DeLorean took a large V-8 engine and squeezed it into a lightweight, compact frame. The result was a fun, powerful car that was also affordable and stylish. As the project progressed, DeLorean and the other executives at Pontiac decided to risk their jobs by not telling anyone outside the division about the GTO's existence.

DeLorean suspected GM's engineering committee would question the use of such a large engine, and would either veto the GTO altogether or delay its production for years. He wrote, "Practically every operational product decision, no matter how small, had to be brought before [the committee]."[24] This included minutiae like bumper design and the tone of the seat belt buzzer. DeLorean remembered how a few years earlier, GM headquarters had vetoed his promising new car, the Grand Prix. Without funding for the necessary tooling, Pontiac decided to produce a simplified version of the car anyway. The Grand Prix sold well for almost a decade. This time around, with what felt like a sure hit on its hands, Pontiac decided to circumvent headquarters. GM's executives were furious when the GTO was introduced, but it became a sensational hit before they could pull the plug.[25]

On a Clear Day You Can See General Motors describes GM's transformation into the kind of frozen bureaucracy that Sloan feared and Drucker anticipated. DeLorean's account of his turnaround efforts at Chevrolet and his brief stint as a senior executive highlighted just how far things had strayed from Sloan's ideals. Life on GM's fourteenth floor was particularly grim. Every morning, DeLorean was given a mountain of reports on trivial issues that never should have made it to his desk. Later in the day, he was expected to attend meetings to discuss these issues. In one episode, he was in a meeting to develop a policy for cost-of-living adjustments for relocated workers. DeLorean was shocked that every single senior GM executive had to participate in this discussion. At the end of the meeting, GM's chairman said, "We can't make a decision on this now." He appointed several people in the room to serve on a task force to study the issue. After an uncomfortable silence, one of the executives pointed out that the chairman had already appointed a task force, and that this meeting was the presentation of its findings. Afterward, DeLorean thought to himself, "What the hell am I doing here? I can't spend the next 17 years of my life up here doing these kinds of things."[26]

When John DeLorean quit General Motors in 1973, the company was still the world's largest carmaker and a financial powerhouse. But GM's glory was fading fast. It was losing touch with its customers and the quality of its products was suffering. The year DeLorean quit, Honda introduced the Civic. The Accord followed three years later. Both cars were industry game changers. They showed how far the Japanese auto-makers had come from their humble beginnings and established them as a legitimate threat to the U.S. auto industry. Instead of planning for the future and responding to competitive threats, GM's senior management was holed up on the fourteenth floor, micromanaging its divisions and debating unimportant issues.

Making an Elephant Dance

In January 1981, Roger Smith became chairman and chief executive officer of General Motors. Just like the previous four CEOs, Smith was an accountant who had been with GM for most of his professional life. He took over at a critical moment in the company's history. The previous year, Japanese automakers surpassed Detroit in total car production, and GM reported its first loss in almost eighty years. Since DeLorean's departure in 1973, the country had suffered two major oil crises that drove up the price of gasoline and pushed consumers to smaller, more fuel-efficient cars. For their part, Japanese carmakers had drastically improved the reliability and styling of their vehicles. Few car buyers returned to an American vehicle after owning a Japanese one.

When Roger Smith got the job, he told the *Wall Street Journal,* "I'd be very surprised if there are any dramatic changes."[27] Behind closed doors, however, he was much more aggressive. Shortly after he became CEO, Smith delivered a brutal assessment of GM to its top five hundred executives. He explained that the company had become too slow and ineffective for the rapidly changing market. He decried the lack of accountability among GM's managers, and said they spent too much time on useless paperwork, rather than pushing decisions lower into the organization, as Alfred Sloan intended. Whereas many of his predecessors ignored foreign competition, Smith said that GM trailed competitors in quality, design, and even management.[28]

Roger Smith was perhaps the first General Motors CEO in the post-Donner era who did not hold the company sacred. He was only fifty-five years old when he got the job, so his tenure would be the longest since Alfred Sloan's. It began with some much-needed relief. In 1981, Japan agreed to limit its U.S. car shipments to 1.68 million, 14% below the number it shipped in the previous, recession-afflicted year.[29] The voluntary export quota lasted three years, during which time the U.S. economy recovered and GM enjoyed record profits. The 1980s were Roger Smith's for the taking. He had billions of dollars of GM's cash to work with, and Japan had mercifully let U.S. automakers pick themselves up off the ground.

ROGER SMITH'S STRATEGY for General Motors focused on two things: restructuring the organization, and massive investments in modernizing systems and equipment.[30] Smith knew that GM's previous CEOs had done very little long-term planning. He wanted to leapfrog the competition by transforming GM into a highly automated, twenty-first-century industrial company. He began looking for ways to acquire state-of-the-art technology. GM had not made a major acquisition since the 1920s, but Smith told Salomon Brothers' John Gutfreund to be on the lookout. Gutfreund came back with the idea of buying Ross Perot's EDS.

EDS did not seem like a logical fit for General Motors. The data services firm had no manufacturing customers, and its culture seemed the complete opposite of GM's. Perot paid his young and energetic workers low salaries, but showered them in bonus money when they produced. GM's computer workers got generous salaries and job security. At EDS you pursued riches; at GM you wanted "thirty and out"—work for thirty years and retire with a pension for life. Perot didn't see how combining the two companies could work, but he was interested in the $3 billion GM spent per year on data processing. He told Smith, "You don't have to buy a dairy to get milk."[31]

Roger Smith saw more in EDS than a way to improve GM's computing operations. He wanted to upend GM's culture, and Ross Perot was the man to help him do it. Smith said, "EDS has the kind of entrepreneurial spirit that we need to develop in GM."[32] To win Perot over, GM structured a unique deal that would let EDS function as an independent unit of General Motors. It would have its own class of GM shares, its own management, and its own board of directors. Smith promised Perot that GM would not interfere in EDS's operations, its compensation policies, or its finances and accounting. Perot would receive $930 million in cash and 5.5 million shares of GM Class E shares. He would join General Motors' board of directors as its largest shareholder. Perot alerted Smith that he intended to further increase his ownership of GM and become actively involved in areas of the company outside of EDS. Smith welcomed him with open arms.

LABOR AS A RESOURCE

Ross Perot got right to work at General Motors. He invited the top two hundred executives to dinners at his house, in groups of eight. He met with more than a thousand of GM's computer workers in groups of fifty.[33] On weekends, he visited GM dealerships in street clothes to test their customer service and see the company's products in the field. He would even show up unannounced at GM plants to have lunch with workers on the factory floor. Perot was trying to understand why one of the world's richest industrial companies couldn't compete against Japanese automakers on shoestring budgets.

When Perot asked a small group of Cadillac dealers how he could help them, one of the men responded, "Get me a Honda dealership!" He wasn't joking. Cadillacs were so unreliable that the dealer had to keep a hundred service bays running two shifts a day just to keep the cars on the road. A Honda dealer could run the same operation with twenty service bays working one shift. The man told Perot, "A Honda dealer sells a product he can be proud of."[34]

Perot found GM's adversarial relationship with its dealers maddening. What bugged him most was that GM wasn't listening to them or seeking their input. This became a recurring theme in his meetings throughout the company. Everyone could list various problems hurting the company. They believed the problems were easily fixable, but the GM system didn't give the right people the authority to fix them. As Perot found out, this dynamic proved especially damaging on the factory floor.

Perot was impressed that Toyota representatives visited each dealer once every three months to solicit feedback on how to improve the cars and what customers were looking for. But this kind of teamwork was nothing compared to how Japanese companies ran their manufacturing operations. Japanese carmakers obsessively leaned on factory workers to refine and improve every manufacturing process. By 1985, Toyota had received over ten *million* suggestions from workers to improve efficiency at its plants. The cumulative impact of all of these tiny process improvements was impressive.

Japanese carmakers could build a plant for a fraction of what it cost GM. Once built, they could keep the plant running 90% of the time versus GM's 60%. They did this with five layers of management versus GM's fourteen, and ended up producing superior vehicles at a significantly lower cost, even after factoring in shipping costs from Japan to the United States.[35] Even the newest American plants with laser scanners and robots were less efficient than Japanese factories using twenty-year-old American-made equipment. Comparing specific production functions often yielded shocking differences. For example, Japanese factory paint jobs saw a 2% defect rate versus 20% to 30% for American cars.[36]

Perot complained that GM was harming itself by neglecting its factory workers. This was eerily similar to one of Peter Drucker's criticisms forty years earlier. Drucker thought GM should "consider labor as a resource and not a cost."[37] He had been greatly impressed by GM workers' ability to take responsibility during World War II, when there was a shortage of experienced supervisors. Drucker thought that after the war, GM should harness the talents of its workers to develop a "self-governing plant community." It was no coincidence that the Japanese car manufacturers embraced this approach—Drucker may have been shunned in Detroit, but he was revered in Japan.

Roger Smith had given up on fostering any kind of constructive relationship with GM's labor force. GM was as hostile to its own workers as it was to its dealers, and part of Smith's obsession with technology arose from his pessimistic view of the company's labor relations. He said, "We have got to have high-tech because we are a high-cost company for labor."[38] Smith envisioned "the lights-out factory of the future" operated by robots, with only a handful of human employees.

GM's lights-on factories of the 1980s, however, were dismal places populated by embittered workers who often lashed out at their employer. Absenteeism was rampant, running as high as 20%. GM autoworkers described alcohol and drug use on the job, as well as gambling and prostitution.[39] Perhaps nobody summed it up better than Deputy Fred, the most interesting character in Michael Moore's 1989 documentary, *Roger and Me*. Fred, who evicted poor families from their homes throughout the film, quit his job at a GM plant in Flint after seventeen years. When someone asked him why he would leave such a good job, he said, "It was like a prison to me. That factory plays tricks on your mind."[40] Was it even possible for GM to build competitive vehicles at its corrupted manufacturing facilities?

THE TESLA MOTORS factory in Fremont, California, is frequently touted as one of the most advanced auto plants in the world. But the quintessential twenty-first-century car factory owes more to Toyota's lean manufacturing than it does to Roger Smith's vision of the automated future. The factory uses versatile, high-tech German robots, but it also relies on a large human component—several thousand workers to make fewer than 50,000 vehicles. Jeffrey Liker, author of *The Toyota Way*, said, "This kind of very flexible, self-contained approach is exactly what Toyota did in the early days of the Toyota Production System."[41] It's fitting that the Tesla factory now occupies the very site where Toyota first revealed the secrets of its manufacturing success to General Motors.

In 1983, GM established a joint venture with Toyota called New United Motor Manufacturing Inc., or NUMMI. The deal made sense for both companies. Toyota had watched Honda successfully open its first U.S. plant the previous year, but it was nervous about managing famously unruly American autoworkers. NUMMI allowed Toyota to test its system on American soil, with American workers, and it also brought the company good publicity. GM would get a marketable small car out of the deal—NUMMI would produce a new Chevy Nova based on the design of the Corolla—as well as an inside look at how Toyota ran such efficient plants. GM contributed its closed Fremont plant to the joint venture, allowing the company to create some value from its unused capacity.

NUMMI proved that Toyota's production system could work not just with American talent, but with unionized General Motors workers. In fact, GM's Fremont workers were notorious as the worst autoworkers in the entire country when the plant was shuttered in 1982. An excellent *This American Life* episode about NUMMI described how workers at the old Fremont plant would routinely deface cars, or leave loose bolts and Coke bottles inside car door panels. Another worker was so mad at being disciplined for drinking on the job that he intentionally left bolts in the front suspension dangerously loose. When NUMMI reopened the Fremont plant, Toyota, against GM's objection, brought in almost all of the same workers who had been there before it closed.[42]

NUMMI was a remarkable success. Its Chevy Novas rolled out of the factory almost defect-free and achieved stellar quality ratings. After just two years, NUMMI's efficiency metrics were significantly better than every other GM plant. They only barely trailed some of the best Toyota factories in Japan.[43] NUMMI proved what Ross Perot and Toyota suspected all along: Japanese carmakers didn't benefit from cultural advantages, secret production techniques, or newer technology; they simply got better performance out of their people by promoting teamwork and cooperation.

When Perot saw how NUMMI produced high-quality cars with very limited resources, he began to question Roger Smith's strategy. Here was GM, spending tens of billions of dollars to attain a vague long-term goal of technological superiority. Yet the company had no near-term goals for becoming more cost-effective. Why wasn't GM curing problems at its existing plants?

After looking at NUMMI, Perot studied the recent turnaround at Jaguar, which was effectively nationalized by the British government in 1975. In 1980, Jaguar brought in a new chairman who worked with unionized workers to make drastic quality improvements with very little capital at his disposal. What most frustrated Ross Perot was that the chairman had recently worked for General Motors.[44] Jaguar showed that GM was not only underutilizing its factory workers; it was squandering its executive talent as well.

Ross Perot spent over a year learning why the world's richest

automaker sold overpriced, inferior cars. He saw that Toyota was doing a masterful job of using its employees' talents, while GM's system
snuffed out the potential of its people. It was also clear that GM's troubles
were only getting worse. Honda and Toyota were investing in domestic
manufacturing bases, they were rapidly growing their dealer networks,
and they were preparing to move into the luxury segment to compete
with Cadillac. GM was spending billions of dollars to win the twenty-
first century, but as Perot complained, its competitors were dominating
the 1980s "using brains and wits as a substitute for capital."[45]

THROWING MONEY AT PROBLEMS

In June 1985, GM agreed to purchase Hughes Aircraft for $5 billion,
pending approval from the board of directors. Roger Smith believed
Hughes's advanced aerospace technology could help GM revolutionize
the auto industry. Perot wasn't so sure. He saw how GM was struggling
to integrate EDS, and he thought tossing Hughes into the mix would
only cause distraction. Besides, GM couldn't even build a quality automobile. Perot didn't understand how acquiring a defense contractor that
made satellites was going to help matters.

Perot decided to air his grievances privately with Smith. His October 23, 1985, letter (page 222) begins by demanding a full briefing about
Hughes and a list of GM's principal reasons for wanting to acquire it.
He then addresses his working relationship with Smith. He writes, "I
will tell you candidly when I think you are wrong. If you continue your
present autocratic style, I will be your adversary on critical issues. . . . I
do not expect that all of my ideas will be accepted. I do insist that they
be heard and thoughtfully considered."

After Perot admonishes Smith for being openly bored in a recent
meeting, he lists the negative effects of Smith's management style,
"Your style intimidates people. . . . You need to be aware that people are
afraid of you. This stifles candid, upward communication in GM. You
need to know that GM'ers at all levels use terms like ruthless and bully
in describing you."

Perot concludes by arguing that GM cannot solve its problems by throwing money at them. After stating that Japanese carmakers are beating GM because of better management, not technology and capital, Perot writes, "This is not a personal issue between us. The issue is the success of GM. I am committed to doing my part to see that we win, and I know that you are, too."

When he did not get a satisfactory response from Roger Smith, Perot decided to vote against the Hughes purchase. He prepared a long speech for the upcoming board meeting, a rallying cry to the other directors to create a sense of urgency to fix GM's problems. EDS's senior managers cringed at the thought of Ross Perot casting the first dissenting vote in GM's boardroom in decades. GM and EDS had been at each other's throats over EDS's billing practices and executive compensation. When Perot's lawyer wondered if opposing Hughes was worth the trouble when GM and EDS were close to negotiating a truce, Perot responded, "That's a hell of a note when your own lawyer advises you against acting as an independent director."[46]

Ross Perot's November 4, 1985, speech to the General Motors board of directors went beyond arguing against the Hughes Aircraft acquisition. It was a summary of everything Perot learned over the previous year, an indictment of Roger Smith's modernization strategy, and a challenge to the board of directors. He said, "We need to become more active in understanding what is really happening inside General Motors. If GM is to change, it must start at the top, and we are the top. . . . We must change the format of board meetings from passive sessions with little two-way communication to active, participatory sessions that allow us to discuss real issues and resolve real problems."

Perot was addressing one of the most prestigious business institutions in the country. GM's board of directors included the chairmen of Pfizer, American Express, and Procter & Gamble, and the retired chairmen of Union Pacific, Eastman Kodak, Merck, and CBS. But even with this much firepower, it was a classic ineffective board. As one of GM's directors said, "Unanimity on this board is assumed."[47] When Ross Perot finished his long and blistering speech, nobody said a word.[48] Roger Smith thanked Perot for his comments, and the board of directors approved the Hughes purchase. Perot later complained, "There's very little ownership among outside board members. . . . They've got noth-ing at stake in the future success of General Motors."[49]

ONE DIRECTOR DISSENTING

"You're kidding," Ross Perot told his lawyer, Tom Luce. But Luce was serious—General Motors' board of directors had just voted to approve a buyout of Ross Perot and three other senior EDS officials. As part of the deal, the four men would get just under $750 million, with Perot himself taking home $700 million. Perot would also have to resign from the General Motors board of directors. Earlier in the day, he told Luce he would sign the deal if the board approved it, but he qualified the state-ment: "Tom, one of those guys has got to stand up and say, 'Guys this is ludicrous.'"[50] Instead, the moment of truth arrived without objection from the board. Perot signed the buyout agreement.

More than a year had passed since Ross Perot's angry letter to Roger Smith. It had been a trying period for everyone. GM's 250-page proxy state-ment explaining the Hughes acquisition contained a very brief disclosure about the board vote, "with one director dissenting." The press quickly realized that Perot must have voted against the deal, and began to cover the rift between him and Roger Smith. GM's operating results only added fuel to the fire. 1986 was a record year for the automotive industry, but General Motors was losing money. Perot's warning to the board that "GM will invest so much in fixed-cost robotics and factory floor automation that we will drive costs up—not down" seemed prophetic. Both Chrysler and Ford surpassed GM in cost efficiency in 1986. Despite Smith's efforts to cut expenses, GM's labor force had grown from 691,000 in 1983 to over 800,000.[51] Perot was all over the newspapers that summer, challenging the GM system and its management. When reporters asked about GM's di-sastrous performance, Perot was always ready with a cunning repartee. "This place cries out for engineers with greasy hands who know how to make cars to be making the policy," he said.[52]

When Luce began discussing a buyout with his counterpart at Gen-eral Motors, Perot was dismissive. "They'll never do it," Perot told Luce. "GM will never admit they had to spend all this money just to get rid of me."[53] Perot remained detached from the negotiations, but he never scuttled them. When it came time to discuss terms, Perot later explained, "I just kept making obscene demands, and they kept agreeing to them."[54] Perot remained dubious until December 1, 1986, when Luce put the approved deal in front of him to sign. Perot later said in court testimony, "My attitude all the way was no one will ever sign this agreement on the GM side, it's not businesslike. I underestimated the desire on the GM board to get rid of me."[55]

Perot received $61.90 per share for his GM stock. It was trading at only $33 in the public market, and would tank to under $30 when the buyout was announced. The nonfinancial terms were also very favorable toward EDS and Perot, with a limited noncompete provision and clarification of EDS's autonomy and service contracts with GM. Shareholders and employees were shocked. In a year when GM's profits were so weak that hourly workers were not going to receive any profit-participation bonuses, the company was buying out Perot for three-quarters of a billion dollars. And rather than leave quietly, as Luce told GM he would, Perot immediately put out an incendiary press release:

> At a time when General Motors is:
>
> —closing 11 plants,
> —putting over 30,000 people out of work,
> —cutting back on capital expenditures,
> —losing market share,
> —and having problems with profitability,
>
> I have just received $700 million from General Motors in exchange for my Class E notes and stock. I cannot accept this money without giving the GM directors another chance to consider this decision. . . . If the GM directors conclude that this transaction of December 1 isn't in the best interests of GM and Class E shareholders, I will work with the GM directors to rescind the transaction.

General Motors was furious with Perot's response to the buyout. The deal was the product of long discussions between both sides; it was generous to Ross Perot and EDS, and yet Perot came out with guns a-blazing the moment he signed it. GM's lawyers felt Perot was going public to protect his image and preempt accusations that the buyout amounted to "greenmail." If Perot was so concerned with how GM was spending its capital, why did he accept the money in the first place?[56]

Shareholders were livid and they immediately responded to Perot's encouragement to speak up. The State of Wisconsin Investment Board (SWIB) wrote a letter to GM directors saying, "Your action . . . severely undermines the confidence we have in the Board and in the officials of General Motors. Not only is the action grossly unfair to other Class E stockholders . . . the payment of 'hush' mail to H. Ross Perot raises serious questions about General Motors' operations and management. His presence on the Board was valuable and perceived as such by the market, as evidenced by the impact on stock prices upon notice of the buyout."[57]

New York City comptroller Harrison J. Goldin invited both Perot and Smith to speak to the Council for Institutional Investors, a group he cofounded the previous year with Big Daddy Unruh to promote better corporate governance. The council's forty members were large pension funds that accounted for a combined 10% of all stock ownership in the country. Though Smith told Goldin he would attend, he ended up sending a delegation of underlings to spar with Perot. Goldin, incredulous that Smith had stood up his largest shareholders, said, "We have a right as major holders of GM stock to hear an explanation from the chairman. If we can't hear it from this chairman, then maybe some other chairman."

Goldin's suggestion that shareholders might boot Roger Smith from the board indicated just how far the Perot buyout had pushed GM's institutional investors. Weary after decades of neglect, they had finally lost their patience. SWIB submitted a shareholder resolution prohibiting discriminatory share repurchases. Goldin's criticisms echoed everyone's dissatisfaction with GM's performance: "A well-run company doesn't have to show quarterly improvements on a regular basis, but when you spend tens of billions of dollars and don't show any improved results, it's time for an accounting."[58]

WHEN THE FUROR over the buyout did not subside, Roger Smith was forced to deal with the shareholders. He apologized to Goldin and embarked on a twenty-two-meeting road show to explain to investors how GM had gotten religion. Smith shared statistics and projections with investment analysts, and discussed cost-cutting opportunities in detail. After his meetings, GM announced a $10 billion cost reduction program and a stock repurchase plan that Smith called "the largest stock buyback ever by a U.S. corporation."[59] He also applied pressure behind the scenes to weaken some of GM's louder critics. Corporate governance gurus Robert Monks and Nell Minow write in several of their books that Smith got SWIB to withdraw support for its shareholder resolution by calling Wisconsin's governor and threatening to cancel planned GM capital spending in the state.[60]

At GM's annual meeting, the shareholder motion to rescind the Perot transaction received 20% of the vote. This was considered an embarrassment for GM—Ralph Nader's Campaign GM was deemed a success in 1970 when it won under 3% of the vote for shareholder initiatives promoting corporate responsibility. But Roger Smith had won: Neither the shareholders nor the directors were going to bring Ross Perot back to General Motors.

With Perot gone and GM's critics temporarily appeased by buybacks and restructuring plans, it seemed like the company was destined to slip into its normal state of submissive directors and shareholders. But beneath the surface calm there were rumblings. When Roger Smith tried to add new directors to GM's board in early 1988, the board rejected the idea. The *Wall Street Journal* reported that the insurgence had shattered a long tradition of passive outside directors at GM. One insider said the board felt it "wasn't as involved in some past decisions as it should have been."[61] An unnamed director added that the board wanted "to be less spoken to and more consulted with."[62] But frustrated directors were soon to be the least of Smith's worries. Even with Perot out of the picture, GM's institutional investors continued to apply pressure. They were not going to disappear into the background, where they had lingered for decades.

Time for an Accounting

When General Motors was at the height of its powers in the 1950s, institutional investors accounted for less than 10% of stock holdings in the United States. By the late 1980s, they owned 50% of the largest fifty companies.[63] Today the broad category of institutional investors, which includes pension funds as well as mutual funds, hedge funds, endowments, and insurance companies, holds 70% of U.S. public equities.[64] In other words, institutional shareholders as a group, at least in theory, control corporate America. But as Ross Perot explained to GM's board of directors, broad institutional ownership had the peculiar effect of disempowering shareholders. By the time GM bought Ross Perot off its board, shareholders had little say in the company's affairs beyond muted grumbling.

General Motors is a good example of how ownership of America's corporations evolved over time. In 1920, most of GM's shares were held by a handful of "owner-capitalists," as Peter Drucker called them. This group included the DuPont Company and men, like Alfred Sloan, who sold their businesses to Billy Durant in exchange for stock. Over the next thirty years, most of the large individual owners retired from GM's board of directors and passed away.[65] In 1957, the United States government forced DuPont to dispose of its large stake in General Motors for antitrust reasons.[66] By the 1960s, General Motors was a modern public company, run by professional managers and governed by a board of directors with little share ownership. From that point forward, institutions would dominate the company's shareholder base.

General Motors itself played a major role in this evolution. Employee pension funds, which form one of the largest groups of institutional investors, are essentially a GM creation. While some pension funds existed when GM president Charles Wilson launched the GM Pension Fund in 1950, they tended to be annuity plans holding fixed-income securities, or trusts invested entirely in the stock of the employer company. Wilson believed pension plans should have significant equity exposure, but he thought it was senselessly risky to bet workers' retirement money on the future of their employer. He mandated independent management of GM's pension funds, little or no investment in the employer company, and a diversified portfolio with no large ownership stakes in other companies.[67] Wilson's guidelines immediately caught on with other employers—eight thousand new plans were launched within a year of GM's—and were codified in the ERISA Act of 1974.

Corporate America's decision to broadly invest its employees' retirement funds in equities gave American workers a huge ownership stake in the country's economic assets. Peter Drucker argued that this made the United States the world's first truly socialist country.[68] But it also placed control of these investments in the hands of conservative, highly regulated fiduciaries who limited their exposure to any single investment. Before Ross Perot pushed them to a breaking point, these kinds of investors were highly unlikely to intervene in the oversight of powerful companies like General Motors.

MANY BOOKS HAVE been written about General Motors' decline, and few parties to the company's fall have been spared blame. GM's executives and directors are obvious targets, but experts have also skewered the United Automobile Workers union, GM's dealers, its white- and blue-collar workers, its corporate culture, OPEC, free trade, and, of course, various government regulators. We can have long arguments about why GM faltered, but one thing is clear: GM's decline was long, slow, and very visible. By sitting idle while the company endured numerous public failures over three decades, the shareholders helped perpetuate GM's struggles. They deserve as much blame for General Motors' decline as any other party.

GM's first major public failure was the Corvair, "The One Car Accident" described in Ralph Nader's *Unsafe at Any Speed*. The 1959 Chevrolet car had serious defects that left it prone to losing control at higher speeds.[69] Despite objections from many of its engineers, GM pushed ahead with the car, which ended up killing drivers in large numbers. When the fourteenth floor rejected Chevrolet's request to add a $15 stabilizing bar to the vehicle, the division head threatened to resign and publicize his dissent.[70] GM's executives relented, but it was too late.

Nader's book was published several years later and caused a wave of negative publicity for GM.[71]

Through the 1970s and early 1980s, General Motors introduced a series of new vehicles that spectacularly bombed. The Vega, X-cars, J-cars, and GM-10 were lambasted by car reviewers and fell flat with customers. We think of Ford's Edsel as the worst car launch in history, but Edsel was an ambitious project that failed to live up to its pioneering marketing blitz. GM's disasters were missed layups, and they were ultimately much more damaging. James Womack, who cowrote *The Machine That Changed the World*, about Toyota's lean engineering, called GM-10 "the biggest catastrophe in American industrial history."[72]

In Charlie Munger's Blue Chip Stamps annual letters, he describes a troubled investment: "We started coping better with reality when it stopped waving the danger flags at us and started using them to poke us in the head and stomach." This is a perfect depiction of what happened to GM's institutional shareholders. The company's missteps received an enormous amount of public attention and scrutiny. Both Ralph Nader's and John DeLorean's books were massive bestsellers. Ross Perot's complaints about GM in the summer of 1986 were covered by all the major business publications. Every bad capital investment and every poor decision was discussed ad nauseam by critics, from the Hamtramck, Michigan, "plant of the future" to the tremendous transfer of wealth to employees through generous long-term benefits. But by paying $700 million to get Ross Perot off its board, GM took the oft-waved danger flag and thrust it in the shareholders' faces. The buyout made shareholders appreciate how much had gone wrong at GM under their watch.

After the Perot buyout, GM's shareholders were even more aggressive than the energized outside directors. In 1990, CalPERS, the California Public Employees Retirement System, wrote a letter to the board asking that Roger Smith be removed as a director after his retirement as CEO. Both CalPERS and the New York State Retirement System pressured the board to be actively involved in choosing the new CEO, rather than leave such an important decision up to Smith. GM's board promoted an engineer to run the company for the first time since the 1950s.

When he did not generate positive results quickly enough, he was fired and replaced by a company outsider.

Just as institutional investors were promoting revolutionary change at General Motors, they were flexing their muscles at other large public companies. The year after Ross Perot's buyout, four pension funds (including CalPERS and SWIB) submitted forty-seven shareholder resolutions on corporate-governance-related issues. These were the first resolutions on governance matters ever filed by public pension funds.[73] The following year TIAA-CREF made history by being the first institutional investor to run a dissident slate of directors.[74] CalPERS CEO Dale Hanson, who battled with GM over its succession plans, stated, "as much care and attention goes to the owning of stock as to the selection of stock. . . . as owners for the last 30 or 40 years, we've been asleep at the switch."[75]

ROSS PEROT WAS reportedly bitter about exiting General Motors with no company of his own to fall back on. But when I recently asked him whether he regretted leaving his beloved EDS in the clutches of GM, he replied abruptly, "I don't need to say any more about that mess. I started a new company. They got rid of me." Ross Perot is not a man to waste his time reflecting on the past. He still has energy to burn, just as he did in late 1986. Several weeks after his buyout was finalized, Perot saw Steve Jobs on television and was so captivated by his enthusiasm that he decided to fund NeXT Computer. When his noncompete with GM expired in 1988, he founded Perot Systems, which quickly became a billion-dollar enterprise. All of this happened before he got into politics and became the most successful third-party presidential candidate in the modern era. But in spite of his many triumphs, one of Ross Perot's finest moments came in defeat when he stood up to Roger Smith and General Motors' board of directors.

Several chapters in this book depict sleepy shareholder bases tolerating entrenched boards and domineering CEOs. Benjamin Graham needed several years and an impassioned plea to the Rockefeller Foundation to free excess capital from Northern Pipeline. In the next chapter we'll see R. P. Scherer's directors try to block Karla Scherer from joining the board, even though she was the largest shareholder and the daughter of the founder. At General Motors, Ross Perot was not just the largest shareholder and a member of the board of directors—he was also Ross Perot! He was a larger-than-life billionaire adored by the masses and media alike. When even the mighty Ross Perot couldn't sway GM's board and management, the company's shareholders realized they had created a monster.

The awakening of institutional investors, prompted by the Ross Perot buyout in 1986, had an immediate impact on public company governance. CEOs and directors were targeted in ways that seemed unthinkable just a few years earlier, as evidenced by CalPERS's campaign to dump Roger Smith from the GM board. But the biggest effect was at first quite subtle—the stiffening resolve of institutional holders behind the scenes. Shortly after the Perot buyout, the head of SWIB said, "If shareholders continue to be passive, they will continue to be shorn like sheep."[76] He meant it. After Perot, you could no longer count on large institutional shareholders to be pushovers. This helped end the corporate raider era, while encouraging the kind of shareholder activism that dominates markets today.

6

Karla Scherer versus R. P. Scherer:
A Kingdom in a Capsule

"In our opinion, it is perfectly clear who are the real beneficiaries of Scherer management's economic policy: **the top executives.***"*
—KARLA SCHERER, 1988

IN 1933, ROBERT PAULI Scherer invented a machine that mass-produced soft gelatin capsules. Some fifty years later, his original prototype was preserved in the Smithsonian Institution, and R. P. Scherer Corporation was the world's largest manufacturer of softgels. But when Robert Scherer's forty-seven-year-old daughter, Karla, joined the board of directors in 1984, she quickly became disillusioned with how the company was managed. R. P. Scherer was a good, cash-generating business protected by patented technology and years of expertise. But for the previous two decades, management had used the softgel profits to diversify into much more commoditized businesses, including paper packaging and hair-care accessories.

There was another problem. R. P. Scherer's CEO was none other than Karla Scherer's husband, Peter Fink. Karla believed her husband was pursuing an aggressive growth strategy that was not in the best interest of shareholders. She was R. P. Scherer's largest shareholder, and most of her net worth was tied up in the stock. She later said, "I was financing the stage upon which management and its cronies danced."¹ Her marriage would not survive this revelation.

While Karla owned significantly more shares than the other directors, the rest of the board refused to acknowledge her concerns. She attributed part of their stubbornness to the fact that she was a woman with no business education on an all-male board. But she also blamed the board members' many conflicts of interest. Karla Scherer described the dynamic: "This was a real old boys' network if there ever was one! These men played golf together, belonged to the same clubs and en-riched each others' coffers."[2]

After a few years on the board of directors, Karla Scherer realized that the softgel business pioneered by her father would be much more valuable if it were separated from its underperforming management team. R. P. Scherer was an archetype of Icahn's arbitrage between as-sets trapped in a public company and those sitting on the auction block. But why should this be so? Northern Pipeline lacked accountability to shareholders because insiders occupied three of five board seats—at R. P. Scherer, management held only two of ten seats. But even when corporate boards are not directly controlled by management, directors tend to be handpicked by the CEO. And even when directors are truly independent, the social nature of the institution makes it hard for them to take adversarial stances. Corporate boards by nature tend to entrench management teams. Karla Scherer's bitter proxy fight against her hus-band is a lesson in such entrenchment.

THE SCHERER SUCCESS STORY

Before Robert Pauli Scherer ascended to his throne as "the capsule king," he was unemployed, with a wife and two small children. But as a 1949 profile in the *Saturday Evening Post* points out, "The Scherer success story has not been a rags-to-riches saga."[3] Bob—and he would want us to call him Bob—was the son of a successful eye doctor in Detroit. He graduated from the University of Michigan in 1930 and quickly found work as a chemical engineer at a Detroit pharmaceutical firm. After four months on the job, Bob decided he needed more than his $125 per month salary to live on. His bosses refused to give him a raise, so he quit his first job just as the country slid into the Great Depression.[4]

Scherer inherited a gift for making machinery from his father, who kept a large metalworking shop in his basement. When Bob was young, he watched his father build a motorized coffee grinder, meat and vegetable slicers, and an ice-cream freezer.[5] After he quit his job, Bob had time and a well-equipped workshop at his disposal. He decided to build a new type of machine to produce soft gelatin capsules.

Bob's old employer was using a cumbersome plate-press method that used two die-cast plates to make batches of softgels. The technology had improved little in fifty years, and its production was slow and imprecise. Each plate was like a large cupcake tin with pill-size indentations. After a thin sheet of warm gelatin was placed over the bottom plate, the liquid medicament—the contents of the capsule—was applied to each pocket, usually just by pouring it over the top. Another sheet of warm gelatin was added, followed by the second plate. It was all squished together like a big waffle iron, and the two plates met to form the capsules.

Bob worked in his parents' basement for three years to create his rotary-die process. The Scherer machine was one self-contained unit that created warm gelatin sheets, injected the medicament in very precise measurements, and used two rolling cylindrical dies to constantly spit out softgels.[6] It was less wasteful than the plate-press method and was significantly faster because it formed the sheets of gelatin and molded the capsules simultaneously. The injection system could accommodate ointments and pastes in addition to liquid, thus increasing the number of substances that could be encapsulated. One machine could churn out well over a million softgels in a single day.[7]

ROBERT SCHERER PATENTED his rotary-die process and went into business in 1933. His old employer gave him his first order that same year, and by 1944, Scherer was making five billion capsules a year. The business was highly profitable, and Scherer reinvested all of the earnings back into the operations. The *Saturday Evening Post* article quoted him saying, "I want growth, not security."

The article also showcased Scherer's work habits, which must have seemed eccentric to the 1949 reader. It describes the typical day of Bob Scherer, "who hates work." He slept late—till about 9:30 a.m.—spent at least an hour reading or thinking, and finally arrived at the office just in time to read his mail and go out for lunch. After a leisurely lunch, Scherer went back to the office and kicked into his workday. If a project grabbed his attention, he would get so focused on it that he would work past midnight. If not, he headed home to his family or went out for dinner, drinks, and cards. For a 1949 business executive, Robert Scherer was a rebel. He even dressed like one: "He goes hatless on the coldest day, and manifests a fine scorn for methodical people who wear rubbers. His double-breasted suits and camel hair coat fit his six-foot-two, 180-some-pound frame to good purpose, but he is forever failing to get his shoes shined."[8]

Scherer insisted, "Nothing I've ever done has been work."[9] This was the key to his success. For his entire career, Bob was laser-focused on refining his softgel manufacturing process and bringing it to new markets. This is what he loved doing, and he rarely strayed from it. By 1940, he was the patent-protected, low-cost producer of softgels, with a 90% market share.[10] He also developed tremendous expertise that widened the competitive moat around his business. In the early days, his customers would bring him medicament, and he would encapsulate it. Within fifteen years of launching his business, most of Scherer's customers had him formulate their capsules as well.

Robert Scherer died of cancer in 1960, when he was only fifty-three years old. Under his leadership, R. P. Scherer maintained a dominant market share and grew rapidly, opening plants in six countries on three continents.[11] After Scherer's death, the company quickly changed course. While Bob was happy to spend most of his time in the shop improving the softgel business, his successors had ambitions for faster growth. For most of the next three decades, R. P. Scherer pursued an aggressive acquisitions strategy.

DIWORSIFICATION

Scherer was succeeded by his headstrong twenty-seven-year-old son, Robert Jr., who became president of the company. Robert Jr. made his first acquisition for R. P. Scherer just one year after assuming leadership. In 1961, he bought E. Morris Manufacturing, a Detroit barber products supplier that got its start importing straight razors from Germany.[12] He proceeded to buy a dental supplies business, a surgical instruments company, a 25% interest in an aloe vera cosmetics maker, a business that made steel cabinets and chairs for ear, nose, and throat doctors, and two companies that made bobby pins and hair curlers.[13] During Robert Jr.'s tenure as president, the company also bought a hardshell gelatin capsule manufacturer in Canada, and entered the hardshell market in several other countries including the United States.

R. P. Scherer became a public company after a successful stock offering in 1971. But the company's core softgel business was struggling to maintain its dominance. It lost one-third of its market share in the 1960s. Former chief operating officer Ernst Schoepe later said, "[T]here was a lack of direction coming from corporate headquarters."[14]

Robert Jr. left the company in 1979 and was replaced by Karla Scherer's husband, Peter Fink, who had served on the board since 1966.[15] As part of Robert Jr.'s departure, R. P. Scherer sold its non-encapsulation businesses to him in exchange for his 20% stake in the company. It was an unusual deal—Robert Jr. was basically keeping all the random acquisitions he'd made over the previous twenty years as president—but it was meant to refocus R. P. Scherer on its core business.[16] Fink vowed to concentrate his efforts on capsule manufacturing, and to consider acquisitions "only if they complement the core business."[17]

R. P. Scherer's commitment to its core business didn't last long. About a year after Fink became CEO, Scherer bought a German company, Franz Pohl, that made "seals and closures for injectable solutions." If you've read a lot of annual reports, you know that company descriptions waver between inscrutable and grandiose. Franz Pohl made aluminum caps for medicine vials. It was a low-return, commodity business with a concentrated customer base.

It was a stretch to argue that Franz Pohl complemented R. P. Scherer's encapsulation business, but the companies at least had some customers in common. Fink's next few acquisitions were even further afield. He bought a company that made disposable dental supplies, an animal testing laboratory, and two eyeglasses and contact lens makers. The company's largest acquisition was Paco Pharmaceutical Services, which made packaging for pharmaceutical products. Like Pohl, Paco might have been loosely complementary to R. P. Scherer's core operations, but it was a bad business. It was a labor-intensive, unionized, paper packaging company with low returns on assets and very low profit margins.

Like Robert Jr. before him, Peter Fink was diversifying R. P. Scherer into businesses that were significantly worse than the core softgel operations. In 1988, R. P. Scherer's capsules business generated a 29% pretax return on assets. This is a lofty figure that would be even higher without the lower-return hardshell business, and the effects of a restructuring in Asia. The acquired businesses, by contrast, managed a paltry 6% pretax return on assets.[18] To make things worse, most of the acquisitions had been *expensive*. Fink paid $64 million in cash for Paco in 1987. Paco's operating income in 1988 was only $830,000.[19] To buy the dental supplies business, the testing lab, and the optical supplies companies, Fink used cash plus more than 1.3 million undervalued R. P. Scherer shares. When Karla's proxy contest drove Scherer's stock price closer to intrinsic value, the folly of Fink's acquisitions became apparent. He had paid well over $40 million for mature businesses that made only $3.2 million in pretax operating income in 1988.[20]

R. P. Scherer was also making questionable investments into its own business. Robert Jr. made the dubious decision to enter the hardshell capsule manufacturing industry in 1968. Hardshells are much more of a commodity product than softgels. They are easier to formulate and manufacture, and generate lower profit margins.[21] With hardshells, R. P. Scherer not only had to compete with other manufacturers, but it sometimes lost business to its own customers, who could easily take production in-house. When Fink became CEO, he pushed forward a $70 million construction plan that included overseas hardshell facilities and a state-of-the-art plant in Utah. Within five years of completing the Utah facility, R. P. Scherer was forced to exit hardshell manufacturing in the United States and Canada. The company suffered a $6.5 million loss shutting down the new Utah plant and a $4.9 million charge for closing its older hardshell facility in New Jersey.[22]

R. P. Scherer had one excellent business—formulating and manufacturing soft gelatin capsules—but it was squandering cash on lesser ventures. The worst of these ventures was the biggest—Paco. Almost immediately after R. P. Scherer bought it, Paco ran into serious troubles.

It narrowly averted a Teamsters strike by agreeing to a three-year con-tract with 8% annual increases in wages and benefits. It also lost a major customer in Puerto Rico, who decided to take its packaging production in-house. Two of the company's plants turned unprofitable, but they re-mained open because labor agreements forced stiff penalties for plant closures. Paco had also established a research-and-development partner-ship focused on ophthalmic drugs and transdermal patches, but several of its partners had defaulted on their contribution requirements. The company needed to fund a shortfall of millions of dollars, or it would have to shut the partnership down and lose its initial investment.[23]

For Karla Scherer, Paco was the last straw. "One more example of extending into businesses which I felt were not appropriate," she said.[24] Karla had virtually all of her wealth concentrated in R. P. Scherer's stock, but she had no confidence in management and the other directors. Her marriage was already troubled, but she knew her doubts about Peter's ability to generate good returns for shareholders were not prompted by marital discord. She had two distinct problems: a crumbling marriage and a precarious financial situation. The first problem made the second one much more vivid.

The Late Awakening

Karla Scherer was Robert Scherer's third child, born five years after he patented his rotary-die machine. Bob's profile in the *Saturday Evening Post* ran before she was a teenager, when she was already a millionaire through her stake in the family business. When she was sixteen years old, Karla met Peter Fink on a sailing date. She started college at Wellesley, but finished her degree at Michigan so she could get married to Peter sooner.[25] In a different era, Karla thinks her parents would have encouraged her to pursue a business education and enter the family business. Instead, at only twenty years old, she went straight from school to being a housewife.

So why did Karla Scherer, who had no business education whatso-ever, want to serve on R. P. Scherer's board of directors? Two events in the early 1980s influenced her to take a more active role in the company. First, her mother passed away. Margaret Scherer was a strong-willed person who not only pulled her family together when Bob died; she also kept all of her children in line.[26] After her mother died, Karla began to ask her husband more questions about the business. Then, in 1982, a large industrial company, FMC Corporation, tried to acquire R. P. Scherer. Peter Fink managed to defeat the takeover attempt with the support of Karla and her younger brother John. But Karla worried that she had further entrenched Fink as CEO out of blind loyalty, without really considering if he was the best person for the job. She decided to ask Peter for a board seat. "It was a late awakening," she said. "I thought, 'you know, I'm the one that owns the stock and I would like to know what is going on.'"[27]

When Karla pressured Peter about a board seat, he was resistant. He told her that the other directors were asking, "What does she know about business?" But Karla persisted. "I grew up with the business," she told Peter. "It's what we talked about around the dinner table." She put an end to Fink's stalling, "So finally I got frustrated and I said—and I remember this conversation like it was yesterday, I remember where I was standing when I said it—I said, 'If I am not nominated for the board, I will nominate myself.' . . . The color drained out of his face and, bingo, I was on the board."[28]

Karla Scherer joined the R. P. Scherer board in 1984. She witnessed the collapse of the hardshell business in 1985, negative earnings in 1985 and 1986, and the Paco acquisition in February 1988. R. P. Scherer had more than doubled its long-term debt to pay for Paco, which began to show signs of trouble almost immediately. While the softgel business continued to perform well, Karla was nervous about the company's future under Peter's watch. In March and April of 1988 she met individually with each director to lobby for putting the company up for sale.

KARLA'S PITCH TO her fellow directors was simple. She argued that with R. P. Scherer profitable after two years of disastrous losses, with earnings in the core business growing nicely, and with a strong market for acquisitions driven by foreign interest in U.S. assets, the company could be sold for a very good price. She believed that a controlled auction of R. P. Scherer would produce a much better outcome for shareholders than continued operation as an independent public company. She had a point—the market was not giving much respect to R. P. Scherer. While the core encapsulation business generated a healthy $35 million in operating income over the previous year, the stock traded at $15⅝, which valued the company at only $230 million. During the past four years, the stock had traded as low as $8⅝ and surpassed $20 in just a handful of months.[29]

Two of R. P. Scherer's directors embraced Karla's idea to sell the company—her younger brother John, who had served on the board since 1961, and Ernst Schoepe, R. P. Scherer's chief operating officer. Schoepe was the only member of management on the board besides Peter Fink. He had climbed up the ranks at the company's German subsidiary and became a director in 1985. He believed Fink was managing the encapsulation business poorly, and he agreed with Karla that the best outcome for shareholders was to find a buyer for the company.

Everyone else on the board of directors refused to support selling R. P. Scherer. Karla remembers that none of them gave her legitimate business reasons for rejecting a sale; instead they focused on loyalty to Peter Fink. One director even told her, "Well, you can't do that. You will emasculate Peter."[30] The board was split 7–3 in favor of remaining independent. Karla, John, and Ernst Schoepe were outnumbered by Fink and the other six directors.

Peter Fink had deep personal ties to his six supporters on the board. They were:

Wilber Mack, retired chairman and CEO of American Natural Resources

Mack was the chairman of R. P. Scherer's board of directors. The company paid him almost $400,000 in cash the year before Karla's proxy fight. In addition to his hefty annual cash compensation, Mack received stock-based rewards as well as generous benefits including club memberships and secretarial support. Upon his death or disability, he was entitled to benefits worth $42,000 annually that were payable to him or his wife as long as either of them lived.[31] According to Karla, Mack acted as a father figure to Peter. He was seventy-seven years old and Karla believed his duties at the company were "largely ceremonial."[32] Mack was recommended by Peter Fink to serve on the R. P. Scherer board.

Peter Dow, president and COO of Lintas: Campbell-Ewald Company

Peter Fink and Peter Dow were childhood friends who both started their careers at Campbell-Ewald, where they were placed on the same four-person training team. Dow maintained a close friendship with Fink after he left Campbell-Ewald. He also lived across the street from the Finks in Grosse Pointe, Michigan.[33] Dow was recommended by Peter Fink to serve on the R. P. Scherer board.

W. Merritt Jones Jr., partner of Hill, Lewis, Adams, Goodrich & Tait

Merritt Jones was a partner at a Detroit law firm that had R. P. Scherer as one of its three largest clients.[34] In the year before Karla's proxy fight, R. P. Scherer paid Jones's firm $496,300 for legal services.[35] He was also married to Peter Fink's sister.[36] Jones was recommended by Peter Fink to serve on the R. P. Scherer board.

Richard Manoogian, chairman and CEO of Masco Corporation

Richard Manoogian was a longtime friend of Peter Fink. Fink served on Masco's board of directors and he sponsored Manoogian for membership in his country club.[37] Manoogian was recommended by Peter Fink to serve on the R. P. Scherer board.

Dean Richardson, chairman and CEO of Manufacturers National Corporation

Richardson ran Detroit-based Manufacturers National Bank, which was a large lender to R. P. Scherer. The year before Karla's proxy fight, R. P.

Scherer paid $528,617 in interest and fees to the bank. Manufacturers National Bank was also trustee to various Scherer family trusts and was transfer agent and registrar for the company's common and preferred stocks. R. P. Scherer chairman Wilber Mack was a former director of Manufacturers National.[38]

William Stutt, general partner of Goldman Sachs

Bill Stutt was a partner at Goldman Sachs, which had a seventeen-year investment banking relationship with R. P. Scherer. Goldman took R. P. Scherer public in 1971. At the time of Karla's proxy fight, Goldman Sachs was the company's financial advisor.[39]

AS YOU CAN see, this was not a group of small-time, self-dealing ya-hoos. Peter Fink's six supporters were highly accomplished business-men. Three of them ran leading Detroit companies while serving on R. P. Scherer's board: Peter Dow led a national advertising agency; Dean Richardson's Manufacturers National Bank was one of the city's largest banks, founded by Edsel Ford; and Manoogian's Masco was a rapidly growing building products manufacturer that is now a Fortune 500 company. Manoogian later became a billionaire and served on the board of Ford Motor Company. The group was rounded out by Mack, the re-tired chairman and CEO of one of Detroit's largest utility companies; Jones and Stutt, partners at Hill, Lewis, one of the city's top law firms, and Goldman Sachs, respectively.

These were capable men with vast business experience, but they were beholden to Peter Fink in critical ways. Four of the six had clear economic incentives to support Fink. Wilber Mack received material compensation from R. P. Scherer well in excess of typical director fees. Dean Richardson, Bill Stutt, and Merritt Jones boasted R. P. Scherer as large clients. Five of the six had deep social bonds with Fink. Except for Stutt, a New Yorker, they were members of the same Grosse Pointe country club.[40] Peter Dow was Fink's boyhood friend, Merritt Jones was his brother-in-law, and Wilber Mack was his mentor.

Four of Peter Fink's supporters owed their position on the R. P.

Scherer board directly to Fink, who hand-selected them. One director, Richard Manoogian, even invited Fink (and later, Peter Dow) to serve on the board of *his* company. With Fink serving on the Masco board, was Manoogian likely to be a difficult and demanding board member of R. P. Scherer? Were these the right men to ask Peter Fink hard questions and hold him accountable for R. P. Scherer's performance? Would any of them want to sell the company out from underneath him if a generous bid surfaced?

On April 26, 1988, and again on June 8, in contested votes won by Fink and his supporters, the R. P. Scherer board of directors passed a resolution that it would not consider any offer to buy the company.[41] It also declared that it was in the best interests of shareholders to reject any sale. That is an obviously ludicrous statement: No business is so good that it is not for sale at any price. I suspect that the captains of industry on the R. P. Scherer board feared that a legitimate bid for the company would force them to choose between their friend Peter Fink and the shareholders.

FIGHTING IN PUBLIC

Karla Scherer decided to take her case directly to the shareholders. On May 20, 1988, nine days after she filed for divorce from Peter Fink, Karla and John Scherer filed a 13D with the SEC disclosing their interest in selling the company for the benefit of all shareholders.[42] In June, they requested the shareholders' list from R. P. Scherer and announced they would wage a proxy fight to change the makeup of the board of directors. Peter Fink and his supporters took the proxy fight seriously. Karla and John were a formidable threat. They controlled 38% of the votes, not including another 9% held in trusts for their benefit formed by their father.[43]

R. P. Scherer immediately fought back with the help of Martin Lipton, the corporate defense lawyer famous for inventing the poison pill. The company refused to provide the stockholder list to Karla and John. The board passed a new stock option plan to accelerate options vesting in the event of a change of control of the company. Peter Fink began to lobby Manufacturers National Bank to vote shares held in trust for Karla and John in favor of management. The board also added a new member, Joerg Siebert, the chairman of Deutsche Gelatine, a German company that sold $12 million of gelatin to R. P. Scherer over the previous year and collected $7 million in other expenses.

Siebert's addition bolstered Fink's defense by bringing the board to eleven members. R. P. Scherer had a "staggered" board consisting of three separate classes of directors who each served three-year terms. This differs from many corporate boards, in which all directors serve one-year terms. The staggered structure prevents a company's shareholder base from removing the entire board of directors in a single election. In 1988, only three R. P. Scherer directors were up for election: Richard Manoogian, John Scherer, and Peter Dow. Karla and John's dissident slate included John and two newcomers, Frederick Frank, an investment banker with experience in the pharmaceutical industry, and Theodore Souris, a former Michigan Supreme Court justice. If the dissident slate prevailed, it would join Karla and Ernst Schoepe to control five board seats. By adding another board member, Peter Fink could protect his majority until the 1989 election and prevent a full year of 5–5 deadlock. This would buy Fink another year to try to improve operations, court shareholders, and keep the company off the auction block.

On July 7, one day before a hearing in Delaware chancery court, R. P. Scherer finally handed over its shareholder list. John Scherer complained that the company's decision to delay and force litigation resulted in substantial legal costs that would ultimately be borne by shareholders. Two days earlier, R. P. Scherer lawyers deposed Karla in Delaware. The questioning was supposed to focus on whether Karla and John had serious intent to wage a proxy battle. Instead, the lawyers grilled Karla in a four-hour session that John described as "inappropriate" and "harassment."[44] Things were getting ugly.

With the August 17 vote looming, both sides began to bombard shareholders with proxy mailings. The company fired the opening salvo on July 11. A letter signed by Peter Fink and Wilber Mack argued that Karla and John were motivated by their own financial interests rather than the welfare of all R. P. Scherer shareholders. Karla followed with a

July 25 letter contending that a sale of the company to the highest bidder would provide maximum value to the stock. She also urged shareholders to vote against the new stock option plan, which she called "golden parachutes" for R. P. Scherer's executives in the case of a buyout. Karla and John named their group the "Karla Scherer Fink Stockholders' Committee."

On July 28, Fink and Mack sent a short letter to shareholders that belittled Karla's "so-called Committee" and claimed she once demanded to be made CEO of the company. On August 4, they followed up with a much longer letter with the same accusation. One of the few bold-print passages in the single-spaced four-page letter reads:

In early March of this year, Mrs. Fink, who has no management experience, demanded she be appointed Chief Executive Officer of your company in the place of Peter R. Fink.

The letter highlights that Karla filed for divorce from Peter shortly before publicly calling for the company to be sold. It again questions Karla's motivations for wanting to sell the company, and argues that her demand to run R. P. Scherer herself contradicted positive statements she made to the media about the company's management and future prospects.

In a section titled "Who Are Karla Scherer Fink's Nominees?" there is a single bullet point about Theodore Souris: "Dissident nominee Theodore Souris, the attorney representing Mrs. Fink, is a member of the law firm handling her divorce proceedings." Of course, Souris himself was not Karla's divorce lawyer. In 1960, he had been the youngest man ever—at thirty-three years old—to be appointed to Michigan's Supreme Court. He served on the high court for nine years before returning to private practice and becoming one of Michigan's most respected corporate lawyers.[45]

In R. P. Scherer's August 4 letter to shareholders, Karla Scherer is portrayed as a fickle Queen of the Night to Fink's calm and collected Sarastro. The fixation on her demand to be CEO is telling. Though Karla vehemently denies that she ever asked to be CEO—and there was certainly no record of a formal request—it wouldn't bother me if she had asked for the job. **Would anyone raise a hyperventilating, bold-faced fuss if a *man* with a 39% voting stake in R. P. Scherer had asked to re-place the underperforming CEO so he could put the company up for sale?** Of course not. Fink and Mack were trying to create the impression that Karla was an irrational, scornful, estranged wife teaming up with her divorce lawyer to ruin her husband's company.[46]

While management's proxy letters had an air of desperation, Karla's were clear and to the point. In her rebuttal to the company's accusation that she demanded to be CEO, which is reprinted on page 227, Karla caught the bold-faced fever. She wrote:

> **We believe management is misleading you in an attempt to prevent the sale of the company so that top executives may con-tinue to benefit personally.** Chairman Wilber H. Mack (whose position, in our opinion, is largely ceremonial) and President Peter R. Fink received total compensation of $3,007,000 between April 1, 1985 and March 31, 1988 . . . over ⅓ the amount of dividend payments to stockholders during that same three period. . . . The issue at hand is **your financial well-being**—not personal attacks management makes to distract your attention.

A WEEK BEFORE the vote, Karla was feeling good about her chances of winning. Several large shareholders had rallied to her cause and bought sizable stakes, including Tony Cilluffo, a well-respected hedge fund manager who was an early partner at Steinhardt, Fine. Then, she re-ceived some unwelcome news: Manufacturers National Bank was going to vote the shares in Karla and John's trusts *against* her slate of directors. This was a major turn of fortunes. Adding the 9% voting stake in Kar-la's and John's trusts to Manoogian's 15% and another 10% from Joerg Siebert's Deutsche Gelatine, management's slate had secured 34% of the vote.[47] This was well within striking distance of Karla and John's 38%.

Remember, Manufacturers National Bank was more than just the trustee for the trusts Bob Scherer set up for Karla and John. It earned half a million dollars a year lending money to R. P. Scherer, and its chairman, Dean Richardson, served on R. P. Scherer's board of directors.[48] The bank had benefited from a long and profitable relationship with R. P. Scherer, and there were deep social ties between the companies' executives. Wilber Mack, R. P. Scherer's chairman, had even served on the Manufacturers National board of directors.

Karla's lawyers had contacted the trust administrator in late July to ask about the bank's intentions regarding the proxy vote. After they argued that positioning R. P. Scherer for a sale was in the best interest of shareholders, they reminded the administrator that Karla and John were the only income beneficiaries of the trusts and they wished the shares to be voted in their favor. The administrator responded that it was a "sensitive" matter that had been "kicked upstairs" to the head of the trust department.[49] Karla was outraged. She was especially frustrated because the bank, over the previous five years, had willingly sold all of the R. P. Scherer shares out of trusts Bob Scherer had set up for his other two children, at their request. In doing so, the trustee had specifically agreed that it was in the best interests of her siblings to liquidate their holdings at lower prices. How could it then argue that it was in Karla and John's best interest to reject a slate of directors seeking an immediate sale of the company?

When Karla and John filed suit over the matter, their lawyers argued, "One would have to be extremely naïve to believe that the Trustee's decision, in voting the Corporation's stock held in the trusts, will not be significantly influenced by the action of Dean Richardson and the incentive for Manufacturers to preserve and promote its rewarding business relationship with the Corporation."[50] It later turned out that the head of the trust department voted for management's slate after letting Peter Fink present his case to the bank at a private dining club. He never met with Karla or her representatives, and he never read her proxy materials or the trust documents contained in Bob Scherer's will.

On the day of the election, the Michigan Court of Appeals ordered Manufacturers National Bank not to vote the shares. The bank had submitted its vote earlier in the week, and brazenly decided not to withdraw it. It didn't matter. Karla's slate was victorious. The company tried to contest the election result based on the trust shares, and another large block of shares voted in favor of Karla's slate on a photocopied proxy that did not capture both sides of the original. The courts sided with Karla, and all of the dissidents were seated on the board by October. In a matter of months, Joerg Siebert flipped to Karla's side, Peter Fink was out as CEO, and R. P. Scherer was on the auction block.

In May 1989, Shearson Lehman Hutton agreed to buy R. P. Scherer for $480 million.[51] Shareholders received $31.75 per share—$28.19 in cash and $3.56 in preferred stock paying a 17% dividend. The stock had more than doubled since Karla began lobbying for a sale fourteen months earlier. By the time the preferred stock was redeemed several years later, R. P. Scherer's shareholders had received $33.21 per share.

Conflicts and Compromises

Most large American public companies feature a wide separation between share owners and managers. The board of directors bridges this gap. In some ways, the board is a middleman, making sure the managers' interests remain aligned with those of the shareholders.[52] But the board is also bestowed with tremendous powers to run the business. It chooses the CEO and provides counsel on major strategic decisions. More than any other party, the board of directors governs the company.[53]

We place a lot of responsibility on corporate directors. We have high expectations both as shareholders and as a society for how they should perform their duties. But are they up to the task? A corporate director must perform so many conflicting duties that it is hard for him or her to be effective. Let's look at two of the most fundamental responsibilities: The board of directors is supposed to select managers and help them guide the company, but it must also evaluate them and hold them accountable on behalf of shareholders. In other words, the board helps define a company's strategy but is then responsible for deciding if the strategy is working. How objective are directors likely to be in evaluating a company's performance if they played a major role in choosing the CEO and advising him or her? We have already seen this form of psychological bias play out in grotesque fashion in the Great Salad Oil Swindle. American Express allowed De Angelis to commit an unbelievable fraud because its managers had already put their reputations on the line by taking Allied as a client. A public company director who turns on a CEO is, in essence, reprimanding himself for choosing the wrong leader.

The dynamics of the corporate boardroom ultimately tighten the bond between management and directors. This widens the very gap between shareholders and managers that the board of directors is meant to bridge. Karla Scherer's battle with R. P. Scherer illustrates many of the ways that directors can enable underperforming managers. Fortunately, the case also gives us some insight into how to resolve some of these problems.

Let's start by listing some of the barriers to healthy dissent among R. P. Scherer's board members. One easily observable problem was the number of financial conflicts of interest on the board. The chairman of the board was paid a huge amount even by today's standards. Also serving on the board were the company's banker, investment banker, lawyer, and one of its largest suppliers. The CEO and COO both served as well, meaning seven of the eleven board members had meaningful financial conflicts: Three received material compensation directly from the company, and the other four were clients or vendors.

Another problem with the R. P. Scherer board was the number of directors picked specifically by Peter Fink to serve. Board seats come with both remuneration and prestige. Especially at larger companies, it's perceived as a great honor to serve on the board of directors. But when CEOs effectively select directors, they personally bestow the honor and board fees upon them. This corrupts the directors' ability to be objective judges of management from the very beginning.

When CEOs play a major role in choosing directors, they might also be biased toward candidates who won't give them trouble in the boardroom. Karla remembers a conversation she had with Peter Fink about a vacancy on the R. P. Scherer board. According to her, Fink filled it with someone, "because he's weak and he'll do what I tell him to do."[54] A great example of this phenomenon was former SEC chairman Arthur Levitt's close call with the Apple board of directors. In Levitt's excellent 2002 book, *Take on the Street*, he writes about the time he thought Steve

Jobs invited him onto the Apple board. Arthur was thrilled—he'd been a genuine Apple junkie ever since he bought his first Macintosh in 1984. He flew out to California the next day, had breakfast with Jobs, and then met with Apple's senior management team. The CFO gave him a presentation on the financial state of the company and the makeup of its board of directors, before sharing the dates of the upcoming board meetings. Arthur gave the CFO a folder of speeches he'd made on corporate governance. While Levitt was flying home, Jobs read one of the speeches and had second thoughts about adding him. He called the SEC chairman and told him, "Arthur, I don't think you'd be happy on our board and I think it best if we not invite you."[55]

Perhaps the most important barrier to dissent on R. P. Scherer's board was the most insidious—the many social connections among the directors. Almost all of them were members of the same country club. The board included Peter Fink's father figure, his childhood buddy, and two of his brothers-in-law. Ironically, if Peter hadn't had his wife as a director, he probably would have had a fully captive board. Deep personal connections between directors and CEOs can't help but affect the oversight function of boards.

One focus for regulators, exchanges, and investors is to promote "director independence." By populating boards with "outside" directors who are not connected to the company, they hope to better ensure that shareholders receive fair treatment. New regulations, including Sarbanes-Oxley, have specifically aimed to increase director independence in an effort to improve board performance. But how do you determine a director's level of independence by using any kind of objective checklist? R. P. Scherer's board is a perfect example of this problem.

Directors are usually deemed "independent" if they don't have business dealings or employment with the company. Prospective director "independence questionnaires" mostly try to ferret out financial conflicts of interest. But social relationships, which can be much harder to define, can have just as big an impact on a director's ability to perform his or her duties. Was Manufacturers National Bank's Dean Richardson any less independent than Peter Dow, Fink's boyhood friend and neighbor? Would you be more worried about the legal fees accruing to Merritt Jones's law firm or the fact he was married to Peter Fink's sister? It is all too easy to populate a board of directors with "independent" directors who, nonetheless, have deep connections to the CEO. At the Walt Disney Company, Michael Eisner had his personal lawyer, his architect, and the principal of his children's elementary school on the board of directors.[56]

I doubt that any formulaic evaluation of director independence could really work to improve boards. One fundamental challenge is that the upper echelon of the business world is so incestuous it's hard to track the many ways that people are socially and professionally connected. The stock exchanges acknowledge this difficulty in their independence standards. Both the NASDAQ and NYSE task the board of directors with using its collective judgment to determine if a particular director is independent.[57] This is yet another situation where the public company board of directors is a "judge in his own cause."[58]

The other challenge is that director independence is an overrated mechanism for improving oversight. Incentives and conflicts matter, but true independence is also a state of mind. Not counting the CEO, guess which R. P. Scherer directors were the *least* independent on paper? They were the dissidents: Karla Scherer and Ernst Schoepe, the CEO's wife and the chief operating officer of the company.

Even if director independence were tremendously effective in improving boards, there's only so long a director can serve before developing a closer relationship with management. We humans are social beings, and the corporate directors and CEOs among us are probably more social than average. Even when boards are not built around social connections, these still develop over time. In 2002, Warren Buffett famously blamed "boardroom atmosphere" for the governance failures of otherwise "intelligent and decent directors."[59] At the 2014 Berkshire Hathaway meeting, he was more specific: "The nature of boards is they are part business organizations and part social organizations. People behave part with their business brain and part with their social brain."

During the 2014 meeting, Buffett answered several pointed questions about Berkshire Hathaway's recent actions as Coca-Cola's largest shareholder. Coke had announced a controversial equity compensation plan that another investor called "an outrageous grab."[60] Buffett agreed that the plan was excessive, but rather than vote against it, he registered his complaint directly with Muhtar Kent, Coke's CEO. Buffett, of course, has a long history with Coca-Cola. In addition to Berkshire being by far the largest shareholder at 9%, Buffett served on the company's board for seventeen years, and his son Howard is a current director. Buffett explained himself: "It was the most effective way of communicating for Berkshire."

Buffett's approach wasn't crazy. Had he voted against the equity plan, it would have still passed 72% to 28%.[61] He said, "We had no desire to go to war with Coca-Cola." Instead of making a public fuss, and embarrassing the company and its directors, he talked to the CEO behind the scenes. It worked: Coca-Cola later revised the plan. But this episode plainly reveals the collegial environment at the top of our largest public companies. Buffett succeeded in changing Coke's equity plan, but he didn't actually vote against it, and neither did anyone on the board of directors. Being effective at a part-social, part-business organization requires that you sometimes play politics.

At the 2014 Berkshire Hathaway meeting, Buffett summed up the issue: "Social dynamics are important in board actions." Carl Icahn disagrees. He wrote about Buffett's abstention, "Too many board members think of the board as a fraternity or club where you must not ruffle feathers. This attitude serves to entrench mediocre management as well as do away with the meritocracy that has endowed our country with the economic hegemony it enjoys to this day."[62] Icahn is right, but as Buffett himself laments when he writes about "boardroom atmosphere," the board *is* a fraternity or club, and ruffling feathers *does* come with negative repercussions. Buffett explains how to impact boards from within: "You have to pick your spots and pick how you do it."[63]

The collegial nature of boards is yet another factor that impairs the oversight capacity of directors and exposes the folly of trying to fix corporate governance with director independence. Over time, most directors fall under management's sway anyway. Often, the directors who are the most removed from the business and its managers are the most susceptible. Enron's board of directors exemplified this dynamic.

When President George W. Bush signed the Sarbanes-Oxley Act into law in 2002, he said, "The era of low standards and false profits is over. No boardroom in America is above or beyond the law."[64] Of course, the irony of the term "post-Enron reform" is that the structure of Enron's board was fully compliant with the new regulations.[65] In terms of board construction, the company was well ahead of the pro-independence era ushered in by its collapse. Before it was despised as an example of bad governance, the Enron board was frequently praised as one of the best in the country. It was filled with luminaries like the former dean of Stanford Business School, who chaired the accounting department, and a former English cabinet member who was also a leader of the House of Commons and the House of Lords. None of these people had special ties to Enron CEO Ken Lay that were worth risking their careers and reputations over. Enron was a veritable model for director independence. It didn't matter.

In this book, we have met a lot of boards that functioned very poorly. What makes a board of directors good? Consider the value and perspective that Karla Scherer brought to the boardroom of R. P. Scherer. First and foremost, she came in with an owner's mentality. Karla owned a significant amount of stock both as a percentage of her net worth and as a percentage of the company. When she joined the board, it was a defensive measure—she knew she had a lot to lose if the company stumbled. Karla also had a well-informed skepticism of the CEO. She was not antagonistic—she insists that she wasn't considering divorce until well after she joined the board—but Karla's thirty years of marriage to Peter Fink certainly gave her a fine-tuned bullshit-detection system.

While Karla Scherer did not have a formal business education, she was smart and she understood R. P. Scherer's business. She was also wise to ally herself with the company's COO, Ernst Schoepe. This gave her deeper insight into the operations and helped her ask the right questions of Fink and the rest of the board. A thorough understanding of the company's business is important to being a good director; it trumps broader business and finance credentials any day of the week. At R. P. Scherer, Peter Fink never could have manipulated the flow of information to Karla and her fellow dissidents.

THERE'S ALWAYS ROOM FOR GELCAPS

R. P. Scherer was tremendously successful in the years after Shearson Lehman Hutton bought the company. The buyout firm teamed up with operators Alex Erdeljan and Jack Cashman, who purchased R. P. Scherer's Canadian hardshell operations in 1986. Erdeljan had worked at R. P. Scherer from 1979 until 1986, and he was well aware that Peter Fink, and Bob Jr. before him, had neglected the softgels business. "They believed the technology had run its course and that they needed to use cash flow from the business to diversify," he said.[66]

Erdeljan and Cashman got rid of all the noncore businesses and focused on promoting the softgel technology to prospective customers. Alex explained why the company had underperformed under Fink: "They really thought of themselves as a contract manufacturer. The mindset was, if someone needs us, they'll call us. . . . They were very inactive in terms of marketing and going after new business." Erdeljan and Cashman put in place new incentives to change workers to "proactive marketers from order takers." They also began to cut costs in the organization, especially at corporate headquarters.

The results were staggering. Encapsulation revenues doubled within six years of the acquisition while operating income tripled in five years. Operating profit margins in the company's core business averaged 11% for the five years before the sale, and 20% for the following five years.[67] The company's new owners made a killing.

R. P. Scherer's incredible success in the 1990s is a testament to the power of good leadership, but it also raises questions about the plight of public companies. Why were R. P. Scherer's original shareholders unable to participate in the enormous upside available to the company? Why did the company suffer poor leadership for twenty-five years, and perpetually forsake an excellent core business for a slew of bad acquisitions? Karla did well by shareholders to take R. P. Scherer out of management's hands and pass it along to someone who would pay a fair price. But could she have done even better for shareholders by bringing in Erdeljan, or somebody else of his caliber, to lead the company?

Alex Erdeljan doesn't think so. "Peter liked being a CEO, but not doing what a CEO has to do . . . and he had all his Grosse Point buddies on the board," he said. Erdeljan explained the benefits of private ownership: "If private equity does one thing well, it's governance. It's their money, they're not afraid to ask tough questions and to really understand the business and make the needed changes. Boards are notorious for waiting too long to get rid of bad people. It's hard to pull the trigger on bad-performing CEOs."

Unfortunately, Karla could not have convinced shareholders to support her proxy fight for any purpose but to sell the company. The only way she could get control of the board was to promise investors a substantial premium for selling the business out from under Peter and the other directors. She would not have garnered much, if any, support from the investment community for a campaign to fire management. Thus Karla Scherer played a curious role in the history of her father's company. To save the business from an underperforming, but deeply entrenched, management team and board of directors, she had to sacrifice much of the future growth and profit potential for herself and other shareholders.

Even today—more than eighty years after Bob Scherer invented the rotary-die encapsulating machine—his technology is dominant and the remnants of his company, now a part of Catalent, are growing and hugely profitable. Erdeljan said, "One of the reasons people underestimated the softgel technology is they tend to look at patents as a proxy for how defensible it is. What people don't realize is that know-how is more valuable." R. P. Scherer had a great business, but its managers didn't understand the value in it. "They were poor managers, and poor managers make poor decisions."[68]

The dramatic case of R. P. Scherer shows us how the board of directors often fails at supervising management on behalf of shareholders. It also hints at a deeper problem with public company governance. The truth is, a board of directors on its own is rarely capable of successfully managing a company for the long term. This is why our fixation on making corporate boards infallible misses the point. Good governance doesn't only require an able board of directors; it also demands the right shareholders and managers. For a public company to run well despite the inherent schism between managers and investors, it needs a fanatical CEO, a long-term-oriented, but attentive, shareholder base, and a vigilant board of directors. We've already seen how hard it is to achieve this mix. Northern Pipeline taught us how managers are easily corrupted, American Express showed us how shareholders can be schizophrenic, and R. P. Scherer revealed that boards of directors often serve merely to further entrench management.

7

Daniel Loeb and Hedge Fund Activism:
The Shame Game

"It seems that Star Gas can only serve as your personal 'honey pot' from which to extract salary for yourself and family members, fees for your cronies and to insulate you from the numerous lawsuits that you personally face due to your prior alleged fabrications, misstatements and broken promises."

—DANIEL LOEB, 2005

IN SEPTEMBER 2013, BILLIONAIRE investor Ron Burkle amended his Schedule 13D statement regarding his firm's investment in a company called Morgans Hotel Group. The 13D is a form filed with the Securities and Exchange Commission—and made publicly available through the SEC's website—that requires 5% shareholders of public companies to, among other things, report recent activity in the stock, their sources of capital, and the purpose of the transaction. Burkle's amendment, his tenth such filing in Morgans since late 2009, included boilerplate passages filled with words like *hereby* and phrases like "such reduction is not determinable." But the purpose of Burkle's filing was not to update the data on his 13D. He reported no change in his holdings or the sources of his funds.[1] Instead, Burkle amended the filing to include a letter he had written a few days earlier to Morgans Hotel's chairman and CEO. He wrote, "Stop acting like a spoiled child. Stop playing with the company as though it's your new toy. Get Morgans on the market and sell it to an appropriate buyer. It's time to sell now for all stockholders benefit. Ask your mother to buy you something else."[2]

When the hostile raider era ended in the late 1980s, management teams of public companies retrenched behind their poison pills and anti-takeover laws like Delaware Section 203. But they did not have free rein. Large institutional investors like CalPERS and TIAA-CREF were more attuned to corporate governance issues, and much less tolerant of underperforming managers. What's more, a group of reformers, opportunists, and gunslingers—a new generation of Benjamin Grahams and Louis Wolfsons and Carl Icahns—emerged in the form of scrappy hedge fund managers with tactics reminiscent of the Proxyteers. What they lacked in capital they made up for with determination and audacity. When they did not have the leverage to influence a management team, they resorted to strongly worded public shamings to try to get their way. One of their best weapons was the pen, and they used the 13D to air their grievances to the rest of the market and win the support of other shareholders. Their methods turned out to be powerful, driving business headlines and shaking up the executive suites of some of America's most iconic companies. Even superstar corporate raiders like Carl Icahn and Nelson Peltz would soon join their ranks.

Hedge fund is a vestigial term that *Fortune* magazine's Carol Loomis used in 1966 to describe A. W. Jones's long-short "hedged" investment partnership. It now applies to a variety of private investment funds that charge their investors an incentive fee carved out of the fund's profits, in addition to a fee based on assets under management. While their investment strategies vary widely, hedge funds tend to share a similar legal structure and a low (but rapidly rising) level of regulatory oversight. Partnerships run by Benjamin Graham, Robert Young, Warren Buffett, and Charlie Munger would today be called hedge funds. In 1990, they occupied a tiny niche in the money management industry. There were only about 600 hedge funds, with a combined $39 billion in assets.[3] Today they number over 15,000 and manage over $3 trillion.

Before the industry matured, hedge funds attracted mostly independent-minded traders and investors with an entrepreneurial streak. Most of them started with very little capital and had to generate good performance to make ends meet. Paul Tudor Jones founded Tudor Futures Fund in 1984 with $1.5 million.[4] Daniel Loeb's Third Point began with $3 million in 1995, and David Einhorn's Greenlight Capital launched with $900,000 in 1996. Though each of these funds went on to manage billions, they started life as small fry. Back in the mid-1960s, Warren Buffett explained to his investors that his "willingness and financial ability" to assume control of his portfolio companies gave him a valuable "insurance policy."[5] But if you only manage a small pool of capital and Michael Milken happens to be banned from the securities industry, what can you do to exert meaningful pressure on a public company? How can a young hedge fund get a management team's attention without an Icahn-style tender offer in its back pocket?

A RADIATING WEAPON

On May 18, 1999, a young hedge fund manager named Robert Chapman wrote a bear hug letter to Corporate Renaissance Group (CRG), a business development company run by Martin D. Sass. The company traded at a steep discount to its assets, which consisted of only cash and three investments. After buying back what shares it could on the open market, CRG announced that it would pursue strategic alternatives including buying an operating business or liquidating the company. When it failed to find a good acquisition candidate, the management team, led by Sass, offered to take the company private for $8 per share.

Chapman owned 6% of CRG, and he thought its cash and investments were worth at least $10 per share. The company's board appointed a special committee to evaluate the management bid, but Chapman worried it would be biased in favor of Sass, who was chairman, CEO, and the largest shareholder. To keep the special committee honest, Chapman submitted a $9 bid while arguing that a liquidation was in shareholders' best interests. He even added his own "highly confident" language. He didn't have the money himself, but he was "highly confident that current discussions regarding financing will prove successful."[6] This wasn't as convincing as a letter from Drexel Burnham, but it sounded impressive. Chapman attached his bear hug as an exhibit to a 13D filing, much as a corporate raider would have done in the 1980s. The gambit worked. After announcing that the value of its assets had increased to more than $12 per share, CRG commenced a liquidation.

Five months later, Chapman attached another letter to one of his public 13D filings. He wrote to the chairman of Riscorp, a collapsed workers' compensation insurance company, four days after the death of its CEO. Riscorp had employed the CEO through a contract with Phoenix Management, which he ran with a younger partner, Riscorp's general counsel. Upon his death, Riscorp continued the relationship with Phoenix, and the younger partner assumed the CEO's duties. Chapman argued that Phoenix was already grossly overpaid, and that the younger partner was not nearly as qualified as the deceased CEO. He added, "I would be remiss not to mention that it was during his role as a legal officer . . . that the company became embroiled in one of the worst legal scandals ever seen by the insurance industry. . . ."[7]

This time, Chapman did not make a formal buyout proposal. He was merely pushing the company to terminate its expensive management agreement with Phoenix. But it was a delicate argument to make—on the one hand, arguing that the CEO was overpaid while, on the other, expressing sympathy for his recent passing. At more than fourteen hundred words, the letter was thorough and well written. Chapman did not have enough shares to vote the directors out of office, but with his creative use of Schedule 13D, he'd found a way to pressure them in full view of the shareholders.

With Robert Chapman's next 13D, the revolution was born. On March 30, 2000, he wrote a letter to J. Michael Wilson, the chairman and CEO of American Community Properties Trust (ACPT). He attacked the Wilson family, which owned 51% of the stock, for plundering the company through related-party transactions and a "consulting-fee gravy train." Chapman added, "If the Trustees desire to continue running ACPT as a real-life version of Monopoly whereby a 32-year old graduate of Manhattan College in the Bronx and former bank loan administrator is named CEO by his father, then I strongly suggest you take the company private, wherein underserved, nepotistic practices are not scrutinized."[8]

Chapman's letters were snarky and irreverent, often combining astute financial analysis with vitriol and humor. He explained his strategy to a Bloomberg reporter: "Ridicule is a radiating weapon."[9] He would end up filing 13Ds on seventeen companies. Some of the letters were outrageous—the term "skin flute" was used once—but he made money on every investment, generating 20% annualized returns on all but one.[10]

Robert Chapman stepped back from the hedge fund industry in 2003 after fracturing his spine bodysurfing. He left just as hedge fund activism kicked into overdrive. A new generation of activist hedge fund managers, wielding 13D letters that sounded like they were written by potty-mouthed teenagers rather than Warren Buffett or Benjamin Graham, began targeting underperforming companies. None did it better than Daniel Loeb from Third Point. As Dan Loeb and his kindred spirits at funds such as Pershing Square, Jana, Ramius and Starboard Value, Greenlight, and ValueAct evolved from gadflies to raptors, they began waging major proxy fights, winning support from large institutional investors, and leading the debate on major corporate governance issues.

The Paddle Out

Daniel Loeb's early years did little to suggest he would become a titan of industry. He graduated from Columbia with a bachelor's degree in economics, but he was not a star student as Benjamin Graham or Carl Icahn had been. He did share one formative experience with Icahn: In his early twenties he made a ton of money speculating in the stock market and then lost everything plus a little more in tax liability. It would take Loeb a decade to pay back his father, who bailed him out of the mess. He told a Bloomberg reporter, "That was a 10-year lesson in the perils of leverage and overconcentrating positions."[11]

After college, Loeb bounced around various jobs in finance, several on the buy side followed by a few on the sell side.[12] In the late '80s, he even worked a brief stint at Chris Blackwell's Island Records. The company had recently suffered a liquidity crisis after sinking so much money into a crime-thriller movie starring Art Garfunkel that it could not pay U2's royalties. Loeb helped Blackwell secure debt financing and resolve a dispute with Bob Marley's estate.[13] Island was one of the great record companies of all time, and an early lesson in hidden value. Though it constantly flirted with liquidity problems and financial trouble, it was an immensely valuable company. When Blackwell sold to PolyGram in 1989 for $300 million, U2, which had converted its royalty receivable into an equity stake, made a killing.

After Island, Loeb worked for three years as a risk-arbitrage analyst at a hedge fund called Lafer Equity Investors. When he couldn't get another hedge fund job after Lafer, he transitioned to the sell side. For many an inspiring investor, moving from a hedge fund to the sell side is a plank walk that leaves you permanently off the ship. But Loeb landed in the right place at the right time—the Jefferies distressed trading desk in 1991.

Jefferies Group was a Los Angeles–based brokerage that built a franchise doing large, off-exchange block equity trades. The firm ran into trouble in the mid-1980s when Ivan Boesky, cooperating with federal investigators, got founder Boyd Jefferies to discuss a stock-parking arrangement on a recorded phone call. The insider trading crackdown threatened the firm's viability, but ultimately boosted its fortunes. Boyd sacrificed himself to save his company, and when Drexel later crumbled, Jefferies Group was there to pick up the pieces.[14]

After Drexel filed for bankruptcy in 1990, Jefferies hired dozens of its people and expanded the brokerage into high-yield and distressed debt. Drexel provided talent for Jefferies's sales and trading desks, which then traded Drexel-issued bonds. Dan Loeb was a distressed analyst and trader, learning how to navigate the bankruptcy code by researching bankrupt Drexel issuers. Having already done so much for Jefferies and Loeb, it seemed like Drexel had nothing left to offer. But there was one last morsel. Loeb began to look at the Drexel bankruptcy itself, and found an obscure security entitled to payments from Drexel's liquidating trust.

Drexel's liquidation plan formed three tranches of "certificates of beneficial interest" (CBIs) for claimants. According to projections in the bankruptcy's disclosure statement, the senior tranche, CBI-A, would receive $646 in payments per unit—more than a billion dollars in total.[15] Many of the CBI-A holders were large European banks that had already written off their Drexel claims. Loeb got a list of owners from the bankruptcy court and found that they were willing sellers at bargain prices. He lined up his best customers to buy the CBI-As, and they were rewarded with a bonanza. Drexel's liquidation ultimately paid out more than $2 billion to creditors.[16]

Loeb did very well at Jefferies and established valuable relationships with a group of rising investors that would come to dominate the hedge fund industry. He also found himself near the epicenter of distressed-debt investing right as it emerged into a viable asset class—a result of the early 1990s recession. After a year selling bonds at Citicorp, Dan Loeb finally started his own hedge fund. In 1995, he launched Third Point from the weight room in fund manager David Tepper's New Jersey offices.[17]

WHY AM I MR. PINK?

Investing communities have always benefited from a healthy exchange of ideas among peers. Robert Beverley, one of the richest men in early America, frequently wrote to a group of buddies who invested in banks and insurers in northern Virginia around the turn of the nineteenth century. They shared notes on the companies' finances, their underwriting and loan quality, as well as their governance and levels of insider ownership.[18] Benjamin Graham nurtured long relationships with like-minded investors, such as Bob Marony, the financial officer of a railroad that Graham savaged in a research report he wrote for his first job. Marony would later cosign Graham's first letter to the Rockefeller Foundation about the pipeline companies. Warren Buffett organized retreats for the Grahamites to caucus with their former teacher. Walter Schloss had decades-long pen pal relationships with fellow stock enthusiasts. Michael Milken supposedly talked to five hundred people on the phone a day.[19] One of them was Ivan Boesky, whose idea exchanges were much more illicit and sometimes involved briefcases stuffed with money.

My point is, there have been very few lone wolves in the investment world.

Part of the education requires discussing your ideas and investment process with others rather than just sprinting onto the battlefield alone. Today, investors swap thoughts on Twitter. Maybe tomorrow they'll strap on a virtual reality headset and chat with AI bots programmed to look and think like Warren Buffett. In the early days of Daniel Loeb's

Third Point, they posted stock recommendations on anonymous Internet message boards.

"Mr. Pink shares his wisdom on such diverse topics as spin-offs, mutual thrift and insurance conversions, merger arbitrage, post-bankruptcy equities and short ideas. Mr. Pink does not lie." In 1996, Loeb appeared as "Mr. Pink" on Siliconinvestor.com and started posting on boards for stocks he had shorted. The next year he launched his own board there, "Mr. Pink's Picks," in which he shared his ideas, long and short, and engaged with anyone who happened by. "Oh Lord He is Wise!" Mr. Pink would proclaim when one of his ideas worked. "Oh Lord He Sucks!" when they didn't. In 1997, he wrote, "Mr. Pink is a pip squeak in the world of hedge funds." It was a curious time in the early days of stock message boards, when investors like Dan Loeb and Michael Burry (profiled in Michael Lewis's *The Big Short*) passed out tips to anybody who would listen. The level of discourse was surprisingly high, as was the quality of the recommendations. Loeb pitched a lot of "special situations"—insurance company demutualizations, spin-offs, broken IPOs, and distressed equities—at a time when they were often grossly undervalued. Reading Mr. Pink's board now would make any investor in today's competitive markets wistful for layups past.

Third Point's early performance was excellent. Loeb did well on both his long and short positions, and by early 2000 his fund had grown to more than $130 million.[20] In five years of buying small capitalization companies, as well as selling them short, Dan Loeb learned just how terrible their governance was. He'd seen long positions blow up because of bad management. He'd also had short targets squander what little money they had left by suing him. When he read Chapman's 13D letter to ACPT, Loeb knew he'd found a useful weapon for his emerging fund. Years of posting strident messages as Mr. Pink informed Dan Loeb's interface with the rest of the market. His 13D letters would read more like targeted flames on anonymous message boards than formal business correspondences.

ON SEPTEMBER 8, 2000, Loeb filed a 13D on Agribrands, a recent spin-off from Ralston Purina. The company had announced plans to merge with Ralcorp, another Ralston Purina spin-off, on terms that Loeb believed shortchanged Agribrands' shareholders. The chairman of both companies was Bill Stiritz, who had been Ralston Purina's CEO since 1981. Stiritz was a well-respected businessman who had created a lot of value for Ralston Purina shareholders during his tenure. He dismantled what was once a bloated conglomerate, kept the best businesses, leveraged them, and then used excess cash to repurchase shares. Once he'd accomplished that, he began to spin off Ralston Purina's constituent parts to shareholders.[21] Ralcorp and Agribrands came out in 1994 and 1998, respectively.

Loeb argued that the deal, which the market valued at about $41 per share, grossly undervalued Agribrands. He then accused Stiritz of once before putting his own interest before Agribrands' shareholders. Though the stock had been "basically flat" since its spinoff—it rose from $35¾ after the spin to $36¼ over two years later, just before the merger announcement—Loeb pointed out that Stiritz was given a mammoth 500,000-share options grant in 1998 when the Asian crisis briefly pushed the stock down to $21. According to Loeb, this happened right before the company announced a large share repurchase and a quarter that beat analyst expectations.

Loeb quoted Stiritz saying the spin-offs had been "successful." He wrote, "But by whose measure? In my business, fund management, we are measured by the rate of return earned for our investors. (Our returns have been quite good, averaging over 35% per annum for over five years notwithstanding the drag from our investment in Agribrands.) From such an investor's perspective the performance of Agribrands and Ralcorp has been dismal. The propitious timing and pricing of your option grants have yielded you a profit of over $14.0 million. It would appear that the success you speak of is your profits on your options, not that of your shareholders."[22]

With his very first 13D, Loeb showed that he was not afraid to disrespect the village elders. Chapman's 13D letters often targeted mediocrities that nobody had ever heard of. But accusing someone like Bill Stiritz of self-dealing was different. Stiritz was an experienced capital allocator who saw an opportunity to fold Agribrands, a mature animal feed

business with excess cash, into Ralcorp, a higher-return consumer products company that wanted to grow by acquisition. There were no syn-
ergies to speak of, but he thought he'd found a way to put Agribrands'
capital to better use for its shareholders. Loeb, of course, disagreed. He
thought the deal harmed Agribrands' shareholders by undervaluing its
core business. Three weeks after his 13D, Cargill made an unsolicited
written offer to acquire Agribrands for $50 per share in cash.[23] Cargill
ultimately paid $54.50, and Loeb walked away with a huge profit.

OVER THE NEXT few years, Loeb filed a succession of angry 13D letters
that, in addition to skewering CEOs for poor performance, were un-
afraid to target board members. One of Loeb's specialties was exposing
directors who padded their professional experience as listed in company
proxy statements. He outed several directors whose sole employment
was at companies that were essentially empty shells. In a 13D letter
to Penn Virginia, Loeb questioned the business experience of a board
member who was "Founder and CEO" of "Woodforde Management,
Inc," a "holding company."[24] Loeb discovered that Woodforde had no
other employees and almost no revenues. The only business the director
engaged in was an ailing detergent company, called Cot'nWash, run out
of the same address as Woodforde. When Loeb addressed the shortcom-
ings of a different Penn Virginia director later in the letter, he began,
"We have placed an order for Cot'nWash that should come in handy for
washing certain articles of clothing soiled when learning that the Company's newest Director . . ."

Loeb also gave a lot of attention to self-dealing and nepotism. In a
letter to the chairman and CEO of InterCept, Loeb complained about
an onerous related-party financing transaction as well as a leasing arrangement for a private jet. He also pointed out that the CEO's daughter
and her husband were both on the company payroll, making nearly a
quarter of a million dollars in combined salary. When Loeb called the
CEO's son-in-law during work hours to learn about his role at the company, he was "on the golf course."[25] In a subsequent letter to InterCept,
Loeb responded to the CEO calling Third Point a "sleazy hedge fund":
"For someone who acquired iBill, a purported 'merchant processing

business' whose real activity is primarily to provide billing services to hard core pornographic websites, your credibility as moral arbiter is not strong. . . . [C]alling your second largest shareholder 'sleazy' in the media is further evidence of your poor judgment and exemplifies the type of behavior that should provide you with ample opportunity to join your son-in-law on the golf course in the not too distant future."[26]

What's notable about some of these personal attacks is that they often weren't that relevant to Loeb's investment, or his motivations for going active in the first place. The second letter to InterCept, for example, served no purpose but to taunt the CEO. It opened by stating, "I am writing to inform you that we agree with the market's determination that InterCept, Inc. (the 'Company') should be worth substantially more with your imminent involuntary extraction from the position of Chief Executive Officer, which we would expect to result from the likely sale of the Company." Loeb was not trying to lobby other shareholders to support him, nor was he hoping to persuade management or the board to do anything different. He was simply kicking the CEO when he was already on the ground. His letter to Star Gas Partners the following year was even harsher. But this time Loeb at least had a purpose: He wanted the chairman and CEO to resign. "Sometimes a town hanging is useful to establish my reputation for future dealings with unscrupulous CEOs," he explained.[27]

A Conservative, Dividend-Paying Stock

Star Gas Partners was a propane and heating oil distributor run by Irik Sevin, a former investment banker who had grown the company rapidly through acquisitions. Star Gas's game was not too dissimilar from the conglomerators'—it used its richly valued stock to help fund acquisitions.[28] But Star Gas did not rely on institutional investors chasing earnings growth to bid up its stock. It used a seemingly rock-solid dividend to seduce income-seeking retail investors into levitating its shares. Taking a page from the corporate raiders' playbook, Star Gas was also not afraid to leverage itself to the hilt.

From its very inception, Star Gas promised investors a healthy dividend of more than $2.00 per share. The stock traded "on yield" as if it were a utility company, and the shares reached the mid-$20 range. But the heating oil and propane distribution business is not a stable utility. It's a seasonal, volatile business with high working capital requirements. In addition, heating oil is in secular decline as a home heating fuel, as homeowners gradually transition to natural gas heat. Star Gas issued shares *every* year between 1998 and 2004 to raise capital. The $335 million in dividends it paid over that period gave the appearance of operating stability, but the company generated $468 million by issuing stock.

In 2002, Star Gas embarked on an extensive restructuring of its heating oil operations. Heating oil delivery seems very similar to propane distribution, but the two businesses differ in fundamental ways. With propane, 95% of homeowners lease their tanks directly from the distributor, and most states let only the tank owners refill them. These "fire safety regulations" entrench incumbent dealers and make their customers essentially captive. With heating oil, customers can switch dealers with relative ease, making it a much more competitive, service-oriented industry. But there's a secret to the heating oil business: If it is operated well, it can generate excellent returns on capital. Some homeowners will always shop around for the best deal, but you can win the lasting loyalty of others with great, personalized service. Many small-town heating oil companies in the northeastern United States have made their family owners very wealthy by doing just that.

In an ambitious attempt to cut costs and improve service, Star Gas decided to deregionalize its heating oil business. It consolidated its operations under just two brands, thus eliminating ninety others it had acquired, many of which were family names that had served local communities for generations.[29] And rather than give customers full service from the twenty-seven local offices it owned, Star Gas dispatched service technicians from only two sites, managed oil delivery from eleven, and started using an outsourced call center in Canada.

Irik Sevin called his plan to create a large, efficient heating oil business in the image of a well-run propane company "very academic and intellectually interesting."[30] But the reorganization was a disaster. It cost almost $30 million without generating meaningful savings. As you might expect, it also alienated customers, who left in droves. Net customer losses in 2004 were five times higher than they had averaged over the previous three years. To exacerbate Star Gas's woes, heating oil prices were rocketing up. The wholesale cost of home heating oil went from $0.78 per gallon in September 2003 to $1.39 in September 2004. This not only affected Star Gas's customers, who consumed less oil; it also threatened the company's liquidity as its working capital requirements increased. As the noose tightened around its neck in 2004, Star Gas made several operating decisions that amounted to taking a directional bet on the price of oil. It delayed hedges and price increases with hopes that heating oil prices might stabilize. Instead, they kept rising, and Star Gas suffered $8 million in unnecessary losses.[31]

On October 18, 2004, Star Gas suspended its dividend to preserve capital. The stock fell 80% in one day. In mid-November, the company sold its propane business for $481 million. Though Star Gas immediately used $311 million to pay down debt, its struggling heating oil operation remained dangerously overleveraged. To make matters worse, because the company was a publicly traded partnership, it passed through a huge taxable gain on its propane sale to shareholders. If you were a retiree who owned Star Gas because it had dependably paid $2.30 in annual distributions for the past five years, you were now stuck with a $5 stock that cost you $20, plus up to an $11 per-share taxable gain. Oof.

On February 14, 2005, Daniel Loeb sent a brutal Valentine's Day letter to Irik Sevin at Star Gas Partners (page 229). He opens by criticizing Sevin for not communicating with shareholders since the collapse of the stock. Loeb then writes, "Sadly, your ineptitude is not limited to your failure to communicate with bond and unit holders. A review of your record reveals years of value destruction and strategic blunders which have led us to dub you one of the most dangerous and incompetent executives in America. (I was amused to learn, in the course of our investigation, that at Cornell University there is an 'Irik Sevin Scholarship.' One can only pity the poor student who suffers the indignity of attaching your name to his academic record.)"

Loeb's letter includes a withering assault on Star Gas's operating performance, Irik Sevin's compensation, and the enormous amount of legal and banking fees the company had incurred. Loeb estimates that the company spent $75 million in fees, or almost half its entire market capitalization. He then questions Sevin's seventy-eight-year-old mother's role as a director: "We further wonder under what theory of corporate governance does one's mom sit on a Company board. Should you be found derelict in the performance of your executive duties, as we believe is the case, we do not believe your mom is the right person to fire you from your job. We are concerned that you have placed your greed and desire to supplement your family income—through the director's fees of $27,000 and your mom's $199,000 base salary—ahead of the interests of unitholders. We insist that your mom resign immediately from the Company's board of directors."

Loeb concludes his letter by letting it slip that the two men know each other socially. He writes, "I have known you personally for many years and thus what I am about to say may seem harsh, but is said with some authority. It is time for you to step down from your role as CEO and director so that you can do what you do best: retreat to your waterfront mansion in the Hamptons where you can play tennis and hobnob with your fellow socialites. The matter of repairing the mess you have created should be left to professional management and those that have an economic stake in the outcome."

THREE WEEKS LATER, Irik Sevin resigned from Star Gas Partners. Within a year the company was recapitalized by Kestrel Energy, a private equity firm affiliated with Yorktown Partners. Kestrel had previously owned Meenan Oil, which was the country's third-largest heating oil distributor when Star Gas bought it in 2001. Star Gas would remain publicly traded after the Kestrel recap, and Meenan's management team, which had never left, would run the whole company. Both the board of directors and the management team had large equity stakes in the business. Management's first move was to return to a localized customer service model.

Star Gas thrived in the years after Dan Loeb demanded the resignation of its chairman and CEO. Despite arguably tougher industry conditions, with wildly volatile heating oil prices that reached $4 per gallon, and a painful economic recession, the company has almost doubled its per-gallon gross profits. Since Kestrel took control in 2006, Star Gas has paid $115 million in dividends and made $249 million worth of acquisitions. It has done this without increasing long-term debt or issuing a single share to raise capital. In fact, the company has spent $83 million retiring 24% of its shares on the open market. The company's pretax, pre-interest earnings over the past year were better than Sevin's Star Gas managed in its best year as a combined propane and heating oil company.[32] And, of course, Star Gas's CEO's salary is 40% lower than Irik Sevin's was.[33]

REDEFINING BUSINESSLIKE BEHAVIOR

At the very end of *The Intelligent Investor*, Benjamin Graham writes, "Investment is most intelligent when it is most *businesslike*." People often refer to this sentence to explain Graham's idea that investors should view shares in a company as fractional ownership interests. But Graham meant so much more than that—the statement is really a philosophy of investing. He is saying that *because* buying shares is the same as buying a fractional interest in a company, an investor should treat the endeavor "as a business venture of his own." Generating superior returns thus requires a prudent businessman's approach to every element of his or her investment process.

Of course, when Benjamin Graham discusses "accepted business principles," he might exclude public letters calling out a CEO's seventy-eight-year-old mother, and referring to soiled underwear or skin flutes. But today's accepted business practices, for better or for worse, tolerate a level of fanaticism that Graham might view as alien. William Thorndike's book *Outsiders* profiles CEOs who excelled through wise capital allocation. But there could be a second volume called *Maniacs*, with chapters on obsessive characters like Steve Jobs, Ray Kroc, Ross Perot, Tom Monaghan, Les Schwab, and Herb Kelleher. In the ranks of these lunatics, we would find many of the characters in this book, from Louis Wolfson to Carl Icahn to some of today's activist hedge fund managers who have taken intelligent investing to extremes.

My favorite book about the hedge fund business is David Einhorn's *Fooling Some of the People All of the Time*. It is a remarkable document—a very detailed account of Einhorn's short position in a small business development company called Allied Capital from 2002 through 2007. It captures the very first conversation Einhorn and his coworkers at Greenlight Capital had with Allied—Greenlight records its research calls—and then walks readers through five and a half years of the fund's quixotic effort to expose Allied's aggressive accounting practices to regulators, analysts, journalists, and other investors.

David Einhorn is one of today's most successful hedge fund managers—Greenlight Capital reportedly manages $10 billion—so his time is incredibly valuable. Being a professional investor, he must also have a keen sense of return on capital. Yet he and his coworkers logged countless hours and days pursuing Allied, which, especially by the end of the saga, could not have been a very big position in the fund. There's a telling moment in the book, when Einhorn visits with Warren Buffett in the first installment of Buffett's annual eBay charity lunch. With his private time with the world's greatest investor, Einhorn can't help himself. He has to pick Buffett's brain about Allied Capital.

David Einhorn's short position in Allied Capital became a holy mission. He wasn't doing it for personal gain: The year he put the position on he pledged half his profits to charity (he ultimately donated them all). And there really is no glory in short selling, even when the target is a scuzzy BDC like Allied. Yet Einhorn not only sunk an ungodly amount of time into the idea, he wrote a four-hundred-page antemortem book about it. The whole thing is a bit mind-boggling.

Whether it was Daniel Loeb attacking Irik Sevin's mother or David Einhorn writing the great American novel about a 3% position in his fund, there was something peculiar about hedge fund managers paying attention to targets in a way that didn't seem to make economic sense. Sevin was by no means the most dangerous and incompetent executive in America. He didn't manage Star Gas's heating oil business very well, but if oil hadn't doubled in price he might still be the company's CEO. As for Allied Capital, it certainly overvalued the assets on its balance sheet, but so did many other companies in the same industry (and some in much larger industries with more damaging effects to the U.S. economy). There is a certain capriciousness to Sevin and Allied becoming top hedge fund targets, and Dan Loeb knew this when he invoked the "public hanging" metaphor. He was warning other public company management teams, "We're watching you, and you might be next." Later hedge fund targets would be much larger and more established companies. Einhorn accused Lehman of aggressive accounting, Loeb exposed the Yahoo! CEO for padding his resume, and Bill Ackman's Pershing Square Capital took on the multilevel-marketing great white whale, Herbalife, in a fight-to-the-death cage match.

WHEREAS CORPORATE RAIDERS busted through gates with hostile tender offers for control and a supporting army of arbitragers, early hedge fund activism was an exercise in persuasion. The ultimate arbiters in many of these disputes were large institutional investors like CalPERS and CalSTERS. It didn't take long for them to start siding with activist hedge funds' campaigns against underperforming management teams. Ridicule as a radiating weapon became unnecessary, and even counterproductive, as hedge fund shareholder activism matured to focus on board representation and proxy fights.

For large institutional investors, their symbiotic relationship with hedge fund activists makes it easier for them to pressure companies behind the scenes. Sometimes they'll even seek out activists for investments they think will benefit from intervention. And, perhaps most important, as activism has become rampant, institutional investors have gotten much better at evaluating campaigns led by hedge funds, and casting their votes wisely. If an activist campaign is based on really stupid ideas, it probably won't gain much support. Thirty years ago, a company under attack from shareholders almost invariably ended up in play. The endgame, where the company was sold even if the timing was bad, was almost inevitable. To quote the great R. Kelly, "it was like Murder She Wrote."[34] As CalPERS's director of global governance, Anne Simpson, told the *New York Times* in late 2013, "shareholder activism is evolving from barbarians at the gate to acting as owners."[35]

This so-called evolution—wherein hedge fund activists are no longer outsiders but, instead, welcomed with open arms by large institutional investors—has had a profound effect on corporate America. *No company is off-limits unless it has locked up its voting control.* Hedge fund activists have waged campaigns in recent years against Apple and Microsoft, the two largest public companies in the world. Carl Icahn pressured Apple to return more capital to shareholders. Even though he didn't rally much support from other investors, it certainly looks like his actions influenced the company to increase its buyback. ValueAct owned less than 1% of Microsoft but managed to place a representative on the company's board of directors. It's hard to imagine hedge funds pulling off a similar feat a decade ago.

Of course, there is one obvious and fundamental flaw with the idea that hedge fund activists will ever be fully aligned with long-term owners. Hedge funds are not structured to run long-term money. Running proxy fights and serving on corporate boards can tie up capital and create a mismatch between the duration of an activist investment and the liquidity terms of the fund. Many hedge funds will tell you that their investors are committed and long term, but that won't be true if their funds' performance starts flagging. As much as hedge funds talk about being long-term owners, it is ultimately an aspirational sentiment.

To successfully run a long-term investment strategy with a hedge fund, you can't just ignore your own short-term business pressures. You must consider catalysts and exit strategies. This is why public company defenders like Martin Lipton are quick to point out that populist statements from hedge fund managers about being long-term owners are more self-serving than accurate. Dan Loeb's investment in Star Gas is instructive here. I wrote earlier about the great success the company has had since its ownership overhaul in 2006. But Loeb actually did not stick around for the turnaround. With Sevin out and the recapitalization completed, the "event" and "catalysts" had come and gone. Investors were tired of Star Gas, and large blocks of shares sat in the hands of participants in the recap. Star Gas was destined to be dead money for a while, and Loeb had better uses for his capital. As he told *New York* magazine's Steve Fishman in 2004, "The only thing I care about is making money for my investors."[36] Mr. Pink does not lie.

The good news for today's investors is that when hedge fund managers like Dan Loeb try to make money in the market, it's usually in their best interest to benefit other shareholders as well. It's much harder for activists to generate good returns for themselves while screwing everyone else, as we saw in the days of greenmail. The awakening of large institutional investors has a lot to do with this dynamic. When passive investors vote shares wisely, it channels shareholder activism in a positive rather than destructive way. For ValueAct to get a great return by owning less than 1% of Microsoft, for example, all Microsoft shareholders need to benefit.

But just as with the Proxyteers and the corporate raiders, we shouldn't get suckered into believing everyone who spouts pro-shareholder populism. A good window into activists' real intentions with regard to other shareholders comes when they get control of a company. Like the Proxyteers and raiders before them, the hedge funds have a spotty record. Perhaps the best example of this is the Sardar Biglari saga at Steak 'n Shake.

AN ETHOS OF CARING

Sardar Biglari is the chairman and CEO of Biglari Holdings, which owns Steak 'n Shake, as well as an insurance company and the magazine *Maxim*. His background is fascinating. The son of a former Iranian military officer who was imprisoned after the 1979 revolution, Sardar lived part of his childhood under house arrest with his mother.[37] He was seven years old when he moved with his family to the United States in 1984. The only words he knew in English were *hi* and *bye*.[38]

When Biglari was nineteen, he read *The Warren Buffett Way* and became interested in investing. He started his own hedge fund after graduating from college, and made a large investment in a restaurant company called Western Sizzlin. After joining the company's board, Biglari helped reorganize the business with a franchising focus and allocated its excess capital into a highly successful activist investment in Friendly's Ice Cream. Biglari's next target was Steak 'n Shake, the iconic midwestern burger chain that inspired Danny Meyer's Shake Shack. Steak 'n Shake had squandered huge amounts of money opening new restaurants while letting performance deteriorate in its existing store base. Biglari was elected to the board of directors in March 2008 and became CEO in early August. Steak 'n Shake was on the verge of default and the country was about to experience a harrowing financial crisis and recession.

Barely thirty years old and with no experience operating restaurants, Biglari pulled off a remarkable turnaround at Steak 'n Shake. After negotiating some wiggle room from his lenders, he aggressively cut costs and simplified the menu. Then, in a gutsy move given the company's precarious financial state, he drastically reduced prices for his customers. Steak 'n Shake saw huge increases in guest traffic and profitability against the backdrop of a struggling economy.

Sardar Biglari created a lot of wealth for Steak 'n Shake's shareholders by saving the company and restoring it to a profitable growth trajectory. But since doing so, he's made a series of controversial moves to entrench himself at the company and maximize his compensation. As one hedge fund manager said to me, "He talks like Warren Buffett but then acts like Ron Perelman!"

Biglari once wrote to Western Sizzlin shareholders, "We intend for the entire organization to exhibit an ethos of caring about its shareholders. . . ."[39] He has since consolidated Steak 'n Shake and Western Sizzlin into a company called Biglari Holdings, which, according to recent SEC filings, has invested $620 million into Sardar's hedge funds. While Biglari's direct ownership in his namesake is less than 2% per his most recent SEC ownership filing, he controls almost 20% through his hedge funds.[40] He stands to earn a 25% incentive fee after a 6% hurdle rate for investing Biglari Holdings' capital.

The hedge fund investments also serve as a powerful entrenchment device, because Biglari Holdings' capital is subject to rolling five-year lockups at Sardar's funds. To further protect his position, Biglari agreed to license his name to the company at a cost of 2.5% of revenues per year should he ever be removed as chairman or CEO, or should he be stripped of capital allocation duties. So if angry investors ever conspire to push out Sardar Biglari, the company will be stuck for years paying him so it can use the phrase "Steak 'n Shake by Biglari" (assuming the agreement holds up in court). Two and a half percent of the company's most recently reported annual revenues comes out to almost $20 million, 70% of the company's 2014 earnings.

Biglari's compensation (excluding any money he makes from the hedge fund arrangement) is also aggressive. Biglari Holdings' last proxy statement showed that he made more than $10 million in each of the previous two years. That's more compensation than the CEOs of much larger companies, including McDonald's, Burger King, Popeyes, and Wendy's. Biglari's payout formula is based on increases in the company's book value. In 2014, Biglari Holdings made a rights offering to shareholders at a 40% discount to the share price.[41] This forced shareholders to pony up more money to prevent their ownership from being diluted. The net effect of the rights offering? Biglari Holdings received an infusion of capital that increased the company's book value, making Sardar's compensation go up. If the proceeds are then invested in his hedge funds, he'll also get 25% of the profits after the 6% hurdle rate.

Because of Sardar Biglari's success creating value for Steak 'n Shake shareholders, investors have mostly tolerated his entrenchment tactics and rich compensation. After a few small shareholders launched a proxy fight for control of Biglari's board, famed value investor and shareholder advocate Mario Gabelli told a reporter for the *Indianapolis Star* that he was likely to support the incumbents.[42] Biglari, for his part, appears to be considering a variant of the "Pac Man" defense. Through his hedge fund, he's bought large stakes in two companies where his dissident shareholder serves on the board.

Sardar Biglari's maneuvers will undoubtedly test institutional investors' patience. If he continues to make money for shareholders through smart investments and good restaurant operations, I suspect he will hold on to his position at Biglari Holdings and prosper. But investors will be wary of his moves on other companies. Despite owning 20% of the stock and exhibiting valuable restaurant operating chops, Biglari has failed to win board representation at Cracker Barrel several years running. He showered shareholders with elegantly written letters skewering the company's operating performance, but they didn't resonate with Cracker Barrel's institutional shareholder base. The poison pen will only get you so far if shareholders don't trust you. In 2007, Biglari wrote a letter to shareholders of Friendly's Ice Cream that stressed "public shareholders' interests should come first." He wrote, "The private jet symbolizes an ongoing culture, one that doesn't care about its shareholders."[43] Restaurant finance writer Jonathan Maze reported in 2014 that Biglari Holdings has registered ownership interests in four jets.[44]

Few hedge fund managers have been as aggressive as Sardar Biglari. When David Einhorn took effective control of Einstein Noah Restaurant Group, he did not rename it Einhorn Restaurant Group and buy four private jets. But Biglari's story, which takes hedge fund shareholder activism to a post-ideological extreme, is instructive. As we have seen, much of the power in our corporate governance system now lies with shareholders. Activist hedge funds were once the pipsqueaks—renegades like Dan Loeb and Bob Chapman who tossed stink bombs into corporate boardrooms—but today they have teamed up with large institutional investors and can win access to almost any boardroom in America. This makes it harder to blame the traditional corporate governance whipping boys (such as captive boards and the separation of management and ownership) when companies stumble. Shareholders must share the blame when governance goes bad. As much as they champion shareholder value and sound corporate oversight, even the most sophisticated investors have a habit of conveniently ignoring warning signs when they are making good money. Unless Sardar Biglari's stock tanks, the market will be permissive of his self-dealings. If he falters, the shareholders will be ruthless.

Investing in public companies is a dangerous pursuit that requires risking real money based on limited information. Even when you are diligent about buying at a margin of safety, you will still make money-losing mistakes. Aspiring investors who require perfection have gotten into the wrong business. Dan Loeb had his Massey Energy, Einhorn his New Century, Seth Klarman his HP, Ackman his JCPenney, and Icahn his Blockbuster Video—all of which suffered steep losses.

Even Warren Buffett had his Berkshire Hathaway, and those pesky Irish banks. When activism goes bad, the glee among rubbernecking investors is palpable. But rather than just point our fingers and gawk, let's dive into some wreckage caused by failed activism and see what we can learn. And don't worry, we can gawk some, too.

BKF Capital:
The Corrosion of Conformity

"A culture of greed and self-dealing has run amok."
—J. CARLO CANNELL, 2005

"Without having the candor to admit it, the opposition is saying 'no' to growth and proposing immediate, drastic cuts to compensation that, if enacted, will inevitably drive away key personnel and diminish the value of our existing business."
—JOHN A. LEVIN, 2005

T HE MOST NOTORIOUS CASE within the canon of failed shareholder activism is Bill Ackman's "Think Big" campaign at JCPenney. Mention the letters J-C-P to money managers and you'll usually get a response that combines rage and schadenfreude. Ackman runs a hedge fund called Pershing Square Capital Management, which has been very successful employing an ultraconcentrated value investing strategy. It now manages more than $15 billion.[1] Once most hedge funds get to this size, they start to tone down their investing style in favor of a more conservative, index-tracking approach. Ackman, to his credit, has stayed true to his roots. A recent SEC quarterly holdings report shows $13 billion spread over just seven stocks.[2] Because he makes relatively few moves, and many of those have been huge home runs, Ackman is closely watched by the whole of Wall Street.

Bill Ackman is known for his silky-smooth delivery of incredibly detailed and lengthy presentations. A 52-page whopper on Burger King, 78 pages on McDonald's, 101 pages on General Growth Properties, and, why not, a 342-page presentation on Herbalife. His 63 pages of thinking

big about JCPenney outlined an ambitious vision for the company's future but the investment thesis was simple. JCPenney owned 49% of its
real estate and leased the rest at below-market rates. The company had
some economies of scale with $17 billion in annual sales and a $1 billion marketing budget.[3] Although even a modest turnaround in its operations would generate good returns for shareholders, Ackman aimed
higher. He saw JCPenney as a blank canvas for the right retailing visionary.[4] He found his artist in Apple's Ron Johnson.

But at JCPenney, Johnson failed to re-create the success he had at
Target and Apple. His effort to wean JCPenney's customers off of big-
discount promotions instead drove them away. Same-store sales plum-
meted 25% and what was once a very low cash-flow business turned
into a very high cash-burning one. The board aborted Johnson's effort to
turn around JCPenney, after just seventeen months. Even Ackman had
harsh words, saying Johnson and his team had made "big mistakes" and
the company's execution had been "very close to a disaster."[5] Within five
months Ackman would sell his entire stake in JCPenney, reportedly for
a loss of more than $450 million.[6]

Despite the crushing result for shareholders, I'm not convinced
JCPenney belongs in the bad-activism canon. When the company's
board unanimously hired Johnson away from Apple, investors were
giddy with excitement. Bill Ackman and the rest of JCPenney's board of
directors took a calculated risk on behalf of shareholders by going with
Johnson, and it was a sensible move despite the outcome. That JCPenney has become synonymous with bad activism shows us the difficulty
of post facto analysis in a results-oriented business.

Judging activism purely based on stock performance can be tricky
and superficial. For example, many interventions result in a sale of the
company that generates positive stock returns. The actual impact of
a sale on long-term shareholders, however, is not so clear-cut. When
it forcibly separates an underperforming, entrenched management
team from a valuable business, shareholders usually benefit. But when
a buyout premium does not fairly compensate shareholders for likely
future gains, then holders have been hurt, even though the stock has
gone up. Recent academic research defending shareholder activism

treats buyouts at a premium as unequivocal positives.[7] They definitely are not. When fund managers talk about their most frustrating experiences as investors, many of them involve low-priced buyouts.

To properly evaluate an activist situation, we need to look beyond the stock price performance and understand what really happened to the business and why. We should also consider what would have transpired had the activists never gotten involved. With this in mind, let's examine the pitiful situation at BKF Capital Group, where an activist campaign in 2005 resulted in total value destruction for shareholders. But for the celebrity status of Bill Ackman, BKF would be the poster child for activism gone awry.

TIMBER I'M FALLING

Baker, Fentress & Company traced its roots back to the 1890s, when it was a Chicago investment bank specializing in the timber business. Starting in the early 1940s, it liquidated its ownership interests in dozens of lumber and logging companies and invested the proceeds in public equities.[8] By 1995, Baker, Fentress was a closed-end fund managing $500 million in passive investments, and a controlling interest in Consolidated-Tomoka Land Company, one of its legacy timber holdings. But the company was a dinosaur. Its portfolio had drastically underperformed the S&P 500 since 1987, when James Fentress, who had run the company for almost twenty years, passed away.[9] Baker, Fentress traded at a steep discount to its assets, so it could not raise capital without diluting existing shareholders. Chairman James Gorter believed that the best way to grow the company was to start managing outside money, but recent underperformance made it hard to attract clients.

In June 1996, Baker, Fentress bought John A. Levin & Company, a money manager that specialized in large-cap value investing. The firm managed over $5 billion, up 40% from the previous year, and had generated strong investment returns since its inception in 1982. John A. Levin's eponymous founder had been director of research at Loeb, Rhoades before leaving in 1976 to become a partner at hedge fund Steinhardt Partners. Levin's own firm started out managing long-only investments for high-net-worth individuals. By the time Baker, Fentress bought it, Levin's institutional clients made up more than 80% of his asset base. He had also recently launched a few hedge fund strategies. The deal gave Levin's firm access to a large, permanent capital base from which it could seed new fund strategies.[10] As part of the deal, John Levin became Baker, Fentress's largest shareholder and CEO.

Levin's company, renamed Levin Management, continued to grow under Baker, Fentress. By the end of 1998 it managed $8.3 billion and was producing healthy growth in its hedge fund assets. The firm's largest hedge fund was its event-driven strategy, co-managed by John's son, Henry. Hedge funds were a valuable growth opportunity for Levin in part because of their aggressive fee structures.[11] In 2000, Levin Management's fee revenue from its traditional long-only assets was $41 million. The hedge funds, which accounted for only about 10% of the firm's total assets, generated $34 million. That year, Henry's fund crossed $1 billion in assets.[12]

Despite Levin Management's growth, Baker, Fentress continued to trade at a large discount to the value of its assets. Closed-end equity funds were out of favor as it was, and Baker, Fentress was a particularly odd duck with stakes in Levin and Consolidated-Tomoka. In 1999, the company decided to deregister as an investment company, liquidate its portfolio, and distribute cash and shares of Consolidated-Tomoka to shareholders. This was an excellent outcome for shareholders, who finally received fair value for Baker, Fentress's equity portfolio. The remaining entity was renamed BKF Capital Group and consisted solely of the Levin business. "I thought that was an incredibly shareholder friendly event," John Levin recently told me.[13] But it also overhauled the stockholder base in a way that opened the door for activist investors.

AFTER MORE THAN a hundred years in existence, Baker, Fentress was about to disappear. Investors who held the dividend-paying, closed-end fund would end up with a small operating business focused on investment management. As Glenn Aigen, BKF's CFO, remembers, "Once we deregistered as a closed-end fund . . . the shareholder base completely changed from a mutual fund and high-net-worth individual base to a more institutional base, being specifically hedge funds."[14] Big structural turnover in a company's shareholder base often results in the stock getting quite cheap, and Baker, Fentress attracted a lot of value investors. Mario Gabelli acquired a large stake. Even Warren Buffett bought shares for his personal account right before the company distributed its assets.[15]

In the early 2000s, BKF Capital Group became a trendy stock pick for value-oriented hedge fund managers.[16] The long thesis was straightforward. Most analysts value money managers at a percentage of assets under management. BKF looked very cheap in this regard—its enterprise value as a percentage of managed funds was lower than other public asset management companies. Adding to the enticement, unlike most of its peers, BKF had a rapidly growing hedge fund business. There were very few public companies with direct exposure to hedge funds. As all the hedge fund managers buying BKF in the early 2000s understood, the industry was experiencing explosive growth.

At the end of 2003, BKF Capital had $13 billion in assets under management. The event-driven hedge fund topped $2 billion and generated $51 million in fees for the year. But despite BKF's rapid growth and its $97 million in fee revenue, its stock was lagging. For most of the year the company was valued at less than $150 million by the market. At one point the market value fell under $115 million, well below what Baker, Fentress paid for John A. Levin in 1996, when it managed significantly less capital. Shareholders began to lose their patience.

When you value a business based on its revenues rather than its cash flows, you are making implicit—and often optimistic—assumptions about its cost structure. But BKF's costs, especially employee compensation, were very high, and there was no indication that John Levin had any interest in moderating them. Many of BKF's investors eagerly awaited the day that the company's hedge funds really took off. But when it finally came, it exposed the flaw in the investment thesis: When BKF's hedge funds earned a large incentive allocation, most of it went to compensate employees rather than shareholders. This highlighted a deeper, structural problem with the company. BKF's employees did not own many shares. John Levin himself only owned about 10%. Their incentives did not line up perfectly with shareholders'.

Levin initially believed that he and his son were so important to the business that nobody would want to make a hostile attack on the company.[17] He also had a star-studded, independent board of directors including James Tisch, Burton Malkiel, Dean Takahashi from the Yale endowment, and investment bankers Anson Beard and Peter J. Solomon. But in 2001, shortly after entities controlled by Mario Gabelli crossed 9% ownership, BKF installed a poison pill with a relatively low 10% threshold. A month later, Gabelli said it would submit a proposal at the upcoming annual meeting that BKF redeem its poison pill unless approved by shareholders.[18]

Stockholder proposals to redeem the poison pill received overwhelming support at BKF's 2002 and 2003 annual meetings. But the proposals were not binding, and the board chose to ignore the recommendations. In September 2003, James McKee, Gabelli's general counsel, sent BKF a spirited letter about the poison pill. He wrote, "It is time to hold companies accountable for their actions and restore the checks and balances in corporate boardrooms and executive suites. This is not the time for companies to build moats around themselves with poison pills and ignore the voice of their shareholders."[19]

Two months later, Phillip Goldstein, a former civil engineer for New York City who embarked on a successful second career investing in undervalued closed-end funds, filed a 13D and submitted a shareholder proposal that BKF sell itself. In his supporting statement he wrote, "BKF's ratio of market capitalization (market price of equity plus debt) to assets under management is just 1.3%. That is significantly lower than the ratio for other investment management companies. For example, Franklin Resources ('BEN') shares trade at a ratio of 4.4%, Janus Capital ('JNS') at 2.9% and Waddell and Reed ('WDR') at 7%. We think the primary reason for BKF's low multiple is its excessive expenses. In 2002, compensation expenses consumed approximately 69% of BKF's revenues vs. 25% for BEN, 30% for JNS and 13% for WDR. . . . In short, we think the surest way to enhance stockholder value is to immediately engage an investment banking firm to evaluate alternatives to maximize shareholder value including a sale of the Company."[20]

Beyond shareholder proposals, McKee's letter on behalf of Gabelli threatened the nomination of directors for the 2004 annual meeting. But the meeting came and went without a proxy fight—just another bid to repeal the poison pill that would be ignored by the board. Despite several years of palpable shareholder discontent at BKF, nobody had been willing to put up a fight for board representation. This was about to change. In April 2004, Steel Partners filed a 13D showing a 6.5% stake.

READY FOR A FIGHT

Steel Partners was founded by Warren Lichtenstein in 1990. It was one of the first firms to utilize an activist investing strategy within a hedge fund structure. Lichtenstein's aggressive style was modeled on Carl Icahn's. Like Icahn, Lichtenstein operated with an urgency to generate immediate results. Many hedge fund activists will fill their proxy materials with nods to long-term value and long-term shareholders. Lichtenstein cut right to the chase: In a letter he wrote to the CEO of SL Industries in 2001, he explained that his slate of directors "will take all necessary action in order to create short-term value for the SL shareholders."[21]

Steel Partners came to BKF with a fourteen-year history of running activist campaigns against small public companies. With Steel involved, there was a certain inevitability to fundamental change at BKF. The company had alienated its investors for three years with high employee compensation and refusal to redeem the poison pill. Steel Partners was a willing fighter, so either the two sides would negotiate a settlement that restructured the board, or Steel would wage a proxy fight and win. The only plausible alternative outcome was the immediate sale of the company. The market responded enthusiastically. Between Steel Partners' 13D in April and its first public letter to the company in December, BKF's stock appreciated 24%.[22]

On December 16, 2004, Steel Partners demanded that BKF immediately add three shareholder representatives to the company's board of directors. Warren Lichtenstein's accompanying letter to the board outlined his case: "Although we believe that John A. Levin & Co. has and continues to serve its clients well, BKF has failed to deliver value to its owners. Frankly, we do not understand how a money management company that manages approximately $13 billion of assets and has over $100 million of revenues can lose money."[23] He continued, "[W]e believe that BKF must adopt compensation arrangements that reward its key employees for performance and align their interests directly with BKF's clients and stockholders. Based on our observation of the long term performance of BKF, we are concerned that BKF's Board runs the Company as if it were a private company that is not accountable to its stockholders. . . . To be clear, our goal is simple and straightforward—to promptly and immediately increase value for ALL of BKF's stockholders."[24]

When John Levin and the rest of the BKF board did not meet Lichtenstein's demand to immediately add new directors, Steel Partners nominated its own slate for election at the upcoming annual meeting. Because of BKF's staggered board, there were only three board members up for election: John Levin, Burton Malkiel, and private equity investor Bart Goodwin. Steel Partners nominated Lichtenstein, investor Ron LaBow, and Kurt Schacht, who had operating experience at several large money managers.

The proxy fight was concentrated into about three weeks, from mid-May until early June 2005. Steel's message strayed little from the charges in its first public letter. It focused on BKF's high employee compensation and low operating margins, as well as entrenchment devices like the poison pill, the staggered board, and anti-takeover provisions in the charter and bylaws. Steel also targeted related-party transactions, including Henry Levin's $9 million in compensation in 2004, and $175,000 in consulting fees paid to John Levin's daughter.

BKF's board argued in its defense that the company's long-term strategy to grow assets necessarily compressed near-term margins. The company's May 18 proxy filing stated, "[W]e feel that our decision to seek to pay compensation competitive with that offered by larger or private investment management firms will provide us with the opportunity to retain and attract the personnel required to bring the firm to a scale at which it can produce higher profits. . . . While we understand that our margins are lower than competitors who are much larger than we are, we do not believe that measures designed solely to improve margins in the short term, or a focus solely on maximizing margins, rather than on absolute profits, in the longer term, will ultimately maximize shareholder value."[25]

The two sides exchanged blows for several weeks. Steel pounded BKF on its corporate governance practices and won support from proxy advisors Institutional Shareholder Services (ISS) and Glass, Lewis. BKF responded by pointing out related-party transactions at companies where Steel served on the board. A May 26 letter from BKF's board said, "On the corporate governance front, Steel Partners has hardly been a role model. . . . Mr. Lichtenstein's hypocrisy in campaigning on a corporate governance platform is breathtaking."[26] BKF highlighted the good performance of its stock, even though much of the rally came after Steel publicly disclosed its stake. Steel called for higher dividends or a share repurchase.

BKF also asserted that Steel Partners might have ulterior motives in investing in a competing money management firm. The board wrote that Steel might move in on BKF's assets to try to generate fees for itself.[27] BKF's board concluded, "Please do not be fooled—Steel Partners is not primarily interested in corporate governance or in representing the interests of all stockholders. It is in this contest to further Mr. Lichtenstein's personal interests."[28] Lichtenstein scoffed at the idea he was interested in pilfering BKF's assets for Steel's benefit. He wrote that Steel's reputation depended on protecting value for all shareholders, and he pointed out that BKF's other angry investors were all in the money management business. He added, "Any inference that we may have ulterior motives has no merit and is a smoke screen to cloud the real issues in this election."[29]

The BKF Capital Group proxy fight was pretty standard fare through the end of May 2005. Steel Partners was having success using its time-tested proxy fight formula. It repeatedly stressed its core argument—that BKF's financial performance was depressed because of excessive employee compensation—while piling on with whatever else it could think of, including corporate governance initiatives, calls for higher dividends, and accusations of insider dealing. BKF Capital was trying its best to deflect Steel Partners' attacks in order to keep shareholders focused on the director election, and the company's success growing assets under management. Then, just eight days before the shareholders' meeting, a hedge fund manager named J. Carlo Cannell surfaced with a 13D letter that distilled all the BKF shareholder discontent into a stinging rebuke of John Levin and the rest of the directors. Levin and his board of luminaries were personally offended, and the embattled chairman responded with his own impassioned plea to shareholders.[30]

A Dynamic Force

In 1992, J. Carlo Cannell launched his hedge fund with only $600,000 in assets. Ten years later, he managed just under a billion dollars and was one of the industry's rising stars. According to *Institutional Investor*, Cannell was the thirteenth-highest-earning hedge fund manager in 2002, with a $56 million haul.[31] This ranked him ahead of big shots like George Soros, David Tepper, Eddie Lampert, and Stephen Feinberg.

Carlo Cannell ran a long-short value strategy focused on obscure, smaller capitalization companies. As he said in an interview in *Value Investor Insight*, "[We] spend our time trying to uncover the promising turnarounds, dullards and assorted investment misfits in the market's underbrush that are largely neglected by the investment community."[32] While many of the fund managers on *Institutional Investor*'s list of top earners built large, multistrategy firms, Cannell kept his organization lean and stuck to his core investing approach. To keep his fund from growing too large, he actually returned $250 million to his investors. "The great disadvantage of our investment approach is that it's not very scalable," he explained.[33] A lot of hedge fund managers would have kept that revelation to themselves and retained the capital (and collected the consequent fees).

Despite reaching the upper echelons of the rapidly maturing hedge fund industry, Carlo Cannell remained something of an oddity. He prided himself on being a loner in the investment world, and he rarely worked alongside other funds. At an investment conference where managers were told to pitch specific stocks, he gave a presentation on the extinction of *Hydrodamalis gigas*, aka Steller's sea cow.[34] In 2004, after several years of returning capital to his investors, Cannell stepped away from his thriving business altogether to sample retirement. "When Cannell Capital was in diapers, I regretted neglecting my family," he announced at the time. "Now that my son is in diapers and the business is not, I have decided to take some time off to be with them."[35]

After six months, Cannell missed the search for investment misfits and dullards. He came back with a renewed focus and found BKF Capital, which he saw as a growing company whose earnings were depressed because of bad management. Given the unhappy shareholder base and the presence of capable activist investors, BKF's problems didn't seem like they would be too hard to fix. Cannell disclosed a 5% stake on February 14, 2005, the same day as Dan Loeb's Valentine's Day massacre at Star Gas. He upped his holdings in BKF to almost 9% as the proxy fight heated up.[36]

While Steel Partners founded its business around activism, Cannell embraced it as a necessary weapon to protect his investors. Years of investing in small public companies hardened him in the same way it had hardened Dan Loeb. Cannell had a strong sense of right and wrong, and felt compelled to act when businessmen with bad intentions harmed his investors. "When I see clearly that people are stealing from my limited partners, it's a breach of duty to do nothing," he told me.[37] In the case of BKF, Cannell objected to Levin's unwillingness to produce profits for his public investors out of the firm's $120 million in fee revenue. "All he needed to do was be self-aware of the structural issues that were inappropriate," said Cannell. "The egregiousness was fairly blatant. It wasn't debatable . . . it wasn't subjective."[38]

Though J. Carlo Cannell is an unconventional money manager, he comes from a storied line of financiers. He's the grandson of investment banker Ferdinand Eberstadt, who had brilliant careers on Wall Street and in Washington, where he was a frequent advisor to the U.S. government. Among Eberstadt's business accomplishments, he founded Chemical Fund, the first mutual fund to reach a billion dollars in assets under management.[39] Carlo's father, Peter B. Cannell, started his career as a copywriter for BBDO, a large advertising agency. Peter's father-in-law pressured him to come to Wall Street, where he later became president of Chemical Fund. Peter started his own firm, Peter B. Cannell, in 1973. It generated 16% annualized returns through his retirement at the end of 2004.[40] Peter's colorful letters to investors, in which he channeled his inner David Ogilvy, were passed around Wall Street much the way Howard Marks's memos are today. Like his son Carlo, Peter Cannell was critical of Wall Street management teams and had a fondness for sharply written copy—he wrote a letter in 2000 titled "Dumb.com" about how Internet companies were wasting shareholder money on terrible ad campaigns.[41]

But Peter Cannell didn't use his poison pen directly on his target companies. As one of his coworkers said in an interview in 1997, "We are plain vanilla investors. We shy away from controversy. If a holding becomes controversial, we sell it."[42] Carlo shares his father's facility with words, but when it comes to underperforming companies he resembles his grandfather, who was described in one book as "the embodiment of dynamic force."[43] His letter to BKF Capital Group on June 1, 2005 (page 236) is proof. It opens:

> "When, O Catiline, do you mean to cease abusing our patience? How long is that madness of yours still to mock us? When is there to be an end of that unbridled audacity of yours, swaggering about as it does now?"
>
> Thus, in 63 B.C., did Marcus Tullius Cicero expose corruption and vice in the Roman Senate in his First Oration Against Lucius Catilina. His words are relevant today as we study the record of BKF Capital Group.

Cannell begins by targeting BKF's low profit margins and high employee compensation: "Costs are exorbitant. . . . Incremental revenues are sucked up by inflated salaries; as a result, BKF continues to lose money, even as assets and revenues have grown 18% and 64%, respectively, over the last five years." He then writes about the rich compensation of Henry Levin and the other senior managers of the event-driven hedge fund: "None of the Managers' compensation is in the form of BKF equity. None of their compensation is in the form of long-term incentives, which would encourage retention. How are these arrangements supposed to align the interests of the Managers with the well-being of your stockholders? All this excess would be dandy in a private company, but BKF is public."

Regarding BKF's expenses, Cannell complains,

> The callous conflagration of shareholder assets by BKF galls us as it would gall Cicero. When we visit companies, we stay at $39.95 motels, not fancy hotels with fruit at the "reception" desk. . . . My visit to your offices on May 26, 2005 left me astounded that such an unprofitable company would house itself in some of the most expensive office space in America. Your 56,000 square foot office in Rockefeller Center immolates cash at the expense of BKF's shareholders. . . . I appreciate the lavish spending of casinos as they lure "whales" to their tables, but this acceptance is predicated upon such adornments being accretive to earnings, to bringing in profitable bacon. Your Rockefeller Center pork just stinks.

While Cannell touched on many of the same issues raised by Steel Partners, he did so in a much more provocative fashion. He singled out board members Barton Biggs, Burt Malkiel, and Anson Beard, stating, "One would expect such deportment from scalawags, but not you noble nabobs of Wall Street." Cannell then urged the board to "(i) take BKF private and squander privately; (ii) appoint an investment banker to conduct an auction of the company, as Opportunity Partner's Phillip Goldstein first suggested in his November 17, 2003 13d filing; or (iii) stand down and pass the baton to a shareholder-friendly board." Cannell concludes the letter, "Cicero ultimately vanquished Catiline despite the latter's attempt to form a rebel force with other rich and corrupt men. . . . You still have time to flee. Go forth, Catiline."

VOTE THE WHITE CARD

As the June 9 meeting approached, momentum was clearly on the activists' side. BKF's previous attempts to curry favor with shareholders, including a 92.5 cents special dividend and a new policy to distribute 70% of free cash flow, didn't have a big impact.[44] Steel Partners' calls for governance reforms, on the other hand, resonated with investors. BKF took drastic action. The company postponed the shareholder meeting for two weeks and caved on all of the corporate governance items. BKF agreed to redeem the poison pill, de-stagger the board, and amend its bylaws to allow shareholders to call special meetings. Lichtenstein scoffed at BKF's too-little, too-late actions in a letter to shareholders:

> Due to your support for our nominees and the corporate governance initiatives that we are advocating, BKF's Board has been dragged kicking and screaming, against their will, into the modern world of corporate governance reform. . . . The fact that BKF has belatedly adopted many of our proposals and positions that we advocated much earlier we believe demonstrates that our advocacy is already yielding benefits for BKF's stockholders. THERE IS STILL MORE TO BE ACCOMPLISHED. BKF'S BOARD STILL DOES NOT UNDERSTAND THAT THE MAIN ISSUES IN THIS ELECTION CONTEST ARE IMPROVING OPERATING PERFORMANCE AND ALIGNING COMPENSATION WITH STOCKHOLDER INTERESTS![45]

To this point in the proxy contest, John Levin had kept a relatively low profile. He had not publicly responded to the personal attacks against him, and the company's previous three proxy letters were signed "The Board of Directors."[46] On June 16, Levin decided to address the shareholders personally. He wrote a powerful rebuttal to Cannell and Steel Partners that implored shareholders to reelect Burt Malkiel and Bart Goodwin. Like William White in the 1954 New York Central proxy fight, John Levin took it upon himself to stand up to "gunpoint capitalism" in the face of near-certain defeat.[47]

Levin opens his letter (page 243) by explaining the decision to rescind the poison pill and de-stagger the board: "The Board of Directors of BKF recently took dramatic action to take off the table for the annual meeting all issues except the central one: which slate of candidates will

produce the best board to foster the growth and success of the company." He points out that while Steel Partners and Cannell made a lot of
mean-spirited noise about reducing expenses, they offered no concrete
plan to do so. Levin then argues that BKF needs to invest in its employee
base so it can properly grow the business to create the most long-term
value for shareholders:

> So while we are comprised of experienced professionals, we are
> also a young public company that is seeking to develop a diversi-
> fied series of investment strategies that have the capacity to grow.
> AT THIS STAGE OF OUR DEVELOPMENT, STOCKHOLDERS
> HAVE THE POWER TO DETERMINE IF WE WILL GROW
> OR FAIL.

After defending BKF's spending policies, Levin then addresses accusations of self-dealing.

> The attack on Barton Biggs, a universally recognized expert on
> the asset management industry, for paying us rent for a limited
> period of time for space inside our offices we weren't utilizing and
> couldn't sublet was always a joke, which people understand when
> we discuss it. We are being attacked for paying a relatively low
> amount of fees to Peter Solomon's investment banking organiza-
> tion while these same attackers simultaneously criticize us for not
> pursuing strategic alternative to realize shareholder value.

Perhaps the most compelling passage in Levin's rebuttal comes when
he discusses his children's compensation:

> With respect to the attacks on my children, I must say they reveal
> much about the nature of the opposition but disclose absolutely
> nothing improper. Much has been said about the compensation
> paid to my son Henry, but I just ask that stockholders evaluate him
> as one of two senior portfolio managers for event-driven strategies
> that have generated a very significant portion of our firm's revenues

and free cash flow over the years. . . . He is paid on the basis of the profitability to the firm of the strategies he manages, which is exactly how our hedge fund manager critics pay themselves. . . . I don't understand why being rewarded based on the profitability of the accounts he manages is no longer a valid way of looking at things. . . . My daughter, Jennifer Levin Carter, has a distinguished academic record, having become a member of Phi Beta Kappa in her junior year at Yale, and having graduated from there with distinction in molecular biophysics and biochemistry, from Harvard Medical School and from the Harvard School of Public Health. She has provided valuable research to our investment professionals on biotech and other companies within her area of expertise, and is viewed as a substantive plus by all who interact with her.

Levin accuses Steel Partners and Cannell of misleading investors by characterizing BKF as a money-losing business, when the company's accounting losses since 2000 stem from $91 million in noncash amortization expenses. He then closes with a last entreaty:

One is supposed to conclude with a wonderful inspirational message of hope, but let me tell you the grim reality. I don't know what any shareholder or group of shareholders is going to say or do next. It is up to the unaligned shareholders of this company to decide what the future is. There is no middle ground. Our slate is composed of outstanding individuals. Burt Malkiel is just the kind of director shareholders should want. He is a former member of the Council of Economic Advisors, a long-standing full professor of Economics at Princeton and a trustee of various Vanguard funds. Bart Goodwin is a quality investor in private equity companies. Both of these gentlemen were directors of BKF before our money management firm merged into it in 1996. They are as independent as directors can be. Vote the white card.

ON JUNE 23, BKF Capital Group shareholders elected Steel Partners' slate of directors by a two-to-one margin.[48] Chairman John A. Levin was voted out, although he was immediately invited back by the new board. When Levin and Lichtenstein took their seats in the same boardroom, however, they did not agree on a plan to move the company forward together. Barton Biggs quit the board on July 12. The company announced Levin's resignation on August 23, though he would keep a "chairman emeritus" title. At the end of September, BKF's assets under management were $9.6 billion, down 29% from the beginning of the year.

The bad news kept coming. On October 18, BKF announced the departure of Henry Levin and the rest of the senior managers of the event-driven team. Their hedge fund would be permanently shut down. On December 20, CFO Glenn Aigen left to go work for Levin's new firm. The company ended the year with only $4.5 billion under management. Anson Beard and James Tisch left the board on January 10 and 11. On April 3, BKF announced that it couldn't come to terms with two managers of $615 million of hedge fund assets. Two weeks later, one more hedge fund manager walked, forcing the liquidation of another $133 million. BKF ended June 2006 with only $1.9 billion in assets. The quarter's revenue was just over $1 million, down 96% from the $30 million it collected a year earlier. In July, the death blow came. BKF lost its long-only manager and announced it would liquidate its remaining assets. By the end of September 2006, fifteen months after the proxy fight, BKF Capital Group had no operating business or assets.[49] The stock price had fallen 90% from the day shareholders voted in the dissident slate of directors.[50]

A Private Business in a Public Company

If activist investors had never meddled with BKF Capital Group, there's no doubt that shareholders would have fared better. Even if John A. Levin had continued paying 80% of revenues to employees until the end of time, the market would have valued the company higher than it valued BKF's empty shell at the end of 2006. But BKF Capital is more than a cautionary tale about failed activism. It raises fundamental questions about the nature of public companies.

John Levin was very clear to shareholders that he was investing in BKF's employee base to prime the company for growth. But shareholders didn't really believe him. They were worried about Levin's sub-10% ownership stake, and they knew there was not a strong incentive for him to tightly manage costs for the benefit of investors. Without perfectly aligned incentives, corporate governance becomes a matter of trust. But in the business world, relying on trust often backfires. BKF's shareholders simply did not trust Levin to look out for their interests versus his employees'. BKF's track record on corporate governance, besmirched by the poison pill and the staggered board, undermined Levin's credibility. In the end, shareholders decided en masse to put three new members on the board of directors. Steel Partners may have been the catalyst, but there was a groundswell of shareholder discontent.

But was the shareholders' mistrust of Levin justified? BKF did utilize anti-takeover devices and Levin did pay millions of dollars to his son, but was he mismanaging the company and abusing shareholders? The first place to look to evaluate charges of self-dealing would be Levin's own salary. He averaged $4 million in total compensation per year for the five years leading up to the proxy fight.[51] That's certainly a lot of money, but it's not even close to out of line for the CEO and portfolio manager of an investment company managing over $10 billion. In 1997, Levin kept about 7% of the business's revenues for his compensation, accounting for 14% of the employees' take. By 2004, his personal compensation was well under 3% of revenues, and accounted for just over 3% of total employee pay. It's hard to argue John Levin was grossly overpaying himself.

Henry Levin's pay attracted a lot of attention from the activists. He earned almost $8 million in 2003 and just under $9 million in 2004. These are big numbers that Steel Partners used to highlight BKF's "lack of accountability."[52] But Levin was one of two senior hedge fund portfolio managers who generated $51 million of fees in 2003 and almost $60 million the following year. The hedge fund industry is famous for its "eat what you kill" compensation structures. Henry's pay for managing a $2.5 billion hedge fund was almost certainly lower than that of most of his industry peers. (Recall that *Institutional Investor* estimated that J. Carlo Cannell made $56 million in 2002.)

BKF let its event-driven team keep two-thirds of its earnings.[53] In the hedge fund world, this was actually a generous deal *for BKF*. Most hedge fund seed arrangements take a smaller 25% cut, and these deals almost invariably get negotiated down if the fund is successful—it's almost a rite of passage to cram down your seed investor once your hedge fund is established. BKF's activists wanted the company to restructure its compensation arrangements with its hedge fund managers, but carving out more than 33% would have been difficult.[54]

IN THE VERY first Steel Partners proxy in December 2004, Warren Lichtenstein wrote, "Perhaps what is most startling is when one compares BKF's financial metrics to those of other publicly-traded money managers. Even a cursory glance at these figures demonstrates that changes are needed to deliver reasonable value to the Company's stockholders."[55] But what happens when a cursory glance is misleading? Comparing BKF to companies like Eaton Vance or Waddell & Reed doesn't make a lot of sense. Those were larger, diversified institutions with established brand names. It would have been impossible for Levin to achieve their level of efficiency without hurting BKF's growth prospects.

Carlo Cannell is a very good investor. But it's hard to overlook how a nonconformist like Cannell, who prospered under the hedge fund pay-for-performance structure, didn't appreciate how BKF was fundamentally different from its industry peers. The great irony of BKF Capital is that the shareholders who pushed the company to reduce its compensation were highly paid hedge fund managers who should have known better. They saw a quick path to increasing earnings by cutting employee compensation, but they ended up driving away the talent. John Levin told me, "We grew from $4 billion to $15 billion. We created $50 million of cash. We distributed $680 million to shareholders, and the whole thing was destroyed by activism."[56]

On the whole, I believe shareholder activism has been very good for the American economy and its public companies. I think that record profit margins achieved by public corporations since the financial crisis are at least partly due to the pervasive threat of activism. But the rise of the shareholder also promotes a bias to conformity among industry peers. Icahn's quote about getting your stock price up before someone does it for you could be rewritten for today's market as "Get your operating margin up to the industry norm or someone will try to do it for you." Many of today's shareholder activists focus their efforts on maximizing operating margins. To a fault, they don't give much credit to uncertain growth prospects, while viewing trailing earnings as future money in the bank. This is a very different kind of activism than Benjamin Graham's, which centered on capital allocation.

IT'S TELLING THAT almost every participant in the BKF proxy fight acknowledged different standards for public and private companies. Phil Goldstein, Steel Partners, and Carlo Cannell all asserted that BKF was being run like a private company. "I'm not judging the greed," Cannell told me. "But that type of structure is best practiced privately."[57] Director Anson Beard, who briefly succeeded Levin as chairman of the board, told Joe Nocera of the *New York Times*, "It shouldn't have been a public company in the first place."[58] Even John Levin alluded to the divide when he wrote about his son Henry, "I understand that being part of a public company must necessarily reduce the cash compensation he can earn. . . ."

Today, John Levin deeply regrets that he did not push for supervoting shares when Baker, Fentress restructured. "I made a horrendous mistake," he said. "This sounds ridiculous, but we thought we had such a great victory in distributing $680 million to shareholders that it would be fine."[59] If Levin had secured voting control of BKF through a dual-class share structure, he would have never been voted off the board for being too generous with his employees. This highlights an interesting bifurcation occurring in the stock market today. On the one side, almost every public company with a one-share, one-vote structure is subject to shareholder activism. On the other side, a large number of companies have opted out of corporate democracy altogether by granting their founders special controlling shares. As a result, large technology companies like Google are completely immune to activism while they sit on huge cash hoards and toss billion-dollar investments into companies like SpaceX.

Google's AdWords is literally one of the best businesses ever to exist, and shareholders have chosen to cede their oversight rights in order to participate in its growth. Google's relationship with its shareholders is thus a matter of trust and not much else. So far, investors have been richly rewarded. Shareholders raised their eyebrows at acquisitions like Android and YouTube, but they have been huge triumphs. Still, it will be fascinating to watch how these benevolent dictatorships work out over time. Google already betrayed its original agreement with shareholders by concentrating ownership back into its founders after generous employee stock and options grants diluted their voting stakes. How long will shareholders continue to trust the company? How long can you really trust anybody that says they aren't evil?

WHEN BKF CAPITAL blew up, John A. Levin landed on his feet. He took $2 billion in client assets to his new company and has grown it to $9 billion, mostly through new relationships. Well over half of the firm's employees worked with Levin at BKF. "We had and have the philosophy of compensating our people very, very well," says Levin. "One of the unique features of our present firm is that more than twenty-five people in operations, investment, and trading have stuck together, which is pretty unusual in this business. That whole culture was effectively destroyed and then transplanted." Levin credits part of his success to not being "challenged by the problems of being public."[60]

Still, one can't help but wonder what would have happened with the business if Steel Partners and John Levin had come to any kind of compromise to work together. Several of BKF's offshoot hedge funds, such as distressed fund Onex, went on to do very well. And Levin's long-only business clearly thrived, with $7 billion of new capital. Cannell attributes BKF's shareholder value destruction to an irrational scorched-earth policy by Levin. "I don't have anything against John Levin, but what he did was stupid," says Cannell. "It hurt him more than anyone else."[61] For his part, Levin believes the company's demise wasn't due to his departure. "I had a reputation, but the real talent was younger. They didn't make any deal with the talent. The big mistake here was, I think they could have hired a lot of people, but they didn't hire anybody."[62]

BKF Capital Group is a catastrophic example of shareholder activism destroying huge amounts of value. But the market doesn't keep track of your mistakes, and Carlo Cannell, John Levin, and Warren Lichtenstein survived to fight another day. They all walked away a little bit wiser, though also a little bit poorer. As for the remnants of BKF, the once-proud Chicago institution with more than a century of history? In 2006, it was reduced to being a shell company with a small cash balance and a large tax-loss carryforward. As you can imagine, a new pack of activist investors began circling.

Conclusion

S HAREHOLDER ACTIVISM IS NOT a passing fad. It is planted in the middle of the corporate governance landscape, with deep roots that have grown for the last century. It has experienced seasonal changes and taken on different forms as market conditions vary. But at its core, shareholder activism is simple. As Carl Icahn pointed out thirty-five years ago, an arbitrage exists when assets sitting in a public company are valued below what they would attract in an auction, or under different management. In Benjamin Graham's time, Mr. Market put a price tag on Northern Pipeline that was significantly lower than the liquidation value of its investment securities. Today, many activists target companies that seem poorly managed compared to industry peers. This approach backfired miserably at BKF Capital, but the pursuit of what Robert Chapman called "the ephemerally salubrious separation of management from ownership" remains a viable investment strategy.[1]

Shareholder activism can produce stellar investment returns by exploiting weaknesses in public company governance. To neutralize activism, boards and managers need to improve their performance enough to eliminate Icahn's arbitrage. But as we have seen at General Motors, R. P. Scherer, and Star Gas, among others, public companies have an unbelievable capacity for ineptitude. The stories in this book can't help but highlight such failures of oversight.

Disasters at public corporations from Enron to AIG to Fannie Mae to BP have defined America's business narrative over the past fifteen years. We tend to view them as isolated grotesques, and when we don't, we lay blame on "corporate greed." But our problems can't be fully explained by capitalistic greed run amok. Given the increasing scale and complexity of today's corporations, this is no small matter. Our large corporations are more intertwined in our lives than ever before, they can be trickier to manage despite all of our technological advances, and when things go wrong, the collateral damage can be awesome.

Tino De Angelis had such a shady past and spotty credit history it was hard for him to open a regular bank account for his business. Yet he somehow convinced American Express to guarantee the value of his inventory. American Express was one of the largest financial institutions in the world, but its senior managers never really understood how much risk they were taking. When nearly a billion pounds of assumed soybean oil turned out to be seawater, the Great Salad Oil Swindle toppled a few brokerage firms and exporters. When a similar lack of oversight occurred at AIG forty-five years later, its financial products unit nearly brought down the entire global economy.

The only people who got rich off Tino De Angelis were Tino and his cronies. Nobody at American Express stood to make a fortune if Tino turned out to be legitimate. Yet American Express single-handedly enabled the swindle. The situation was eerily similar when a small division of AIG sold trillions of dollars of credit default swaps on subprime mortgages. Even at the height of the fiasco, AIG Financial Products' credit default swaps business accounted for less than 10% of the division's profits.[2] As Michael Lewis pointed out in his *Vanity Fair* profile of AIG FP, the division's compensation structure focused on long-term incentives, and employees lost more than $500 million of their own money when AIG collapsed. Some key employees at American Express and AIG assumed a huge amount of professional, personal, and financial risk, without meaningful upside. That's not what reckless greed looks like.

Public company disasters are often symptoms of a chronic lack of accountability and oversight, enabled by disinterested shareholders, disengaged directors, and unfocused management teams. Shareholder activism exists to profit from this dynamic. To this end, activist investors often prey on inefficient management teams in a way that benefits the company and its other shareholders. But as we have seen, when activists spot an opportunity, they will gladly take advantage of disinterested stockholders for their own benefit. As much as activists talk about creating value for all shareholders, we should not forget their true motive—profits for themselves and their financial backers.

JUDGMENT OVER CHECKLISTS

Many smart people have pondered corporate governance since Adolf Berle wrote in 1932 about the dangers of separating ownership and control. But it's easy to get mired in theoretical details that don't teach us how public companies actually work. In 2012, Cornell professor Lynn Stout wrote a thought-provoking book, *The Shareholder Value Myth*, which explains, "U.S. corporate law does not, and never has, required public corporations to 'maximize shareholder value.'"[3] She also argues that shareholders' rights are so limited that they do not really constitute "ownership" of the company.[4] But even if Stout is technically correct on both counts, can a board of directors in the real world promote a corporate purpose that subordinates voting shareholders' interests to other pursuits?[5] Many of the "Dear Chairman" letters in this book explicitly refer to shareholders as the rightful "owners" of the business. This is for all intents and purposes true, because shareholders provide capital to public companies and are the only constituents who can vote for directors. An abstract discussion about the nature of ownership doesn't address the practical realities that make corporate governance such a knotty problem. It ultimately doesn't matter whether or not shareholders "own" the company, and whether or not companies are legally required to maximize shareholder value. As long as investors are motivated by financial gain, and as long as they determine the makeup of boards of directors, public companies will prioritize shareholder profits.

When academic corporate governance experts promote actual reforms, the results can be perverse. Between 2011 and 2014, for example, a group of Harvard professors made a mission of targeting "staggered boards," which feature multiyear terms for directors, rather than one annual election for the whole board. Think of staggered boards as Senate-style governance with overlapping terms, versus the House of Representatives, where everyone stands for election at the same time.

The Harvard group succeeded in declassifying the boards of almost one hundred S&P 500 and Fortune 500 companies.[6] This is an incredible result that shows the impact a few loud voices can have in areas where shareholders are somewhat ambivalent. I don't know whether the group really thinks staggered boards are a legitimate problem, or if they simply found a soft target that would generate the most attention, but the plain truth is, staggered boards are no big deal. Not only is there value to having some continuity in directors during a board overhaul; a staggered board rarely entrenches anybody. When smart activists come in with the right plan of action, it usually wins over the rest of the directors within one election cycle. Two of the most contentious proxy fights in this book, R. P. Scherer and BKF Capital, featured staggered boards. All it took was one election for the activists to get their way.

Perhaps the best example of favoring checklist-style governance over common sense is the proxy advisory business. The largest proxy advisor, Institutional Shareholder Services (ISS), was started with good intentions in the mid-1980s, and now advises a large number of institutional investors on voting matters. Regulations that require investment firms to have robust proxy voting policies have had the peculiar effect of pushing more of them to outsource the responsibility to ISS or its competitor, Glass, Lewis. As hard as they might try, these firms don't have the resources to properly track the board's performance at every public company. They are forced to resort to standardized evaluations, and the resulting recommendations can be shockingly imprudent.

In 2014, shortly after I joined the board of a company called Tandy Leather Factory, ISS advised investors to withhold votes from *every single director* except for me. Tandy operates a quirky little business that dominates the leather-crafting industry, and my fund had purchased 30% of the stock on the open market. I thought that other investors didn't understand the quality of Tandy's business, so for several years I was happily buying as many shares as I could, at what I thought was a large discount to the company's intrinsic value. When the board realized I was literally two phone calls away from getting control of the company without paying a premium to shareholders, they installed a poison pill blocking me from buying more shares. While I was angry at the poison pill and pulled a minor hissy fit, it was a reasonable course of action for the board. In fact, the Tandy director leading the charge, Michael Nery, was not an entrenched executive—he was a value fund manager with a 10% ownership stake in the company. Because Tandy installed the pill without a shareholder vote, ISS recommended withholding votes from Nery, as well as management insiders who had more than one hundred years of collective operating experience at the unique, niche company. This makes no sense at all.

ISS's shortsighted advice is not restricted to small, under-the-radar companies. In 2004, they advised Coca-Cola shareholders to withhold votes from Warren Buffett because of conflicts of interest related to his ownership of Dairy Queen. In an angry op-ed in the *Wall Street Journal*, fellow Coke director Herbert Allen sarcastically wrote, "Maybe ISS has a strong point that Mr. Buffett's vote on the board can be swayed because a company that he probably forgot that he owned has a small contract with Coke that could add up to as much as three cents of his $50 billion fortune."[7]

Conflicts of interests are a fact of life in the boardrooms of large public companies. It's a mistake to put ourselves in a situation—either through regulation or the dominance of ISS-style "best practices"—where any potential conflict disqualifies director nominees. When a corporate director has deep industry knowledge and experience, he or she is likely to have conflicts. For shareholders to elect a good group of directors, they need to use their judgment to decide which conflicts matter and which don't. ISS's formulaic evaluation penalized Buffett even though his ownership of DQ was tiny compared to his $10 billion of Coca-Cola stock. Apparently there was also no question on ISS's checklist that asked, "Is the candidate the greatest capital allocator to ever live?"

By studying real activist situations and seeing their economic consequences, I hope this book has demystified corporate governance enough to help readers think in a clear, businesslike fashion about the questions at hand. To wit: If you had a large percentage of your net worth tied up in Coke stock, would you withhold votes from Warren Buffett because he owns Dairy Queen? Of course not!

If we apply the same commonsense analysis to other popular

corporate governance initiatives, we find that many of them, like the Harvard crusade against staggered boards, don't make a lot of sense. The separation of the chairman and CEO roles, for instance, wouldn't really have an impact on a company's governance as long as the CEO remains an active board member. The way most companies are structured, the chairman has few, if any, privileges not afforded to other directors. Another idea that gets kicked around a lot is granting special voting rights to longer-tenured shareholders. But it seems inevitable that this reform would divide the shareholders into haves and have-nots, giving well-established funds tremendous advantages. This would result in strengthening existing activist investors and giving them a competitive edge over smaller, newer funds.

The hottest topic in corporate governance is proxy access, and many public companies vehemently oppose it. The idea is to allow qualifying shareholders the ability to nominate directors, and for those nominees to appear on the ballot in the company's proxy statement. A common variant of proxy access would give shareholders who own at least 3% of the stock for three years the right to nominate 25% of the directors. On the surface, proxy access seems unimportant. Running proxy fights is ultimately not that expensive, and it is well within the means of the large institutional investors promoting these reforms. But while it seems trivial, proxy access would have the profound effect of destigmatizing dissident slates. If major holders could nominate directors, and have them be viable candidates without a hostile campaign, this would bring a new level of accountability to management teams. Proxy access would practically institutionalize shareholder activism—you can see why companies are so afraid of it.

PREDATORS BECOME PREY

Dear Chairman contains some of the best shareholder letters to public companies. As the curator of these fine works, I must confess to my own place in the firmament of shareholder activism: I once wrote the *worst* "Dear Chairman" letter in history. In May 2009, I wrote a public 13D letter to a small company called Peerless Systems, which was trading for less than the value of its cash balance. In only 175 words, I created an appalling homage to the passive voice with a gruesome grammatical error. Fortunately, my fund's 20% stake spoke louder than a badly written letter, and the company quickly nominated my partner and me to the board. Peerless was a software company that had improbably become the investment vehicle of a smart and aggressive activist named Timothy Brog. Within five days of our 13D, Peerless had filed its own 13D on another company, Highbury Financial. Highbury was itself an acquisition vehicle that had purchased a stake in a growing mutual fund company. Unlike BKF Capital, Highbury's management was not involved in its money management operations. It was searching for new acquisitions while paying a related entity, run by Highbury's chairman, hefty consulting fees. Brog saw that Highbury's shareholders could profit immensely just by removing the unnecessary layer of senior executives. He also coveted the mutual fund business for Peerless. At one of my first Peerless board meetings, I remember we read through a draft of Tim's harsh 13D letter to Highbury and discussed the spelling of *cojones*.

The situation was absurd. My fund was an activist investor in Peerless, which was an activist investor in Highbury, which was looking to make another acquisition. In the end, Highbury sold itself to a strategic acquirer, netting big profits for Peerless. Peerless did a large self-tender that returned capital to shareholders and bought out my fund. Brog took what was remaining of Peerless and more than doubled the stock through share repurchases and one more crafty acquisition. Then he sold the company off to another activist investor.

Peerless's fate highlights a curious fact about public companies controlled by activist investors: They often fall prey to other activists. Investment vehicles controlled by Carl Icahn, Boone Pickens, and Harold Simmons were all targeted by activist shareholders. Robert Young's Alleghany and Ben Heineman's Northwest Industries were eventually swallowed by other takeover artists. The business world consumes its own, and the life's work of great investors is inevitably reabsorbed into the industrial complex with little acknowledgment of their accomplishments. If these men are remembered at all, it will probably be for how they spent their fortunes, rather than how they made them. Which brings us to Warren Buffett.

Buffett's legacy is Berkshire Hathaway. The vast majority of his wealth is going to the Bill and Melinda Gates Foundation, and Buffett requires that his annual donations be spent within one year.[8] So we won't be seeing his name on a lot of libraries, museums, or hockey arenas. Berkshire Hathaway is of course a monumental achievement. It is a vast, decentralized conglomerate, far more unwieldy than many of the companies we have seen implode in the pages of this book. Berkshire has compiled an astonishing fifty-year record of success, but, like other large diversified holding companies, it is prone to undervaluation. As recently as 2011 and 2012, Berkshire Hathaway stock was obscenely cheap.

Shareholder activism spares no one, no matter how high their pedestal. Berkshire Hathaway is a public company, and as far as we know, Buffett has not chosen to entrench his successors with new supervoting shares or anything of the sort. How long will his life's work survive in an era of pervasive shareholder activism? It seems almost inevitable that Buffett's company, like the public vehicles of so many other successful investors, will become a target. It will be up to Berkshire Hathaway's shareholders to defend it.

A FIXTURE IN THE MARKET

John A. Levin wrote at the end of his letter to BKF Capital shareholders, "One is supposed to conclude with a wonderful inspirational message of hope." This is where I'm supposed to offer prescriptions for the future, but I have none to give. I don't have any easy fixes for our governance problems. Instead, I hope this book has given you some valuable perspective on shareholder activism, so you can be a better judge of the factions fighting for control of our public corporations, and a wiser voting stockholder.

As shareholder activism has become ubiquitous, it looks less and less like a defined movement, as it was in the Proxyteer or corporate raider eras. Instead, it is a fixture in the stock market—it is the reality that when enough shareholders are upset at a board or management team, one of them is almost certain to intervene.

When Carl Icahn surfaced as a large shareholder of Phillips Petroleum in early 1985, he was sued in a matter of days. Nowadays his targets often greet him with board seats. Public company management teams and boards have learned that circling the wagons under activist threat just alienates the shareholders. The best corporate defense requires anticipating your areas of weakness and educating your investors about them. For example, if operating margins are lower than industry norms, or if the company uses less leverage, it's better to explain why *before* an activist comes calling. Because ignoring the shareholders is such a losing strategy, activism has made public companies much more responsive. The system will work even better if the shareholders return the favor.

It's naïve to think every individual shareholder has the bandwidth to thoughtfully evaluate activist campaigns and vote his or her shares accordingly. This is one of the reasons why fiduciary investors have dominated the stock market over the past sixty years. But many of these fiduciary entities, despite having the resources to become informed voters, are, from a governance perspective, essentially absent. It is worth their time and effort to change their ways. Even passive investors such as index funds and quantitative investment managers can boost their performance by voting their shares wisely to promote good governance.

The purpose of our governance system is to harness the talents of professional managers, while ensuring they are faithful and honest stewards of outside shareholders' capital. We've learned that sound corporate oversight requires a team effort from able managers, demanding directors, and engaged shareholders. When the system fails, as it so often does, the consequent loss of accountability can lead to disastrous results. We've seen in this book how quickly a company can cross the line. On one side stood General Motors, with Alfred Sloan as CEO, and an active board of directors consisting of large individual shareholders and representatives of DuPont, a 23% owner. On the other side was General Motors, with a succession of weak CEOs, a quiescent board with little share ownership, and a diffuse, disconnected shareholder base.

Business history teaches us that the pursuit of profit brings out an extreme and obsessive side of people. When we harness it well, we get Wal-Mart, Les Schwab Tires, Southwest Airlines, and Apple. When we don't, we get salad oil swindles, junk bond manipulations, and Steak 'n Shake funneling its cash to its CEO's hedge fund. The publicly owned corporation has been a remarkable engine for progress and economic growth because it can place large amounts of capital in the hands of the right people with the right ideas. Without proper oversight, however, public companies can squander unimaginable amounts of money and inflict great harm on everything around them. The emergence of the shareholder as the dominant force in corporate governance has bestowed a tremendous amount of power and responsibility on investors—the electorate—to channel public companies to produce great outcomes rather than destructive ones.

Appendix:
Original Letters

Note: These letters are reprinted with permission and appear as originally written. I have not corrected any errors.

CHAPTER I LETTER—GRAHAM

June 28, 1927.

Mr. John D. Rockefeller, Jr.,
Mr. Raymond D. Fosdick,
Mr. Frederick Strauss,
Finance Committee of the Rockefeller Foundation,
New York City.

Dear Sirs:

Your attention is respectfully directed to certain elements in the position of the various Pipe Line companies, formerly Standard Oil subsidiaries, which urgently require specific action in the interest both of the Rockefeller Foundation and of the other stockholders. The writers have a substantial interest in most of these enterprises, and one of them is—next to the Foundation—by far the largest stockholder of record of Northern Pipe Line. Moreover, we have been in touch with numerous smaller stockholders, and may properly claim to represent their views as well as our own.

Since the inception of the Rockefeller Foundation's investment in these companies in 1915, their industrial and financial situation have both changed materially. The result is that certain policies which were reasonable and satisfactory twelve years ago, being still maintained under greatly modified conditions, have given rise to an absurd and unfortunate state of affairs. With the exception of the Prairie and Illinois concerns, the going value of these companies' pipe line investment has greatly diminished in recent years, while concurrently their holdings of marketable securities have been substantially increased. Hence, while in 1915 their assets were fairly divided between plant and cash, for the past few years the cash assets have so over-shadowed the going value of the pipe lines as to create an entirely new and anomalous corporate set-up.

At the present time these companies partake far more of the nature of investment trusts than of industrial enterprises, for the greater part of the stockholders' money is invested in gilt-edged securities, yielding an extremely low net return. Permit us to point out that this state of affairs is quite disadvantageous to the Rockefeller Foundation, and far more so to the other pipe line stockholders. The larger portion of the securities' fund consists of railroad bonds, the interest on which is subject to the corporation income-tax of 13½%. If the Foundation owned these securities directly, instead of through the medium of its investment in the pipe line stocks, the income therefrom would be free of corporation tax, and the net return would thus be substantially higher. In order to avoid this heavy tax, a good part of the companies' cash has been places in government and municipal bonds. The same argument holds, however, with respect to these, for the direct yield theron is far lower than the average obtained by the Foundation from its own investments, which it may select without reference to the element of tax exemption.

We ask that you also give serious consideration to the much greater disadvantages under which the other stockholders are laboring, due to the extraordinary fiscal situation of these companies. Because of its ownership of the largest interest therein, and because of the prestige represented by its name, the

Rockefeller Foundation must be considered to some extent in the ethical position of trustee for the smaller participants. We are hopeful, therefore, that its high-minded and generous solicitude, evident in so many fields, will be manifested to some degree in the Foundation's attitude towards its fellow shareholders.

Investors in these companies now find themselves possessed of a hybrid security, of a type entirely outside the range of accepted financial practice. Each share of stock represents the ownership of a large amount of high-grade bonds, conjoined with a smaller interest in a highly fluctuating, and apparently declining, industrial enterprise. Under these conditions the undoubted investment value behind their shares is largely obscured by the speculative character of the pipe line assets. Furthermore, the income derived from the gilt-edged investments is much too low from the standpoint of a stock investment, especially one identified with the pipe line industry. Hence, the effective value of these investments is subject to an absurd depreciation in the minds of the public, and of the stockholders themselves—an unfortunate situation which is greatly intensified by the meagre details given the owners of these properties as to their real assets and earning power.

That the disadvantages suffered by the stockholders from this state of affairs are not imaginary, but entirely real, appears strikingly from the following single instance. At the end of 1926 there were 1,909 stockholders of Northern Pipe, compared with 2,154 at the end of 1924. This means that in two years, at least, 12% of the total number of stockholders disposed of their shares. <u>Practically every one of these stockholders received for his stock less than the amount of free cash assets represented thereby</u>—allowing no value at all for the pipe line which was earning a substantial sum. Some of these stockholders received only 80% of the cash assets alone behind their shares.

As concrete illustrations of the conditions prevailing, we append a few figures relating to three of these concerns:

December 31, 1926	N.Y. TRANSIT	EUREKA PIPE LINE	NORTHERN PIPE LINE
Cash & Investments Per Share (Market Value)	$52.40	$49.50	$89.60
Pipe Line & Other Assets Net Per Share (Book Value)	77.60	101.20	21.30
Total Assets Per Share	$130.00	$150.70	$110.90
Market Price 12/31/26	31¼	50½	72½
Present Market Price	35	57	85

The relief, so urgently required in the interest of the Rockefeller Foundation as well as the other stockholders, is simple and obvious. The cash capital not needed by these pipe line companies in the normal conduct of their business, or to provide for reasonable contingencies, should be returned to the stockholders, whose property it is, in the form of special dividends and/or reductions of capital. Steps in this direction have already been taken by two of the companies—namely, Southern Pipe Line (capital distribution of $50 per share), and Cumberland Pipe Line (special dividend of $33). But the stockholders of the other companies have no assurance or even indication that similar action will be taken in their behalf within a reasonable period. The mere hope of eventual relief is certainly an insufficient remedy for their present disabilities, especially when speedy action could so easily be effected.

The writers have discussed the question with the president of both the Northern and Southern Groups at various times during the past two years. We have been given to understand that the Rockefeller Foundation itself several years ago made a suggestion similar to our own, but that action was deferred thereon because of the pendency of government tax claims. These have since been settled, for the most part on very favorable terms, and we respectfully suggest that the matter should again be given careful consideration.

We believe we may point out without impropriety that the initiative in this direction should properly come from the shareholders rather than the management. This is true for both legal and practical reasons. The determination of whether capital not needed in a business is to remain there or be withdrawn, should be made in the first instance by the owners of the capital rather than by those who are administering same. Accordingly, the undersigned, as substantial stockholders themselves, and speaking on behalf of many others, urgently request that an opportunity be given them to discuss the situation with representatives of the Rockefeller Foundation, to the end that a comprehensive plan may be devised to remedy the present unsatisfactory situation and to improve the position of all the shareholders.

Respectfully yours,

Benjamin Graham
60 Beaver St., New York City.

R. J. Marony
42 Broadway, New York City.

CC: Mr. John D. Rockefeller, Jr.,
     Mr. Raymond D. Fosdick,
     Mr. Frederick Strauss.

CHAPTER **2** LETTER—YOUNG

To Shareholders of
    The New York Central Railroad

Dear Fellow Shareholder:

Put us to work to make your stock more valuable. We have bought stock with a present market value of $25,000,000 in the faith that we can.

Robert R. Young.

For the Nominees of

The Alleghany-Young-Kirby Ownership Board

April 8, 1954

PLEASE RETURN YOUR PROXY IN THE ENCLOSED ENVELOPE
NO STAMP REQUIRED

**Why New Top Direction of Your Company
Is So Urgently Needed**

Before the New York Security Analysts on March 15 the best hope Mr. White held out for Central shareholders was a *possible* $2 annual dividend within four or five years, or a little less. If this had been our view we would not have acquired our stock holdings.

The net income of New York Central in 1929, after all taxes and charges, was $77 million. In that year it paid dividends of $8 a share or the equivalent of $5.75 a share on its present number of shares. In 1953 its net income was $34 million or a decline of 56% from 1929, while all other Class I railroads as a group earned 102% as much as in 1929. Central's earnings thus declined even though during this period it had spent on capital improvements more than three-quarters of a billion dollars.

The Moody's Index of railroad stock averages at the lowest point in 1929 was $96.92. The low for New York Central stock was 160. On April 2 of this year Moody's Index stood at $46.33, a decline of 52%, while Central's stock closed at $23.62, a decline of 85%. Thus Central's stock during the last 25 years has declined marketwise 33 percentage points more than the averages. Had Central's stock merely kept pace with the averages, instead of turning in a below-average performance, it today would be selling $53 higher, or at a price of roundly $77.

This then is the result achieved under the financial management of the Vanderbilt family, First National Bank, J. P. Morgan & Co., and allied banking interests represented on the board of New York Central during the last 25 years.

What Good Management Can Do

We ask you particularly to observe in this connection the table on pages 4 and 5 [see table on page 217] reciting the comparative market history of Alleghany and its affiliates for the years 1938 to 1954. During these years security prices generally experienced a rising market due to the expanding earning power of industry.

A test of good management is the extent to which increased earnings are used to rehabilitate the companies in question, and this is usually reflected in the subsequent market prices of their securities. C&O, alone of the major railroad and industrial stocks in Alleghany's portfolio, was in good financial condition in 1938. Therefore it had neither declined as much as the other railroad stocks in the portfolio, nor increased as much thereafter.

Mindful of the declining competitive position of coal Alleghany sold out 1,941,033 shares, or 100% of its C&O holdings, from 1938 to 1954 for a total of approximately $83 million. This was at an average price of $42.88 per share compared with a high for this year of 36⅞ and a low of 33⅛.

The Poor Operating Record

Of the 19 largest railways in the Eastern District, the Pocahontas and Southern Regions, as selected and tabulated by the Bureau of Transportation Statistics of the Interstate Commerce Commission, the New York Central ranked, with one exception, the poorest in 1952 in operating ratio (expenses to revenues) for freight service. The ratio for the Central was 73.85% compared with an average of 66.72% for the other 18 railroads.

These figures, in our opinion, utterly demolish the myth that the relatively higher proportion of passenger traffic carried by the New York Central is solely responsible for its poor operating record.

Yet Central is situated in the best traffic territory in the world and has the most preferred water level routes.

It should also be noted that the Lackawanna, from which Mr. White was transferred in 1952 after 11 years as President, was left in such condition that it operated in 1953 at the highest transportation expense ratio of all the 77 railroads in the East with the exceptions of the bankrupt Long Island, the Canadian government's Grand Trunk Western, and the little Susquehanna.

Why the Sorry State of Central Affairs?

This sorry state of New York Central affairs, in our opinion, is basically due to the fact that its present Board together owned, according to last year's proxy statement, only 13,750 shares of stock or less than ¼ of 1%.

Just ask yourself why the four bankers on the present board, together owning only 450 shares of Central, are so determined to hang on to your company. Is it not because of the substantial benefits which have accrued to their four banks through cash deposits, trusteeships and countless other ways?

The directors and officers of these four banks interlock with 50 other industrial companies and 14 other railroads having assets of more than $107 billion. How much of the undivided loyalty of these four men do you think your Central enjoys?

The Passenger Deficit

One of our first moves will be to address ourselves vigorously to Central's passenger department which last year lost more than $50 million.

C&O is developing (with the help of the Pullman Standard Car Manufacturing Company) Train X, a new, modern, low-to-the-ground, lightweight train. Train X, according to engineers' estimates, will meet Interstate Commerce Commission safety standards and will cost only half as much to operate as present equipment, and one-third as much to build. It can go a long way, we believe, toward eliminating Central's loss in the passenger department.

Without the cooperation of connecting railroads C&O could not, practicably, install Train X. The Central can.

The New York City Real Estate

Since 1947 C&O has been urging Central to sell its New York City real estate carried on its books at $48,760,000 and which we estimate to represent $150 million in present values. Today this estimated value yields less than 5%. By using the proceeds of sale to buy up New York Central bonds now quoted at a 30% discount, we believe a substantial improvement in the Company's financial condition can be achieved. Under our persistent pressure the Central board finally took action by suing J. P. Morgan & Co. and four other banks as Trustees under the bonds, and the New Haven Railroad to establish through the courts by declaratory judgment what might be done with funds derived from the sale of certain of the real estate.

Senator Langer on Banker Control

That we are not alone in our concern over banker control of our 130 Class I Railroads is shown by the following paragraphs taken from a letter written on March 18, 1954 by Senator William Langer (Republican, North Dakota), Chairman of the United States Senate Committee on the Judiciary, to Colonel J. Monroe Johnson, Chairman of the Interstate Commerce Commission.

"For some time as Chairman of the Senate Judiciary Committee I have been engaged in a study of the control of the railroads of our country by a small group of financiers and bankers located in New York, Pittsburgh and Philadelphia. Because of my concern over the concentration of control in the hands of a few, I have been hopeful that some person or group of persons would break up the control of the Morgan, Kuhn Loeb and Mellon interests which long have dominated our railroads.

"It was, therefore, a source of personal gratification to me to read that Mr. Robert R. Young was undertaking this task by seeking control of the New York Central. I think it is high time that the New York Central be removed from the control of the banking group and be returned to control by its stockholders of whom, I understand, Mr. Young and his proposed Board of Directors are the largest. If Mr. Young and his associates are successful in the present contest, it is my view that a long step will have been taken toward breaking down the present monopoly control in the railroad field."

The Lawsuit in Your Behalf

The present board is not entitled to have unlimited access to the treasury of your Company in an effort to maintain themselves as directors to the exclusion of our nominees who have no such conflicts and who own more than a million shares of Central stock. Yet the present board has said it intends to wage an all out campaign in the press, radio, television and magazines.

They have hired Robinson-Hannegan Associates, Inc. a high powered publicity firm, and Georgeson & Co., professional proxy solicitors, to sway your vote in their favor. They apparently believe that the stockholders cannot stop them from spending your money for their own electioneering or from ordering any of your one hundred thousand officers and employees to do proxy service for them.

In behalf of the Company, and of yourself, we have commenced suit in New York against the present board of directors to stop these expenditures and recover them for the stockholders.

The Lifetime Contracts of White & Metzman

Ask yourself for what reason Mr. White, when he was promoted from the related Lackawanna, got a contract at $120,000 a year until at age 65 he retires, $75,000 a year until age 70, and $40,000 a year thereafter. Certainly, such a contract can remove much of the incentive for hard work, and in our opinion is inimical to your interests.

Your present board of directors did not submit to you for approval this contract or another lifetime contract for your former President, Mr. Gustav Metzman, at $25,000 a year. Mr. Metzman's contract is over and above his full and liberal pension of $26,000 a year, to say nothing of the strange salary of $60,000 a year he is said to receive at his present age of 68 from the American Railway Car Institute, a trade association of car builders who sell equipment to the railroads, including the Central. (Your former President, Mr. Williamson, received an inheritance of $100,000 from a supplier in 1942.) Did Mr. Metzman's service to *you* merit all these awards?

Other employees of the Central, not being directors of J. P. Morgan & Co. or of the First National Bank of New York, as are

Mr. Metzman and Mr. White respectively, have received no such recognition. If these contracts had been submitted to you, the C&O would not have voted its Central shares in favor of the action of the present board in thus attempting to make these two men secure for life at your expense.

Article 7 of your By-Laws reads: "The Board of Directors shall have power at any time to remove any officer and this By-Law shall form a part of the contract with every officer." It is the opinion of our counsel, Lord, Day & Lord, that Mr. White's term of office as President is subject to the will of the Board at any time.

You can be sure that if your new Board continues his present salary of $120,000 a year it will be only if he revises his pessimistic view about the earnings possibilities of your Company and only so long as he turns in a good day's work.

The undersigned will offer his services to the stockholders for one dollar a year as Chairman of the Board, but not as principal operating officer.

Competition Cuts Costs

Alleghany-Young-Kirby furthered the principle of competitive sealed bidding for railroad bonds which spread to the telephone and public utility industries and saved hundreds of millions of dollars for shareholders, consumers and shippers at the expense of the bankers.

Before the introduction of the competitive bidding rule by the ICC, the Central, its officers and bankers went out of their way to oppose this fundamental American principle of competition as applied to their friend, Morgan Stanley & Co.

Only by an alert, vigorous top direction by owners determined to bring competition into every phase of the company's affairs can the cancer of an excessive transportation ratio left us by the banker-dominated Central's board be cut out. In our opinion, Mr. White cannot possibly take a vigorous stand for competition in the company's many relations with suppliers, concessionaires and contractors under the present board.

Why Are We Spending Our Money
and Energies on Your Behalf?

First, because we have bought over a million shares of Central stock in the full faith that under sound management it can again sell far above its present price and pay far in excess of its present dividends.

Quite aside from your and our interest as shareholders in dividends and appreciation, we believe that our control of the Central will work to the vast benefit of the railroads, the travelling public and of the shippers.

Robert R. Young.

For the Nominees of
The Alleghany-Young-Kirby Ownership Board
4500 Chrysler Building
April 8, 1954   New York 17, N. Y.

Warning

If any banker, lawyer, shipper, supplier or other person solicits your proxy for the present Board, ask him what his special interests are, or what your Company is paying for his services. Like the bankers now on your Board, he, too, may be hoping to receive special favors from your railroad or from the bankers.

If your stock is held in a broker's or other nominee's name, take special care to see that he follows your instructions and that we receive your proxy.

YOUR PROXY IS ENCLOSED.
PLEASE SIGN IT NOW AND RETURN IN THE ENCLOSED
ENVELOPE.
NO STAMP REQUIRED.

Comparative Market History of
Alleghany and Affiliates 1938–1983

Although Robert R. Young and Allan P. Kirby both went on
the board of Alleghany in May, 1937, the former becoming
chairman at that time, they constituted with their then partner,
Kolbe, only three of the nine directors. They were thereafter
faced with a hostile president and board majority until January
5, 1938, when they procured the resignation of the incumbent
president and his replacement by Kirby. At the same time they
caused the enlargement of the board to ten members, and for
the first time achieved majority control of said board. The bonds
of Alleghany were then quoted at 71 for the earliest maturity
(due in 1944) to 37½ for those due in 1950. The Common was
selling for 1½. Young first served as a member of the Nickel Plate
board on January 19, 1938 on which day its common stock sold
at 18½ and its 6% Gold Notes due in October, 1938, sold at 60¾.
He became a director of the Pere Marquette on May 3, 1938 on
which day its common stock was quoted at 10 and its various
maturing senior obligations between 56–66. Alleghany's board
control also carried with it control of Pittston, a subsidiary of
Alleghany, and of the Missouri Pacific Railroad, debtor company,
in Section 77 reorganization proceedings. With respect to
Missouri Pacific, Alleghany led the successful opposition to
three successive reorganization plans sponsored by banking and
insurance interests, making possible in each instance a further
improvement of the treatment of all classes of security holders.

Comparative Market Prices

	High - 1938	Low	High - 1953	Low
ALLEGHANY				
Prior Preferred	21	8		80†
Series A Preferred	17	5	152	130
Common	1⅝	⅞	5	3
			Redemption Price	
Coll. Conv. 5s 1944	85	45	102½*	
5s 1949	76	44	102½*	
5s 1950	51	25	102½*	
NICKEL PLATE				
1947				
Preferred	38	12	123‡	
Common	23	7	34‡	
			Redemption Price	
6% Gold Notes 1938-1941 a	106 a	30	100 a	
1st 3½s 1947	95	65	101*	
Ref. 5½s 1974	74	30	103½*	
Ref. 4½s 1978	62	27	102*	
CHESAPEAKE & OHIO			High - 1953	Low
Common	38	22	42	33

Comparative Market Prices

	High - 1938	Low	High - 1953	Low
PERE MARQUETTE				
Prior Preference	43	17	99	91 b
Preferred	38	15	85	67 b
Common	18	5	21	16 b
			Redemption Price	
1st 5s 1956	81	53	105*	
1st 4s 1956	75	50	100*	
1st 4½s 1980	76	50	105*	
MISSOURI PACIFIC			High - 1953	Low
First & Refundings	25	14	118	102
Gen. 4s, 1975	8	4	117	84
Conv. 5 1/2s, 1949	6	3	101	69
Preferred	4	1⅛	58	33
Common	2	½	14	6
PITTSON				
Common	¾	⅛	31	18
INVESTORS DIVERSIFIED SERVICES c			High - 1953	Low
Common	18¼ d		98	82

† The majority of this stock was exchanged in 1953 for new $4 Prior Preferred Convertible Stock. That not exchanged was redeemed at $80 a share.

* All issues marked with an asterisk (*) have been redeemed at the call price in the years 1943–1945.

‡ Prices on November 10, 1947 when C&O distributed its Nickel Plate holdings to C&O shareholders as an extra dividend.

a. Those 6% gold notes, due October 1938, which were not paid off in 1938, were extended until 1941. They were then exchanged for 20% payment in cash and the remainder in 6s, due 1950, which were redeemed at 100 in December, 1943.

b. Since Pere Marquette was absorbed into C&O in 1947, these prices represent the present equivalent on the basis of quotations for C&O shares received in exchange.

c. I. D. S. is Investment Manager for three domestic open-end investment company affiliates: Investors Mutual, Investors Stock Fund and Investors Selective Fund, which have a widespread portfolio of securities including railroad stocks and bonds.

d. Acquisition cost of controlling stock purchased in April and May 1949.

CHAPTER 3 LETTER—BUFFETT

June 16, 1964

Mr. Howard L. Clark, President
American Express Company
65 Broadway
New York, N.Y. 10006

Dear Mr. Clark:

Our Partnership has recently purchased approximately 70,000 shares of American Express stock. This purchase was made after extensive investigation among Travelers Cheque users, bank tellers, bank officers, credit card establishments, card holders and competitors in these various lines of endeavor. All confirmed that American Express' competitive vigor and preeminent trade position had not been damaged by the salad oil problem. While I am certain that management must feel at times like it is in the midst of a bottomless pit regarding the field warehousing activities, it is our feeling that three or four years from now this problem may well have added to the stature of the company in establishing standards for financial integrity and responsibility which are far beyond those of the normal commercial enterprise.

There is something a bit presumptious in offering a suggestion to management while the ink is hardly dry on the certificates representing recent purchases. I would like to respectfully suggest that perhaps a midyear letter to shareholders would be in order, stressing the points mentioned at the annual meeting which illustrated how the competitive position of the company had been maintained. I don't think the long-term shareholder is overly concerned as to the exact net dollar settlement of salad oil claims, or for that matter, the exact net earnings for the first six months (which you may very well not wish to comment on because of seasonal variations, world-wide accounting problems, etc.), but he is very interested in whether Travelers Cheques sales, card holders, card changes, foreign deposits, etc., are all maintaining the growth of the pre–salad oil days.

We have read where a shareholder has instituted suit to prevent voluntary assumption by the parent company of the subsidiary's obligation in the salad oil problem. I am a member of the Financial Analysts Federation and serve on the Corporate Information Committee. Prior to a few months ago we had no connection whatsoever with American Express Company or its stock. I would be quite willing to testify, at my own expense, to the fact that we would not have purchased our 70,000 shares of stock if we had thought the parent company was going to ignore the claims against the subsidiary because our feeling would be that the long-term value of the enterprise would be very substantially reduced. In other words, it is our judgment that American Express by making a fair and perhaps even generous offer is an enterprise that is worth very substantially more than American Express disclaiming responsibility for its subsidiaries' acts. We have backed up this viewpoint by the investment of some $2.8 million. I have no idea whether any of this is relevant to a court of law in determining whether the management is acting properly in making a settlement offer, but if it should be, let me again state my willingness to so testify.

These must be trying days for you and the rest of the management. Let me assure you that the great majority of stockholders (although perhaps not the most vocal ones) think you have done an outstanding job of keeping the ship on an even keel and moving full steam ahead while being buffetted by a typhoon which largely falls in the "Act of God" category. The typhoon will pass, and I think history will show that the ship has continued to make real progress.

Cordially,
Warren E. Buffett
WEB

CHAPTER 4 LETTER—ICAHN

William C. Douce
Chairman of the Board
Phillips Petroleum Company
Phillips Building
Bartlesville, Oklahoma 74004

Dear Mr. Douce:

I am the beneficial owner of 7-1/2 million shares of Phillips Petroleum which makes me one of the Company's largest shareholders. I have examined the material you have sent me concerning your offer and find it to be grossly inadequate. I have received an opinion letter from Donaldson, Lufkin & Jenrette Securities Corporation (one of the foremost oil analysts in the country), in which they opine that the package is worth approximately $42 per share.

I am, therefore, writing this letter to propose that all of the shareholders of Phillips be given an opportunity to choose an alternative transaction which I believe would better serve their interests when compared to the proposed recapitalization.

Under my proposal, I would acquire 100% of Phillips for $55 per share of Phillips common stock, payable $27.50 per share in cash and a subordinated note which in the opinion of independent nationally recognized investment bankers will carry a value of $27.50 per share on a fully distributed basis.

The financing for my acquisition will be arranged by Drexel Burnham Lambert Incorporated who has informed me that if Phillips is agreeable to this transaction and cooperative in facilitating it, and based on current conditions, Drexel is highly confident it can arrange the necessary financing by February 21, 1985, assuming it can begin its financing efforts no later than the close of business on February 6, 1985. My offer is not subject to due diligence. It is subject only to the Board agreeing that provided our financing is in place by February 21, Phillips will postpone the special meeting of stockholders scheduled for Friday, February 22 and schedule another meeting at which shareholders can choose between our offer and yours.

It is important that you note that I have absolutely no objection to the EISOP purchasing Phillips Petroleum. However, what I strenuously oppose is the Board not allowing the shareholders to receive a fair price for all their shares. If I can do a Leveraged Buyout for Phillips at $55 per share, a group which has the tax advantage of an EISOP should easily do as well. If you raise your offer so that you acquire all the outstanding Phillips shares for a package worth $55 per share, I will gladly step aside.

The time constraints resulting from the early date of your special meeting require me to request that you accept or reject this proposal by the close of business on Wednesday, February 6, 1985.

I propose to you that you alter your plan to provide a value of $55 per share or better for all of Phillips' shareholders. I wish to state emphatically that under no circumstances will I accept an offer from you or any of your representatives to buy any or all of my shares unless such offer is extended on precisely the same terms to all of Phillips' public shareholders. If the recapitalization proposal is not altered as I have suggested, I intend to solicit against your proposal. I also plan to promptly commence a tender offer for 51% of the outstanding Phillips shares at $55 per share, with the remainder of the shares to be acquired with securities valued at $55 per share. As noted in the attached letter, Drexel is confident it can arrange financing for this offer.

Very truly yours,

/S/   Carl C. Icahn

CCI:slb
Enclosure

CHAPTER 5 LETTER—PEROT

October 23, 1985

CONFIDENTIAL

Mr. Roger B. Smith
Chairman of the Board
General Motors Corp.
14130 GM Bldg.
3044 W. Grand Blvd.
Detroit, MI 48202

Dear Roger:

In order to resolve my concerns about the Hughes transaction, we need to address two areas:

—The economic and business aspects;
—The negative impact of GM's management style on advanced technology companies, and the long-term implications to Hughes.

The business aspects of Hughes can best be resolved by having the outside

—lawyers
—accountants
—investment bankers

give me a full briefing. Telephone calls to Detroit and return telexes are not adequate.

I will require a due diligence–type briefing, highlighting Hughes' problems as well as its strengths. Specifically, I do not want a Hughes sales presentation.

This briefing should include a factual analysis on Hughes' profit decline and the write-offs.

In addition, I would like to have GM's principal reasons for acquiring Hughes, in outline form, ranked in order of their significance to GM.

I can complete these briefings in a day or two. I am available to start immediately.

If this is acceptable, please have Elmer, or the appropriate GM executive contact me to set it up.

The next step is to openly address and solve the problems between us. Failure to do so will allow the same problems to adversely impact Hughes.

The only issue is the success of GM. Our compatibility is not the issue.

In the interest of GM, you are going to have to stop treating me as a problem, and accept me as -

—A large stockholder
—An active board member
—An experienced businessman

You need to recognize that I am one of the few people who can and will disagree with you.

—they feel you need to know;
—are concerned that you won't want to hear;
—that they are afraid to tell you.

I will tell you anything that can build and strengthen GM, whether you want to hear it or not.

For example, Hughes is not generally considered by senior GM'ers to be a significant contributor in making GM quality and cost competitive. Acquiring Hughes does not resolve the fundamental management issues that place GM at a competitive disadvantage. This is the foundation for my business concerns.

In our relationship -

- —I will support you when I believe you are right.
- —I will tell you candidly when I think you are wrong.
- —If you continue your present autocratic style, I will be your adversary on critical issues.

I will argue with you -

- —Privately.
- —If necessary, I will argue with you publicly before the Board, and the shareholders.

You and others at GM may think that I will simply get frustrated and go away, if you continue to make life unpleasant enough. You need to understand that I cannot leave because of my obligations to -

- —EDS' customers,
- —EDS' people
- —the Series E stockholders.
- —My responsibilities as a GM Director.

My agenda has one item on it—to see GM succeed. I have no interest in a line management role in GM.

I do not expect that all of my ideas will be accepted. I do insist that they be heard and thoughtfully considered.

I will be constructive in all of my efforts to see that GM succeeds, and I will expect the same from others.

Let me be more specific about the problems between us.

For example, during the recent meeting in Detroit, you were

- —Obviously bored.
- —Barely tolerated what others said.
- —Your attitude and comments stifled open communication.

—For example, "GM has no corporate strategy"—whether you like it or not, many senior level GM'ers do not know what GM's corporate strategy is. Senior people believe we are "getting out of the car business".

You need to understand that -

—Your style intimidates people.
—Losing your temper hurts GM.
—Your tendency to try to run over anyone who disagrees with you hurts your effectiveness within GM.
—You need to be aware that people are afraid of you. This stifles candid, upward communication in GM.
—You need to know that GM'ers at all levels use terms like ruthless and bully in describing you.
—There is a widespread feeling throughout GM that you don't care about people.
—You cannot correct GM's problems by focusing on single issues as they are brought to your attention. Your tendency to do this is of widespread concern within GM.

The business issues can be resolved if we approach them openly, candidly and in good faith. UAW style confrontation, misinformation, and misleading statements are unacceptable to me from this point forward, as a GM Director.

Past examples include:

—Initial trading of Series E shares.
—Mort's salary—Claim that GM didn't know about it; Mort is overpaid, therefore, everybody in EDS is overpaid.
—Claims that failure to put Mort's compensation calculation in prospectus is an SEC violation.
—Holding up SIP shares for months using technical issues as the reason, when the real reasons were never discussed.
—Claims that GM can't delay Hughes closing; can't let interest accrue to Hughes after a certain date.

—Failure to keep commitments made at the time of purchase.

—Using the fairness issue only when it serves your purposes.

Finally, I do not believe that GM can become world class and cost competitive by throwing technology and money at its problems.

—The Japanese are not beating us with technology or money. They use old equipment, and build better, less expensive cars by better management, both in Japan and with UAW workers in the U.S.

—We are not closing the quality and price gaps in spite of huge expenditures on automating plants. The fact that we have not set a date to have competitive prices indicates the prevalent attitudes about our will to win.

The foundations for a future relationship are honesty, openness and candor—or simply put, mutual trust and respect. From this point forward, actions count—words do not. We must focus all of our energies on helping GM win.

Roger, my goal is to successfully resolve these problems. I have tried to define them as a first step. This is not a personal issue between us. The issue is the success of GM. I am committed to doing my part to see that we win, and I know that you are, too.

I suggest that you and I visit about these issues.

Let me know when you want to meet.

Sincerely,

Ross
/sb

CHAPTER **6** LETTER—SCHERER

August 4, 1988

Dear Fellow Stockholder:

The Chairman and the President of R.P. Scherer Corporation
sent you a letter dated July 28, 1988, which distorts what
the Karla Scherer Fink Stockholders' Committee For Sale
of R.P. Scherer Corporation wants to accomplish.

The Committee wants just two things:

> —To sell the corporation for its maximum cash value for the
> benefit of all stockholders;
> —To oppose "golden parachutes" for top executives who we
> believe are already lavishly paid—at your expense.

The letter's assertion that I, Karla, demanded to be made CEO
of the corporation is **absolutely false.** No such demand was ever
made. Also false is the claim that the letter was sent to you on
behalf of the board of directors. We, who are both directors, were
unaware of the letter until company management delivered it to the
news media. The last board meeting was June 8, 1988.

**We believe management is misleading you in an attempt to
prevent the sale of the company so that top executives may
continue to benefit personally.** Chairman Wilber H. Mack (whose
position, in our opinion, is largely ceremonial) and President Peter
R. Fink received total compensation of $3,007,000 between April 1,
1985 and March 31, 1988, including cash, the value of incentive stock
awarded and realized net values on the exercise of stock options,
but not including the cost to the corporation of their retirement
benefits—over ⅓ the amount of dividend payments to stockholders
during that same three year period, which totalled only $9,002,000.

In our opinion, it is perfectly clear who are the real beneficiaries of Scherer management's economic policy: **the top executives**.

Since we made public our resolution to sell the company on May 23, 1988, your R.P. Scherer stock on June 24, 1988 reached a high of $28.75 per share, an increase of approximately 80% in anticipation of the company's sale. The issue at hand is **your financial well-being**—not personal attacks management makes to distract your attention.

It is not enough simply to agree with us. Please **support** us by **signing, dating,** and **returning** the enclosed green proxy card **today.**

KARLA SCHERER FINK   JOHN S. SCHERER

CHAPTER 7 LETTER—LOEB

VIA FACSIMILE & U.S. MAIL

February 14, 2005

Mr. Irik P. Sevin
Chairman, President and CEO
Star Gas Partners L.P.
2187 Atlantic Street
Stamford CT 06902

Dear Irik:

Third Point LLC ("Third Point") advises certain entities that hold 1,945,500 common units in Star Gas Partners L.P. ("Star Gas" or the "Company") (NYSE: SGU). Our 6% interest in the common units of the Company makes us your largest unitholder. Unlike the poor, hapless retail investors "stuffed" with purchases at the $24 level (many of whom are party to class action lawsuits against you personally and against the Company), we purchased our stake around these levels and took profits on about 500,000 shares near the $7.00 per unit level.

Since your various acquisition and operating blunders have cost unit holders approximately $570 million in value destruction, I cannot understand your craven stance with respect to shareholder communications. We urged you to hold a conference call to discuss the Company's plight and to set forth a plan of action.

We have also tried to reach you on innumerable occasions only to be told that your legal counsel advised you against speaking to bondholders and shareholders due to the torrent of shareholder litigation currently being brought against senior management and the Company. We did receive a call from Company CFO Ami Trauber (who I was interested to learn previously worked at Syratech (NASD: SYRA) which currently trades at 6 pennies a share and is undergoing a restructuring of its debt). How peculiar that Ami, who is named in virtually all the same shareholder class action complaints that have been filed, is not subject to the same gag order mandated by Company counsel. Since you refused for months to take our numerous calls, I must regrettably communicate with you in the public forum afforded us by Section 13(d) of the Securities Exchange Act of 1934.

Sadly, your ineptitude is not limited to your failure to communicate with bond and unit holders. A review of your record reveals years of value destruction and strategic blunders which have led us to dub you one of the most dangerous and incompetent executives in America. (I was amused to learn, in the course of our investigation, that at Cornell University there is an "Irik Sevin Scholarship." One can only pity the poor student who suffers the indignity of attaching your name to his academic record.)

On October 18, 2004, Star Gas announced the suspension of its common unit dividend, causing an 80% crash in unit price from $21.60 on October 17th to $4.32 on October 18th and destroying over $550 million of value.

On November 18, 2004, after a modest recovery in the stock price, Star Gas announced the sale of its propane business, causing the common units to decline in price from $6.68 on November 17th to $5.55 on November 22nd. Management evidently felt this would create shareholder value when in fact it did the exact opposite. The Company apparently did not feel a fiduciary obligation to maximize value for unit holders, and elected not to return calls from major unitholders prior to the sale of the propane segment. Had you been more responsive, we could have warned you that this that action would not create value. Shockingly, the Company also indicated that unitholders would be "passed through" a taxable gain on sale of up to $10.53 per share even though unitholders may have suffered a loss of over $15.00 a unit.

To add insult to unitholder injury, and to ensure you a dazzling place in the firmament of bad management, we learned that two members of the Company's special committee assigned to evaluate the sale of the propane business, Stephen Russell and William P. Nicolletti, received a one-time fee of $100,000 each! Was that really necessary given that you paid advisory fees to Lehman Brothers (your former employer), paid additional advisory fees to KeyBanc Capital for advising the special committee and paid significant legal fees associated with the transaction? The dereliction of fiduciary duty is truly astounding and we demand that all fees paid to the special committee be repaid immediately by Mr. Russell and Mr. Nicolletti.

On December 17, 2004, Star Gas closed on a $260 million JP Morgan working capital facility. As of December 31, 2004, the Company was already in violation of its fixed charge coverage ratio of 1.1x to 1.0x. As a result, the Company has been forced to use $40 million of the $143.5 million in excess proceeds from the propane business sale for working capital purposes in order to maintain minimum availability on the working capital facility of $25 million to prevent a violation from occurring under the credit agreement. Clearly, JP Morgan did not expect EBITDA of $0 million (before non-recurring items) for the quarter ending December 31, 2004 given that the deal closed December 17, 2004. I also presume that Peter J Solomon (the Company's restructuring advisor) was not marketing a refinancing based on such projections.

In its Form 10-K filed December 14, 2004 (with 17 days left in quarter), the Company that stated heating oil volumes were down 7.2% year-over-year for the two months ended November 30, 2004. However, in its Form 10-Q for the quarter ended December 31, 2004, the Company indicated that heating oil volumes were down 15% for the entire quarter. This would mean one of three things: (i) volumes were down over 50% in the last part of the year (hard to believe), (ii) management does not have an accurate picture of where the business is heading or (iii) management felt it was unnecessary to update its unitholders on material information regarding its customers heading into the all-important winter season.

As mentioned above, for the quarter ended December 31, 2004, EBITDA declined to $0 million from $26 million the prior year. Heating oil volume was down 15%, gross margin per gallon was down over $0.05 or approximately 10%, but fixed costs (delivery, branch, G&A) were up 8%. This is unacceptable and will cause a death spiral. How are you rationalizing the cost structure of the business? Ami Trauber indicated to us that the Company believes it can improve EBITDA margin per gallon to historical levels of $0.12 (some of your competitors are at an approximate 50% premium to that). As your largest common unitholder, we insist that you provide a plan of action on how you will achieve that goal.

Furthermore, we would also like to understand why, even at its peak performance, the Company's margins are significantly lower than those of your competitors. We do not see any reason why a properly managed heating oil distribution business should not operate at least at your historical margin levels, if not at levels similar to the 17% margins enjoyed by your competitors. We would like to form a special committee of unitholders and would like to retain an independent consulting firm to evaluate the Company's operations and management performance; we are prepared to sign a confidentiality agreement in order to have access to the necessary Company data.

The Company received $153.5 million of net proceeds from the sale of the propane business. Star Gas has indicated it has until the end of the year to make use of this cash. However, the Company must pay interest on the MLP Notes of 10.25% per year, amounting to $15.7 million in annual costs (or almost $0.50 a unit) if the Notes are not repurchased immediately. We urge you not to destroy more value for unit holders than you already have; we believe that, unless there is a better use for the cash, the Noteholders should be repaid as soon as practicable before that cash is burned away.

However, if you think there is a better alternative than repaying the Noteholders, such as tuck-in acquisitions, we would like to understand that strategy before cash is deployed.

The Company's expenditure on legal and banking fees is completely inexplicable and out of proportion to the Company's size, resources and scant earnings. We estimate the Company has spent approximately $75 million in fees over the last four months (approximately 50% of SGU's market capitalization) related to make-whole payments, bridge financing, debt refinancing, advisory professional fees and legal costs. Furthermore, a careful reading of the small print in the Company's most recent Form 10-K reveals a further record of abysmal corporate governance. In particular, your $650,000 salary for a company your size is indefensible given the spectacular proportions of your failure as an executive.

Furthermore, given the magnitude of your salary, perhaps you can explain why the Company paid $41,153 for your professional fees in 2004 and why the Company is paying $9,328 for the personal use of company owned vehicles. We questioned Mr. Trauber about the nature of this expense, and I was frankly curious about what kind of luxury vehicle you were tooling around in (or is it chauffeured?). He told us that you drive a 12 year old vehicle. If that is so, then how is it possible that the company is spending so much money on the personal use of a vehicle that is 12 years old? Additionally, your personal use of a Company car appears to violate the Company's Code of Conduct and ethics which states that "All Company assets (e.g. phones, computers, etc.) should be used for legitimate business purposes." We demand that you cease accepting a car allowance for personal use of a Company vehicle, in apparent violation of the Company's Code of Conduct and Ethics. We also demand that you voluntarily eliminate your salary until dividend payments to common unit holders are resumed.

The Company's Code of Conduct and Ethics also clearly states under the section on Conflics of Interest, that

A "conflict occurs when an individual's private interest interferes or even appears to interfere in any way with the person's professional relationships and/or the interests of SGP. You are conflicted if you take actions or have interests that may make it difficult for you to perform your work for SGP objectively and effectively. Likewise, you are conflicted if you or a member of your family receives personal benefits as a result of your position in SGP. . . . You should avoid even the appearance of such a conflict. For example, there is a likely conflict of interest if you:

1. Cause SGP to engage in business transaction with relatives or friends; . . .

By this clearly stated policy, how is it possible that you selected your elderly 78-year old mom to serve on the Company's Board of Directors and as a full-time employee providing employee and unitholder services? We further wonder under what theory of corporate governance does one's mom sit on a Company board. Should you be found derelict in the performance of your executive duties, as we believe is the case, we do not believe your mom is the right person to fire you from your job. We are concerned that you have placed your greed and desire to supplement your family income—through the director's fees of $27,000 and your mom's $199,000 base salary—ahead of the interests of unitholders. We insist that your mom resign immediately from the Company's board of directors.

Irik, at this point, the junior subordinated units that you hold are completely out of the money and hold little potential for receiving any future value. It seems that Star Gas can only serve as your personal "honey pot" from which to extract salary for yourself and family members, fees for your cronies and to insulate you from the numerous lawsuits that you personally face due to your prior alleged fabrications, misstatements and broken promises.

I have known you personally for many years and thus what I am about to say may seem harsh, but is said with some authority. It is time for you to step down from your role as CEO and director so that you can do what you do best: retreat to your waterfront mansion in the Hamptons where you can play tennis and hobnob with your fellow socialites. The matter of repairing the mess you have created should be left to professional management and those that have an economic stake in the outcome.

Sincerely,

/s/ Daniel S. Loeb

Daniel S. Loeb

CHAPTER **8** LETTER—CANNELL

June 1, 2005

John A. Levin, Chairman and CEO
J. Barton Goodwin, Director
Burton Malkeil, Director
Barton Biggs, Director
David Grumhaus, Director
James Tisch, Director
Anson Beard, Jr., Director
Peter Solomon, Director
Dean Takahashi, Director

BKF Capital Group, Inc.
One Rockefeller Plaza, 25th Floor
New York, NY 10020

"When, O Catiline, do you mean to cease abusing our patience? How long is that madness of yours still to mock us? When is there to be an end of that unbridled audacity of yours, swaggering about as it does now?"

Thus, in 63 B.C., did Marcus Tullius Cicero expose corruption and vice in the Roman Senate in his First Oration Against Lucius Catilina. His words are relevant today as we study the record of BKF Capital Group.

Fund management should be a challenging yet simple business—control costs, manage investments intelligently, and fees will flow to the bottom line. Revenues from incremental assets should require little additional expense.

But that is not BKF. Costs are exorbitant. A culture of greed and self-dealing has run amok. Incremental revenues are sucked up by inflated salaries; as a result, BKF continues to lose money, even as assets and revenues have grown 18% and 64%, respectively, over the last five years. Management has frittered away its gains in revenues, producing greater losses, while distributing, at shareholder expense, a staggering 78% of revenues to the executive cabal. Meanwhile, the Board of Directors, whose job it should be to protect the rights of shareholders, and not protect entrenched management, has failed to discharge its fiduciary duties by reigning in run-away compensation and other costs.

$Million	2004	2003	2002	2001	2000
Revenue	$120.7	$98.6	$89.3	$91.4	$76.6
Employee Costs	93.8	77.8	61.8	60.1	57.4
% Revenue	77.7%	78.9%	69.2%	65.8%	74.9%
Net Income	-1.8	-8.4	-2.5	1.5	2.1

Source: 2004 BKF 10-K

BKF's richly-compensated employees, egregious occupancy costs and ill-defined "other operating expenses" are not in the best interest of shareholders. BKF's operating metrics (operating margin, revenue-per-employee, etc.) are abysmal. Comparisons to similar publicly-traded companies reveal the mismanagement.

$Million	Company Name	Assets under Management	Revenues	Operating Margin	Employees	Revenue/ Employee	Cost per Employee
CLMS	Calamos Asset	$38,000	$342.8	45%	264	$1,298.5	$248.9
GBL	Gabelli Asset Mgmt.	28,700	255.2	39%	188	1,357.4	553.7
HNNA	Hennessy Advisors	1,261	9.5	50%	10	954.5	201.6
TROW	T. Rowe Price	45,200	1,277.0	41%	4,139	308.5	110.6
LIO LN	Liontrust Asset Mgmt.	£5,035	£24.5	35%	43	£569.4	£369.3
BKF	BKF Capital	$13,604	$126.5	4%	151	$837.7	$634.1

Source: Factset, 2004 SEC 10-Ks

BKF's April 22, 2005 Form 8-K discloses the compensation arrangements for the managers of the event-driven portfolios, Messrs. Frank Rango and Henry Levin (the son of BKF's Chairman & CEO). The Board's passivity allows the Managers to pay their team up to 67% of the event-driven group's revenue. The Managers are entitled to a base salary of $800,000 and are incentivized with 67% of the group's remaining net profit. The gravy train doesn't end there, however. If BKF terminates Rango and Levin without cause, each will enjoy severance payments of between $2 million and $4 million. There are no restrictions on their ability to solicit BKF's investors or employees if they leave. None of the Managers' compensation is in the form of BKF equity. None of their compensation is in the form of long-term incentives, which would encourage retention. How are these arrangements supposed to align the interests of the Managers with the well-being of your stockholders? All this excess would be dandy in a private company, but BKF is public.

BKF's May 10, 2005 10-Q, states: "As a result of this dependence on key personnel, and the ability of investment personnel or groups of investment personnel to start their own independent businesses, management may be constrained in its ability to negotiate compensation with senior personnel." That's ridiculous. I own Cannell Capital LLC, which has served as General Partner of Tonga Partners LP since 1992. No one has provided me with a guaranteed minimum base salary. No one will pay me severance if my firm is liquidated. I focus on profits. My only security is maintaining the better than 30% gross compound annual return that my firm has achieved over the last 12 years for its investors.

BKF's list of "related party transactions" reads like comic monkeyshines. If the compensation committee must bless paying 78% of the Company's earnings to Mr. Levin, his relatives and intimates, at least pay them in stock. This would align the interests of the business operators with the business owners. It would also provide employees greater after-tax benefits. I suspect most BKF employees labor under the oppressive yoke of federal, state, and New York City income and sales taxes. Long-term capital gains rates of 15% on stock-based compensation would offer them far greater economic benefit. Please us by pleasing them.

The callous conflagration of shareholder assets by BKF galls us as it would gall Cicero. When we visit companies, we stay at $39.95 motels, not fancy hotels with fruit at the "reception" desk. If the bathroom glasses are not wrapped in paper, we flee. We are not squired about in Lincoln Town cars driven by perfumed menservants (although admittedly, Cannell Capital LLC squandered $1,200 on The Donkey Van, http://donkeynation.com, a used 1995 Ford Econoline van, purchased from See's Candies, Inc. in 2004).

My visit to your offices on May 26, 2005 left me astounded that such an unprofitable company would house itself in some of the most expensive office space in America. Your 56,000 square foot office in Rockefeller Center immolates cash at the expense of BKF's shareholders. Why dedicate half a floor to "test" Dell computers? Not all meretricious trappings are poor business expenses, however. I appreciate the lavish spending of casinos as they lure "whales" to their tables, but this acceptance is predicated upon such adornments being accretive to earnings, to bringing in profitable bacon. Your Rockefeller Center pork just stinks.

The BKF Board would benefit from exposure to one of my heroes, Alan "Ace" Greenberg, Chairman of Bear Stearns, Inc. ("BSC.").[1] Greenberg's careful management and cost controls yield 24% pretax margins at BSC. And yet BKF maintains in last week's Form DEFA14A that "BKF Capital will not be improved through [a] strategy of deep cost cutting"—an audacious claim.

Were "Ace" to ascend to the chair of BKF's board, a prospect over which we drool, he might ask the following;

- Why does BKF pay Jennifer Levin Carter, Mr. Levin's daughter, $174,600? The claim that she provides "consulting

services rendered to various alternative investment strategies
of the company" smells. What are these services?

- How does BKF justify paying $8.7 million to Henry Levin, son of
  the CEO and Chairman, given the terrible operating margins at
  BKF?
- Is senior management invested in BKF's funds? If yes, how much?
  If not, why not? Why do you, the directors, own so little stock in
  BKF? Do directors maintain significant accounts at the Company?
  Please try to eat your own cooking. Shareholders like that.

One would expect such deportment from scalawags, but not you
noble nabobs of Wall Street. I hoped for better from Mr. Biggs,
who built an illustrious career offering advice to investors—
which BKF so plainly needs. I hoped for better from Professor
Malkiel, who has directed Vanguard Group as a paragon of
financial probity and responsibility. I hoped for better from Mr.
Beard. It's hard to believe that this is the same Beard who, in a
May 12, 2005 letter to Morgan Stanley shareholders wrote:

"Shareholders deserve better. We strongly believe that new
leadership is critical to the success of the Firm and to the creation of
shareholder value."

The boards' lack of credible hedge fund experience is a hindrance
to BKF. Though burnished, bespoke and credentialed, I see little
in the directors, save James Tisch, which suggests any operating
experience in its quiver. I am not interested in managing BKF
or any of its assets. (In fact, Cannell Capital has distributed over
$250 million back to investors in recent years in order to remain
nimble.) But BKF's board should include people with credible
hedge fund management expertise and long term track records.

BKF has grown since the November 1995 merger of Baker
Fentress with John A. Levin & Co., but in the last five years,
BKF has generated $464.6 million in revenues, but no profits.
Indeed, BKF has racked up $62.4 million in losses. Mr. Levin

operates BKF like a private playpen. He does not appear to value stockholders as important partners or constituents.

I therefore urge the Board either to: (i) take BKF private and squander privately; (ii) appoint an investment banker to conduct an auction of the company, as Opportunity Partner's Phillip Goldstein first suggested in his November 17, 2003 13d filing; or (iii) stand down and pass the baton to a shareholder-friendly board.

We today speak with many interested parties who are on deck to increase the efficiency and productivity of your operations, energize the investment team to spark greater performance and substantially increase assets under management. Please consider this latter "dream team" option.

Cicero ultimately vanquished Catiline despite the latter's attempt to form a rebel force with other rich and corrupt men.

"The city should rejoice because it has been saved from a bloody rebellion. He asked for nothing for himself but the grateful remembrance of the city for what he has done. He acknowledged that this victory was more difficult than one in foreign lands, because the enemies were citizens of Rome."

You still have time to flee. Go forth, Catiline.

Sincerely,

J. Carlo Cannell

Managing Member

---

1. A used copy of Memos from the Chairman, Alan C. Greenberg, is being sent to you by 2nd rate, the postal classification reserved by the USPS for printed matter. Here are some of my favorite excerpts:

- "I have just informed the purchasing department that they should no longer purchase paper clips. All of us receive documents every day with paper clips on them. If we save these paper clips, not only will we have enough for our own use, but we will also, in a short time, be awash in the little critters. Periodically, we collect excess paper clips and sell them (since the cost to us is zero, the Arbitrage Department tells me the return on capital will be above average)."

- "The only statistic I care about is return on equity. After many sessions with some of our business school graduates (yes, we do have some), I think they have helped me understand the secret to improving our R.O.E. It seems that if we increase revenues and cut expenses, return on equity goes up and that is what makes me happy."

- "Bear Stearns will no longer purchase rubber bands. If we can save paper clips from incoming mail, we can save rubber bands, and my hope is that we can become awash in those little strechies."

- "When you are a private enterprise, savings on expenses go to the bottom line. When you are owned by the public, savings still go to the bottom line, but they are in turn magnified by the multiple the stock carries."

June 16, 2005

Dear Fellow Stockholder,

The Board of Directors of BKF recently took dramatic action to take off the table for the annual meeting all issues except the central one: which slate of candidates will produce the best board to foster the growth and success of the company. The Board (1) rescinded the poison pill, (2) modified its proposal to de-stagger the board so that all directors will be up for election in 2006 and so that directors may be removed by majority vote, and (3) amended the by-laws so that holders of 25% of the shares will have the right to call a special meeting of stockholders (to remove directors or for any other purpose). Furthermore, the Company disclosed that it had retained two investment banks to explore transactions to realize shareholder value. Why were these steps taken? TO MAKE IT PERFECTLY CLEAR TO STOCKHOLDERS THAT THIS ELECTION IS NOT ABOUT SELLING THE COMPANY OR ANTI-TAKEOVER DEVICES, BUT ABOUT HOW TO BUILD UP A PUBLIC COMPANY. Since the opposition slate has not offered any sort of credible business plan, stockholders should be asking them: "What's going on?"

In our view, the letter recently filed by Carlo Cannell accurately reflects the intentions of the dissident stockholders. Through a noisy, mean-spirited public campaign, they were seeking to force the Company to take itself private or to force a sale to a third party. In fact, both these avenues have been seriously examined and pursued, but to date, neither of these options has proven to be viable. As a third option, the Cannell letter asks stockholders to put their faith in an undisclosed "dream team." It would have been nice if Mr. Cannell shared with other shareholders just who these "dream team" members might be and just what it is they are planning to do.

On June 9, 2005, Steel Partners, after our series of requests that they disclose their business plan, has made a proposal that reflects their stubborn refusal to understand the business they are seeking to control. THEY HAVE DEMANDED THAT BY THE CONCLUSION OF THIS YEAR, WE ACHIEVE PROFIT MARGINS COMPARABLE TO THOSE ACHIEVED BY A NUMBER OF MUCH LARGER COMPETITORS WITH VERY DIFFERENT BUSINESSES. Steel Partners, which does hire sophisticated financial analysts, makes arguments to stockholders that ignore basic issues such as scale, business mix, distribution models, the amortization of intangible expenses and a series of other issues that are essential to understanding the financial results of our business.

Unlike some of the competitors cited by Steel Partners, we do not operate closed-end funds that have locked-up capital or large mutual fund complexes that can absorb their administrative costs. In addition, such publicly traded investment vehicles are often less reliant on and identified with particular portfolio managers. In contrast, we derive our revenues from fundamentally based long-only and alternative investment strategies in which clients are particularly focused on the identity of the portfolio manager and other investment team members. With respect to the alternative investment strategies in particular, we believe that they are valuable assets that are housed at our firm because of the research, distribution and operational platform we can provide, but they do tend to run at lower margins.

As we have often explained, we are trying to build up our firm so it can be more comparable in size to our competitors and so that we can earn greater profits. To that end, we have seeded a number of long-only and alternative investment strategies, but as they develop their track records, the associated compensation costs have impacted our margins. Over the past three years, we have started from scratch two long/short equity strategies that in the aggregate currently have approximately $900 million in assets under management, and in the past 18 months we have launched three more long/short equity strategies that are being incubated, and a small cap value product. If a reasonable percentage of such new products succeed, the investments should produce important returns to stockholders.

So while we are comprised of experienced professionals, we are also a young public company that is seeking to develop a diversified series of investment strategies that have the capacity to grow. AT THIS STAGE OF OUR DEVELOPMENT, STOCKHOLDERS HAVE THE POWER TO DETERMINE IF WE WILL GROW OR FAIL. Without having the candor to admit it, the opposition is saying "no" to growth and proposing immediate, drastic cuts to compensation that, if enacted, will inevitably drive away key personnel and diminish the value of our existing business.

Since Steel Partners began its attacks on the company, we have been forced to spend a great deal of time and energy with clients, employees and potential employees, trying to give them some hope that the company they have selected or are considering will be there for them. While we have needed a senior executive to strengthen our management team and increase our profits, the actions by Steel Partners have made the recruitment of such a person extremely difficult. Of course, Steel has avoided addressing the consequences of its actions, and we remain gravely concerned that a group of competitors will not be focused on developing value for all stockholders and may be interested in replacing our products with theirs. WE JUST DO NOT BELIEVE THAT A NEW MANAGEMENT COULD REPLACE OUR SENIOR PORTFOLIO MANAGERS AND STILL RETAIN OUR CLIENTS. The stockholders opposing us may be skilled portfolio managers with impressive track records, but the fact is that our clients have chosen our people to manage their money in a particular style. If they wanted Mr. Lichtenstein or Mr. Cannell to manage their money, they could have chosen them, and we would not at all be surprised if some of our clients do in fact have their money invested with them. But even if some of our clients have chosen Mr. Lichtenstein or Mr. Cannell to manage their money for them, it does not mean they would want them to manage a greater portion of their assets.

We think that the portfolio managers attacking us well understand the difficulty of retaining existing client assets, so we must ask whether these portfolio managers think that they can take advantage of a possible decline in our stock price (perhaps brought on by the disruption they engender) by merging one or more of their entities into our publicly traded company. Or maybe Mr. Lichtenstein sees his investment as being hedged because BKF is a potential source of direct revenues for his management business (which is owned by him, not his investors). SEC filings disclose that Mr. Lichtenstein's management company has received significant management and consulting fees from public companies where he has become Chief Executive Officer; we think that is something stockholders ought to know.

If you wonder where this distrust of the opposition slate comes from, please look at the quality of the arguments being used to attack us. The attack on Barton Biggs, a universally recognized expert on the asset management industry, for paying us rent for a limited period of time for space inside our offices we weren't utilizing and couldn't sublet was always a joke, which people understand when we discuss it. We are being attacked for paying a relatively low amount of fees to Peter Solomon's investment banking organization while these same attackers simultaneously criticize us for not pursuing strategic alternative to realize shareholder value.

With respect to the attacks on my children, I must say they reveal much about the nature of the opposition but disclose absolutely nothing improper. Much has been said about the compensation paid to my son Henry, but I just ask that stockholders evaluate him as one of two senior portfolio managers for event-driven strategies that have generated a very significant portion of our firm's revenues and free cash flow over the years. The strategies have long, established track records and importantly have attracted investors that later invested in other firm strategies. He is paid on the basis of the profitability to the firm of the strategies he manages, which is exactly how our hedge fund manager critics pay themselves. While I understand that being part of a public company must necessarily reduce the cash compensation he can earn, I don't understand why being rewarded based on the profitability of the accounts he manages is no longer a valid way of looking at things, especially when he must perform many of the same client servicing, marketing and personnel management functions that his counterparts at privately held firms perform.

My daughter, Jennifer Levin Carter, has a distinguished academic record, having become a member of Phi Beta Kappa in her junior year at Yale, and having graduated from there with distinction in molecular biophysics and biochemistry, from Harvard Medical School and from the Harvard School of Public Health. She has provided valuable research to our investment professionals on biotech and other companies within her area of expertise, and is viewed as a substantive plus by all who interact with her. She is paid consulting fees at an hourly rate, and in all likelihood is receiving less than she otherwise would because of sensitivity to public perception.

With respect to the "losses" being generated by our business, I only ask that investors look at our business as any reasonably sophisticated investor should—and you can be sure that the portfolio managers attacking us are sophisticated investors. Steel Partners has repeatedly stated that it does not understand how we lose money, and in the Cannell letter, the author makes the point that our business has generated over $62 million in losses since 2000. Both Mr. Lichtenstein and Mr. Cannell conveniently forget to note that the company has recorded over $91 million in expenses over that same period relating to the amortization of intangibles arising from the 1996 transaction involving our money management business and a closed-end fund. In other words, the "losses" just do not reflect the way in which our business has been managed, and they obscure the cash flow actually being generated. We understand shareholders who make inquiries as to why our cash flow is not higher, but attacks on our "losses" by sophisticated money managers betray their tendency to obscure the relevant facts to achieve their aims.

Once again: What's going on? Is BKF now in a terrible predicament because Steel Partners is looking past the potential value destruction in our particular situation in order to burnish its "activist" credentials, intimidate existing and future targets and thereby enhance its overall portfolio returns? If Steel wants to claim credit for our corporate governance reforms, then it has already done all it can. If Steel wants to force through a compensation program that drives out key personnel, then what is the real business strategy? After having brought our money management business public in a transaction that generated significant value for stockholders by distributing approximately $700 million in assets, I am particularly pained as I watch this pack of hedge funds, pretending to be suffering and abused shareholders, continue on their destructive path, more concerned with the image that they project than with the interests of other BKF shareholders. Ever since we became a public company, we've stated that a supportive shareholder base was important to our business. I've thought that shareholders who are disappointed with management could always sell (in fact our stock has done exceedingly well), and those who have constructive proposals or valid criticisms could always make them. I can accept and understand criticism, but I don't understand attacks that so clearly destroy value.

At this point, I expect you might be wondering what is motivating me to continue to fight. Indeed in the recent period, I have wrestled hard with that question. A number of my key long-term partners have pressured me to hang in there so as to not allow a small number of our shareholders to destroy the firm. Their encouragement has kept me going for now. This is a great firm with great people. We made a lot of good decisions and we made some bad ones, as have many successful investment firms. But managing a public company with hostile shareholders is not an enviable task, particularly for someone like me who is more interested in managing money than in anything else.

One is supposed to conclude with a wonderful inspirational message of hope, but let me tell you the grim reality. I don't know what any shareholder or group of shareholders is going to say or do next. It is up to the unaligned shareholders of this company to decide what the future is. There is no middle ground. Our slate is composed of outstanding individuals. Burt Malkiel is just the kind of director shareholders should want. He is a former member of the Council of Economic Advisors, a long-standing full professor of Economics at Princeton and a trustee of various Vanguard funds. Bart Goodwin is a quality investor in private equity companies. Both of these gentlemen were directors of BKF before our money management firm merged into it in 1996. They are as independent as directors can be. Vote the white card.

Sincerely,

/s/ JOHN A. LEVIN

John A. Levin

Chairman and CEO

Acknowledgments

DEAR CHAIRMAN AROSE FROM two ideas. The first one was pretty good—to use original letters from public company investors to tell a short history of shareholder activism. The second idea was really bad—that I should be the one to write it. Besides the obvious problem of not being a writer, I have a demanding full-time job and a young family in no particular need of neglect.

There were several critical events that pushed the project forward when I was very close to giving up on it. First, Warren Buffett sent me his letter to American Express. Buffett probably spent thirty seconds reading my letter explaining the project, plus another fifteen seconds telling someone to find his letter and send it to me. That forty-five seconds of his attention resulted in my spending a sleep-deprived year at this keyboard. Not only did I have to write the book, but I needed to do my very best job. Thank you, Warren Buffett.

A few weeks after receiving Buffett's letter, I went to a Brooklyn Nets game with my friend Christian Rudder, who was in the middle of writing his own book. I told him my book idea and explained my plan to write the whole thing before finding a publisher. He groaned, "Dude, don't do that." The next day Christian introduced me to his agent, Chris Parris-Lamb, and before long I had the necessary deadlines and commitments to make this book a reality. Thank you, Christian Rudder.

After getting some pointers from Chris about how to structure a book proposal, I sat down to write. The first five pages I sent him took forever to write and were a real disaster. If he had lost my phone number at that point, I would have never resumed writing. Instead, he pointed me in the right direction, helped me craft a good proposal, and then convinced Hollis Heimbouch at HarperCollins to buy the book. Thank you, Chris Parris-Lamb and the Gernert Company.

I owe many thanks to Hollis at HarperCollins for publishing and editing *Dear Chairman*. Her edits made the book so much better and more focused. Without Hollis, this book would be a rambling mess with a lot of ridiculous music references (though I stand by comparing the third merger wave to third-wave ska). Thanks also to Stephanie Hitchcock and the rest of the team at HarperCollins.

John Vengilio helped me tremendously as my research assistant. He kept me organized and helped get permission to publish many of these letters. He brought R. P. Scherer and Bill Shlensky to my attention, among many other juicy tidbits. He also endlessly pestered the SEC for copies of many old filings.

Thanks to Kevin Barker for doing the endnotes for me. Kevin's wife, Amy Miller, was one of two smart lawyers who read much of the material and shared valuable comments. Nick Joseph was the other. Thank you Kevin, Amy, and Nick.

Eddie Ramsden helped me kick around the book idea at its very inception and added many excellent insights. I would also like to give special thanks to Natalie Banas, Andy Shpiz, Jon Fasman, and Fred Kovey, who read several early versions of the proposal and some of the chapters, and gave very helpful feedback.

Jason Zinoman helped me make sense of the publishing world and offered great advice throughout the process.

I have so many other people to thank for helping me: Terry Kontos, Martin Lipton, Thomas Kennedy, Bradley Radoff, Barry Steinhart, Gil Weisblum, Peter Decker, James Pappas, Norbert Lou, Bill Martin, Peter Cecchini, Timothy Brog, Steven Wolosky, Robert Holton, Steven Bronson, Herbert Winokur, Harvey Goldschmid, Brian Cheffins, Damien Park, Winthrop Smith, Natalia Da Silva, Jim Heimbach, Elizabeth Heimbach, Ross Perot Jr., Carol Hoffman, Jack Mitchell, and George Konomos.

Special thanks to all of the subjects of the book for letting me republish your wonderful letters. These are your stories and I tried my best to do them justice.

I want to thank my business partner of almost a decade, Gregory Bylinsky. Greg, the son of a great business writer, not only tolerated this project; he offered assistance and provided valuable input. Thanks to my other coworkers, the aforementioned Natalie, Robbie Beers, Richard Baluyut, and Gregory Shrock. Greg No. 2 has been incredibly patient listening to all my random thoughts about public companies and then explaining how things really work.

Thank you to the investors in my fund. Your patience and commitment to long-term investing provide me a job that I love, and writing our quarterly letters is really what inspired me to think about this book. I hope to channel the lessons I learned from researching and writing this book as best as I can into providing good returns for you in the future.

The closest thing I have to a mentor is Arthur Levitt. He and Joel Greenblatt have made my career possible, and I'm eternally grateful.

My family deserves many thank-yous, especially my parents, to whom this book is dedicated. My father provided constant pressure as usual, combining inspirational messages like "this book is not an economically rational use of your time" and "you better not screw this up because your name is going to be on this forever." My mother not only offered book-saving child care at a critical moment; she also has a deeper understanding of corporate governance than I'll ever have, and she's been an excellent sounding board.

Thanks to my brother Marshall and his wife, Teresa, both economics professors like my parents. I've leaned quite heavily on Marshall for feedback since I started thinking about this book and he has always been quick with smart advice.

Thank you to my lovely and loving wife, Susie Heimbach, and our boys, Gilbert and Benji. Susie is an ace transcriber who also helped me edit many of the chapters. For a full year, she and the boys have suffered more than Bill Shlensky at an afternoon Cubs game. Gilbert and Benji, I am now officially done; we can plug in the karaoke machine.

All the people listed above—and certainly many others whom I have mistakenly left out—have made this book better than I could have managed on my own. Any decent insight in these pages probably came from one of them. As for my mistakes, inaccuracies, misjudgments, and general failures in duties of care and loyalty in the composition of this book . . . well, I've assembled a seven-person board of directors and we have taken out a large directors and officers insurance policy. The board will be happy to meet with you once a year, in Nome, Alaska. Please limit yourself to one question.

Notes

INTRODUCTION

1. Jimmy Greenfield, *100 Things Cubs Fans Should Know Before They Die* (Chicago: Triumph Books, 2012), 66.
2. All these number are from court filings in Appellate Court of Illinois Case #51750, *Shlensky v. Wrigley*.
3. Johan Matthijs de Jongh, "Shareholder Activists Avant La Lettre: The 'Complaining Participants' in the Dutch East India Company, 1622–1625," in *Origins of Shareholder Advocacy*, edited by Jonathan G. S. Koppell (New York: Palgrave Macmillan, 2011), 61–87.
4. Ross Perot, speech to the General Motors board of directors, November 4, 1985.
5. Alice Schroeder, *The Snowball: Warren Buffett and the Business of Life* (New York: Bantam Books, 2008), 486.
6. Steven M. Davidoff, "Nader, an Adversary of Capitalism, Now Fights as an Investor," *New York Times*, DealBook, January 14, 2014.
7. Steve Fishman, "Get Richest Quickest," *New York*, November 22, 2004.
8. William "Mickey" Harley, letter to Nelson Marchioli, Denny's CEO, and Charles Moran, Denny's chairman, February 23, 2004. Mickey signed the letter, but I wrote it with sensible input and editing from my direct boss, Greg Shrock.
9. Warren Buffett speaking at Berkshire Hathaway Shareholders' Meeting, 1998.

1: BENJAMIN GRAHAM VERSUS NORTHERN PIPELINE: THE BIRTH OF MODERN SHAREHOLDER ACTIVISM

1. *Benjamin Graham: The Memoirs of the Dean of Wall Street*, edited by Seymour Chatman (New York: McGraw-Hill, 1996), 200.
2. Ibid., 200: "They were duly brought me, and I soon found I had treasure in my hands."
3. John H. Armour and Brian R. Cheffins, "Origins of 'Offensive' Shareholder Activism in the United States," in *Origins of Shareholder Advocacy*, edited by Jonathan G. S. Koppell (New York: Palgrave Macmillan, 2011), 257.
4. "Cent. Leather Proxy Fight," *New York Times*, January 31, 1911.
5. Armour and Cheffins, "Origins of 'Offensive' Shareholder Activism," 257.

6. T. J. Stiles, *The First Tycoon: The Epic Life of Cornelius Vanderbilt* (New York: Vintage Books, 2010), 439, 449–65.

7. Jones is commonly credited with starting the world's first hedge fund in 1949. Graham founded Newman & Graham in 1936. Alice Schroeder, *The Snowball: Warren Buffett and the Business of Life* (New York: Bantam, 2008). Newman & Graham, like A. W. Jones, had a limited number of partners, paid a performance allocation, and employed shorting and hedging strategies. See *Benjamin Graham: The Memoirs*, 268.

8. *Benjamin Graham: The Memoirs*, 180.

9. Regarding the "investment partnership": Technically Graham-Newman was a corporation. When the IRS questioned the tax status of the Benjamin Graham Joint Account, Graham's accountant recommended they incorporate to avoid further taxes if they were later determined by regulators to be a corporation. See *Benjamin Graham: The Memoirs*, 268. According to Joe Carlen, Graham's average annual performance was 17.5%, versus 14.3% for the S&P. Also, when the fund liquidated, investors got GEICO stock, which did well. Joe Carlen, *The Einstein of Money: The Life and Timeless Financial Wisdom of Benjamin Graham* (Amherst, NY: Prometheus Books, 2012), 262.

10. The annual return figures come from the memo "47 Year Results of Walter & Edwin Schloss Associates," memo, Walter Schloss Investing Archive, Heilbrunn Center for Graham & Dodd Investing, Columbia Business School, New York.

11. Benjamin Graham, *The Intelligent Investor* (New York: Harper, 1973), 107: "[T]he investor who permits himself to be stampeded or unduly worried by unjustified market declines in his holdings is perversely transforming his basic advantage into a basic disadvantage. That man would be better off if his stocks had no market quotation at all, for he would then be spared the mental anguish caused him by *other persons'* mistakes of judgment."

12. Ibid., 109.

13. Ibid., 281.

14. John Micklethwait and Adrian Woolridge, *The Company: A Short History of a Revolutionary Idea* (New York: Modern Library, 2003), 62.

15. Ibid., 62.

16. *Benjamin Graham: The Memoirs*, 142.

17. Ibid., 142.

18. Ibid., 143.

19. The title of *The Intelligent Investor* is a nice example of Graham's scholarly nature. While the publisher has updated the subtitle several times ("The Classic Text on Value Investing" to "The Classic Bestseller on Value Investing" to "The Definitive Book on Value Investing"), Graham's original subtitle was simply "A Book of Practical Counsel."

20. *Benjamin Graham: The Memoirs*, 200.

21. Ibid., 201.

22. Ibid., 203.

23. Ibid., 207.

24. He wrote the letter with Bob Marony, who was a shareholder and director of Graham-Newman. Graham met Marony in 1919 when he was analyzing the Chicago, Milwaukee & St. Paul Railroad. He ended up writing a research report saying that the St. Louis & Southwestern Railroad was a much more attractive buy.

Marony was the financial vice president of the Chicago, Milwaukee & St. Paul, but he did not disagree with Graham's assessment. The two men became friends and began to share investment ideas. Marony knew Bertram Cutler and Tom Debevoise personally. After receiving Graham's letter, Cutler wrote a note to Debevoise about Marony, " . . . [H]he is going to be a nuisance I am afraid."

25. *Benjamin Graham: The Memoirs*, 210.
26. Ibid., 211.
27. Joe Nocera, "The Board Wore Chicken Suits," *New York Times*, May 27, 2006.
28. Leonard Marx, letter to Warren Buffett dated April 15, 1957, Walter Schloss Investing Archive, Heilbrunn Center for Graham & Dodd Investing, Columbia Business School, New York.
29. This is a rite of passage for value investors—holding on to a position even after people with more information tell you how you would sell the stock if you only knew what they knew.
30. I cross-referenced the director names in the proxy mailings with the ICC employee list. The assertion about "affiliated directors" is from *Benjamin Graham: The Memoirs*, 211.
31. Jonathan Macey discusses Federalist No. 10 in his inaugural lecture as the Sam Harris Professor of Corporate Law at Yale Law School, October 9, 2006. Jonathan Macey, "Where's the Theory in Corporate Governance?," https://itunes.apple.com /us/itunes-u/corporate-law/id387940792?mt=10, released August 6, 2007.
32. Thomas Debevoise's son Eli Whitney Debevoise cofounded Debevoise & Plimpton in 1931. The General Education Board was a philanthropic organization started by John D. Rockefeller Sr. His donations to the board in the early twentieth century were, at that time, the largest philanthropic donations in the history of the United States. Quotation from Thomas M. Debevoise, letter to Wickliffe Rose dated April 16, 1925, Folder 181, Box 18, Rockefeller Family Collection, Rockefeller Archive Center.
33. Northern Pipeline proxy mailing dated January 12, 1928, Folder 912, Box 121, Rockefeller Family Collection, Rockefeller Archive Center.
34. See Robert A. G. Monks and Nell Minow, *Case Studies: Corporations in Crisis*, June 30, 2011, http://higheredbcs.wiley.com/legacy/college/monks/0470972599/supp /casestudies.pdf, 84–85. The justification for building the museum was that it would generate goodwill and name recognition for Occidental. *Time*'s review? "Most of it is junk." The $150 million figure comes from a shareholder filing. Even if that estimate is too high, the original guidance in Occidental's proxy was $50 million plus $24 million of future funding.
35. Lucian A. Bebchuk and Jesse M. Fried, *Pay Without Performance: The Unfulfilled Promise of Executive Compensation* (Cambridge, MA: Harvard University Press, 2006), 113.
36. Countrywide was of course bought by Bank of America. ABN-Amro was bought by a consortium led by Royal Bank of Scotland, Fortis, and Banco Santander. Not long after dividing up the assets, both RBS and Fortis were pushed to insolvency by ABN-Amro's liabilities.
37. There's been a lot of research on this phenomenon, most recently Michael Mauboussin and Dan Callahan, "Disbursing Cash to Shareholders: Frequently Asked Questions About Buybacks and Dividends," Credit Suisse report, May 6, 2014,

http://www.shareholderforum.com/wag/Library/20140506_CreditSuisse.pdf.

38. Winn Dixie paid hefty dividends for many years prior to its bankruptcy and woefully underinvested in its stores.

39. Within seconds of descending into the cave, you also had to contend with an army of annoying salesmen telling you about incomprehensible features like Dolby noise reduction.

40. *Benjamin Graham: The Memoirs*, 205.

41. The Rockefeller Archives have no minutes of meetings with Northern Pipeline, but there are some documents regarding later distributions that refer back to previous discussions with Northern Pipeline management.

42. *Benjamin Graham: The Memoirs*, 187.

43. Schroeder, *Snowball*, 186.

44. Graham, *The Intelligent Investor*, 269.

45. Berkshire Hathaway annual letters, 1976 and 1996. The 1976 number takes equities at cost and adds $45.7 million in unrealized gains.

46. This assumes exercise of its option to purchase Bank of America shares.

47. *Benjamin Graham: The Memoirs*, 208.

2: ROBERT YOUNG VERSUS NEW YORK CENTRAL: THE PROXYTEERS STORM THE VANDERBILT LINE

1. Joseph Borkin, *Robert R. Young: The Populist of Wall Street* (New York: Harper & Row, 1947), 50.

2. Ibid., 50. The original Alleghany block was 43%, so 41% of the remainder is slightly over 70%.

3. Matthew Josephson, "The Daring Young Man of Wall Street," *Saturday Evening Post*, August 18, 1945.

4. David Karr, *Fight for Control* (New York: Ballantine, 1956), 99.

5. DJIA promotional flyer, Dow Jones Indexes, December 31, 2011, http://www.djindexes.com/mdsidx/downloads/brochure_info/Dow_Jones_Industrial_Average_Brochure.pdf.

6. Karr, *Fight for Control*, 93.

7. J. C. Perham, "Revolt of the Stockholder," *Barron's*, April 26, 1954.

8. Connie Bruck, *The Predators' Ball: The Inside Story of Drexel Burnham and the Rise of the Junk Bond Raiders* (New York: Penguin, 1989), 157, and Mark Stevens, *King Icahn: The Biography of a Renegade Capitalist* (New York: Dutton, 1993), 96. Also, the Alamo and bat incidents weren't actually simultaneous.

9. Borkin, *Robert R. Young*, 178. Young spent $1.3 million, New York City spent $900,000.

10. Robert Young, letter dated April 8, 1954, Robert Ralph Young Papers (MS 1738), Manuscripts and Archives, Yale University Library.

11. Robert Young, unfinished memoirs, Robert Ralph Young Papers (MS 1738), Manuscripts and Archives, Yale University Library, 4. I changed some unnecessary capitalizations.

12. At Equishares, Young immediately became frustrated with Raskob's weakness for speculative investments. While Young was bearish on equities—he even persuaded Du Pont to move $15 million of his personal holdings out of stocks in June 1929—Raskob piled into the frothy market with abandon. Young later wrote,

"These mistakes of Raskob's were due largely to his unjustified faith in other men, coupled with an unquenchable bullish outlook. They were mistakes which I admired and loved him for. . . . At no time from October 1929 to March 1933 would he admit that the next month held promises of anything but a great boom." Young, memoirs, 5.

13. Young, memoirs, 9–11.
14. Borkin, *Robert R. Young*, 35, 41.
15. Ibid., 98.
16. Ibid., 102.
17. Ibid., 108.
18. Ibid., 141.
19. Karr, *Fight for Control*, 11.
20. John Brooks, *The Seven Fat Years: Chronicles of Wall Street* (New York: Harper & Brothers, 1958), 6.
21. Ibid., 10.
22. Borkin, *Robert R. Young*, 142. The actual quote ends, "as chief executive officer, nor that the responsibility of management be divided."
23. Ibid., 144.
24. Karr, *Fight for Control*, 7.
25. Borkin, *Robert R. Young*, 146.
26. Brooks, *7 Fat Years*, 12. Also see Diana B. Henriques, *The White Sharks of Wall Street: Thomas Mellon Evans and the Original Corporate Raiders* (New York: Scribner, 2000), 133.
27. Karr, *Fight for Control*, 15.
28. Ibid., 32.
29. Borkin, *Robert R. Young*, 151, citing *New York Times*, February 16, 1954, 35.
30. Ibid., 154.
31. Ibid., 152. The full quote reads: "It's a good bet . . . that as it goes, so goes the Central."
32. Robert Young, letter to the New York Central shareholders dated March 5, 1954, Robert Ralph Young Papers (MS 1738), Manuscripts and Archives, Yale University Library.
33. Northern Pipeline proxy mailing, January 12, 1928, Series 87.1N3, Box 121, Folder 912, Business Interests—Northern Pipeline, Rockefeller Family Collection, Rockefeller Archive Center.
34. Borkin, *Robert R. Young*, 203.
35. Ibid,. 170, from Associated Press (AP) interview.
36. Ibid,. 151.
37. Ibid,. 137.
38. Ibid,. 171, from AP debate.
39. Ibid,. 171, from AP debate.
40. Ibid,. 196–97, citing *New York Times*, February 17, 1954.
41. Ibid,. 201.
42. Ibid,. 162.
43. Ibid,. 162.
44. Brooks, *7 Fat Years*, 28.
45. Borkin, *Robert R. Young*, 202.

46. Karr, *Fight for Control*, 33–34.
47. Robert Young, letter to Henry Luce quoting *Fortune* article from May 1954, Robert Ralph Young Papers (MS 1738), Manuscripts and Archives, Yale University Library.
48. Brooks, *7 Fat Years*, 25.
49. Ibid., 32.
50. Ibid., 32.
51. Ibid., 35.
52. Karr, *Fight for Control*, 111.
53. Robert Young, "Little White Lies," proxy mailing, Robert Ralph Young Papers (MS 1738), Manuscripts and Archives, Yale University Library. For the Minneapolis & St. Louis, see Karr, *Fight for Control*, 109.
54. Karr, *Fight for Control*, 114.
55. "Soon-to-be-boss of North Western Collector of Two Kinds of Trains," *Toledo Blade*, February 23, 1956.
56. "Business: Challenge to Management—The Raiders," *Time*, July 25, 1955.
57. Henriques, *White Sharks*, 199, quoting Dero A. Saunders "How Managements Get Tipped Over," *Fortune*, September 1955.
58. Ibid., 99.
59. Ibid., 172.
60. Karr, *Fight for Control*, 151.
61. His decline was dramatic. The SEC targeted him for stock manipulation at American Motors, as well as a stock-parking scheme at Merritt-Chapman, an investment vehicle he controlled. Wolfson's public fall also brought down a Supreme Court justice, Abe Fortas, who had agreed to be a paid advisor of the Wolfson family foundation.
62. "Dissolution Approved by Merritt Chapman," *Milwaukee Journal Business News*, May 11, 1967.
63. Henriques, *White Sharks*, 307.
64. Borkin, *Robert R .Young*, 223.
65. Perhaps the best investment he and his wife ever made was in her sister Georgia O'Keeffe's artwork. Their collection included some of her most famous paintings and was auctioned off in 1987 for millions.
66. Borkin, *Robert R. Young*, 47.
67. Henriques, *White Sharks*, 243–44.
68. Ibid., 264.
69. Ibid., 206–7.

3: WARREN BUFFETT AND AMERICAN EXPRESS: THE GREAT SALAD OIL SWINDLE

1. L. J. Davis, "Buffett Takes Stock," *New York Times Magazine*, April 1, 1990.
2. Warren Buffett, letter to Mr. M. Rubezanin, April 10, 1957, Walter Schloss Investing Archive, Heilbrunn Center for Graham & Dodd Investing, Columbia Business School, New York.
3. Appendix to Buffett Partnership Ltd., 1963 Annual Letter to Partners, January 18, 1964.
4. Ibid.
5. Buffett Partnership Ltd., First Half 1963 Update Letter to Partners, July 10, 1963.

6. Alice Schroeder, *The Snowball: Warren Buffett and the Business of Life* (New York: Bantam Books, 2008), 230.

7. Ibid., 232.

8. Ibid., 232.

9. Norman C. Miller, *The Great Salad Oil Swindle* (Baltimore: Penguin, 1965), 79–80.

10. Ibid., 90.

11. Ibid., 80.

12. Ibid., 81–83.

13. Ibid., 80.

14. Peter Z. Grossman, *American Express: The Unofficial History of the People Who Built the Great Financial Empire* (New York: Crown, 1987), 312.

15. Ibid., 312.

16. Miller, *The Great Salad Oil Swindle*, 88.

17. Ibid., 15.

18. Ibid., 16–17.

19. Ibid., 22–23.

20. Ibid., 23.

21. Grossman, *American Express*, 306.

22. Miller, *The Great Salad Oil Swindle*, 60–61.

23. Ibid., 104–5.

24. Grossman, *American Express*, 313.

25. Ibid., 309.

26. Miller, *The Great Salad Oil Swindle*, 82.

27. Ibid., 83.

28. Ibid., 83–84.

29. Ibid., 134.

30. Ibid., 179.

31. Ibid., 179–80.

32. Ibid., 163–68.

33. Ibid., 178.

34. Schroeder, *Snowball*, 558.

35. Ibid., 264.

36. Buffett Partnership Ltd., 1962 Annual Letter, January 18 1963.

37. Buffett Partnership Ltd., 1963 Annual Letter, January 18 1964.

38. Buffett Partnership Ltd., Partnership Letter, October 9, 1967.

39. Schroeder, *Snowball*, 260.

40. Ibid., 151.

41. "How Omaha Beats Wall Street," *Forbes*, November 1, 1969.

42. Grossman, *American Express*, 327.

43. Ibid., 328.

44. Davis, "Buffett Takes Stock."

45. Stanley H. Brown, *Ling: The Rise, Fall, and Return of a Texas Titan* (New York: Atheneum, 1972), 56.

46. Bruce Wasserstein, *Big Deal: The Battle for Control of America's Leading Corporations* (New York: Warner Books, 1998), 58.

47. John J. Nance, *Golden Boy: The Harold Simmons Story* (Austin, TX: Eakin Press, 2003), 182–93.

48. Ibid., 202.
49. Ibid., 205.
50. Jim Mitchell, "The Inside Story of Harold C. Simmons from Huck Finn Looks to High-Rolling Investments," *Dallas Morning News*, October 1, 1989.
51. Peter Tanous, "An Interview with Merton Miller," Index Fund Advisors, February 1, 1997, http://www.ifa.com/articles/An_Interview_with_Merton_Miller.
52. Moira Johnston, *Takeover: The New Wall Street Warriors* (New York: Arbor House, 1986), 22.
53. John Brooks, *The Go-Go Years: The Drama and Crashing Finale of Wall Street's Bullish 60s* (New York: Wiley, 1999), 238.
54. Ibid.
55. Ibid., 258–59.

4: CARL ICAHN VERSUS PHILLIPS PETROLEUM: THE RISE AND FALL OF THE CORPORATE RAIDERS

1. Mark Stevens, *King Icahn: The Biography of a Renegade Capitalist* (New York: Dutton, 1993), 133.
2. Ibid., 134.
3. Ibid., 150.
4. Ibid., 150.
5. Ibid., 159.
6. Bruce Wasserstein, *Big Deal: The Battle for Control of America's Leading Corporations* (New York: Warner Books, 1998), 78.
7. Hostile takeovers were not by any means an invention of the 1980s. They were increasingly common through the 1960s and 1970s. In mistaken business lore, Inco's ill-fated takeover of ESB in 1974 was the first major hostile takeover.
8. Connie Bruck, *The Predators' Ball: The Inside Story of Drexel Burnham and the Rise of the Junk Bond Raiders* (New York: Penguin, 1989), 117.
9. Ibid., 169.
10. "US Bond Market Issuance and Outstanding (xls)—annual, quarterly, or monthly issuance to December 2014 (issuance) and from 1980 to 2014 Q3 (through November 2014)," Securities Industry and Financial Markets Association, accessed December 27, 2014, http://www.sifma.org/research/statistics.aspx.
11. Well, maybe the unwitting bondholders of Iceland's banks.
12. Stevens, *King Icahn*, 168.
13. T. Boone Pickens, *The Luckiest Guy in the World* (Washington, D.C.: BeardBooks, 2000), 17–24.
14. Ibid., 31.
15. Moira Johnston, *Takeover: The New Wall Street Warriors* (New York: Arbor House, 1986), 53.
16. The buyout was more than 10% higher than where the stock closed the day before the announcement, and 30% higher than where it closed the day after.
17. While the raiders got most of the blame, my sympathies lie with them versus management. They owe their allegiance to their own shareholders and investors, not those of their target company.
18. Pickens, *The Luckiest Guy in the World*, 224.

19. Ibid., 229.

20. Ibid., 233.

21. Debra Whitefield, "Unruh Calls for Pension Funds to Flex Muscles," *Los Angeles Times*, February 3, 1985.

22. Johnston, *Takeover*, 60.

23. Ibid., 70–71.

24. Stevens, *King Icahn*, 149.

25. Ibid., 14.

26. Ibid., 18.

27. Ibid., 28.

28. Ibid., 31.

29. John Brooks, *The Takeover Game* (New York: Dutton, 1987), 86.

30. Stevens, *King Icahn*, 43.

31. Ibid., 43.

32. Ibid., 111.

33. Ken Auletta, "The Raid: How Carl Icahn Came Up Short." *New Yorker*, March 2006.

34. Bruck, *The Predators' Ball*, 247.

35. James Stewart, *Den of Thieves* (New York: Touchstone, 1992), 136.

36. Bruck, *The Predators' Ball*, 17.

37. Ibid., 163.

38. John Taylor, *Storming the Magic Kingdom: Wall Street, the Raiders, and the Battle for Disney* (New York: Ballantine, 1988), 108.

39. Bruck, *The Predators' Ball*, 165.

40. Ibid., 166.

41. Pickens, *The Luckiest Guy in the World*, 234.

42. Front-loaded, "two-tier" tender offers divide the tender into two stages. The first tier usually targets 51% of the shares. The second tier, for the remaining 49%, generally offers less beneficial terms. For example, the first tier might be all-cash versus a second tier that offers debt securities. This pressures shareholders to participate in the first 51% for fear that they will be stuck accepting a lesser offer on the back end.

43. Stevens, *King Icahn*, 163.

44. Carl Icahn, letter to William C. Douce dated February 7, 1985, quoted in Phillips Petroleum Proxy Statement, February 8, 1985.

45. Intentionally triggering the poison pill seemed crazy, but not *totally* crazy. If Icahn bought 30%, the poison pill would essentially replace the other shareholders with debt, giving him full control for $2.5 billion. The total consideration for the deal would be about $59 per share, not that much higher than his proposed $55 per share.

46. William C. Douce, letter to Icahn dated February 4, 1985, quoted in Phillips Petroleum Proxy Statement, February 8, 1985.

47. Robert J. Cole, "Phillips, Icahn Argue on Note Plan," *New York Times*, February 9, 1985.

48. Douce, February 4, 1985, letter to Icahn.

49. Bruck, *The Predators' Ball*, 166.

50. Daniel Rosenheim, "Recess Called, Phillips Shakes Bushes for Votes," *Chicago Tribune*, February 23, 1985.

51. Robert J. Cole, "Phillips Meeting Recessed for a Day," *New York Times*, February 23, 1985.

52. Johnston, *Takeover*, 86.
53. Ibid., 86–87; also Cole, "Phillips Meeting Recessed for a Day."
54. Cole, "Phillips Meeting Recessed for a Day."
55. Johnston, *Takeover*, 87.
56. Pickens, *The Luckiest Guy in the World*, 235.
57. Steven Brill, "The Roaring Eighties," *American Lawyer*, May 1985.
58. Robert Slater, *The Titans of Takeover* (Washington, D.C.: BeardBooks, 1999), 85.
59. Brill, "The Roaring Eighties."
60. Stevens, *King Icahn*, 187.
61. Ibid., 304.
62. Brill, "The Roaring Eighties."
63. Robert A. G. Monks and Nell Minow, *Corporate Governance*, 5th ed. (Hoboken, NJ: Wiley, 2011), 288.
64. T. Boone Pickens, *Boone* (Boston: Houghton Mifflin, 1987), xii–xiii.
65. The 1990–91 recession ran from July 1990 to March 1991. The S&L crisis went from 1986 to 1995.
66. "The Milken Sentence; Excerpts from Judge Wood's Explanation of the Milken Sentencing," *New York Times*, November 22, 1990.
67. Kurt Eichenwald, "Wages Even Wall Street Can't Stomach" *New York Times*, April 3, 1989.
68. Robert Sobel, *Dangerous Dreamers: The Financial Innovators from Charles Merrill to Michael Milken* (New York: Wiley, 1993), 94.
69. Stewart, *Den of Thieves*, 259.
70. Harvey Silverglate, *Three Felonies a Day: How the Feds Target the Innocent* (New York: Encounter Books, 2011), 101.
71. Carol J. Loomis, "How Drexel Rigged a Stock," *Fortune*, November 19, 1990.
72. Benjamin J. Stein, *A License to Steal: The Untold Story of Michael Milken and the Conspiracy to Bilk the Nation* (New York: Simon & Schuster, 1992), 113.
73. Sobel, *Dangerous Dreamers*, 207, and Stein, *A License to Steal*, 114.
74. Stein, *A License to Steal*, 105.
75. Sobel, *Dangerous Dreamers*, 88.
76. See William K. Black, *The Best Way to Rob a Bank Is to Own One: How Corporate Executives and Politicians Looted the S&L Industry* (Austin: University of Texas Press, 2006).
77. "Drexel Burnham Lambert's Legacy: Stars of the Junkyard," *Economist*, October 21, 2010.
78. Brill, "The Roaring Eighties."
79. Ibid.
80. Ibid.
81. Ibid.
82. Bruck, *The Predators' Ball*, 172.
83. Stevens, *King Icahn*, 170.

5: ROSS PEROT VERSUS GENERAL MOTORS:
THE UNMAKING OF THE MODERN CORPORATION

1. The saga was described in Ken Follett's book *On Wings of Eagles* (New York: Signet, 1984).

2. Doron Levin, *Irreconcilable Differences: Ross Perot Versus General Motors* (Boston: Little, Brown, 1989), 34–38. When the aircraft was turned away, he protested outside the North Vietnamese embassy in Laos with a bullhorn.

3. Ibid., 24.

4. Albert Lee, *Call Me Roger* (Chicago: Contemporary Books, 1988), 17.

5. Ibid., 175. In 1980 a GM car cost $300 less to build than a Ford and $320 less than a Chrysler. By 1986, GM's cars were $300 more expensive to build than either Ford's or Chrysler's.

6. J. Patrick Wright, *On a Clear Day You Can See General Motors: John Z. DeLorean's Look Inside the Automotive Giant* (Grosse Point, MI: Wright Enterprises, 1979), 191.

7. Lee, *Call me Roger,* 110.

8. Ibid., 144.

9. Thomas Moore, "The GM System Is like a Blanket of Fog," *Fortune*, February 15, 1988.

10. Lee, *Call Me Roger,* 156.

11. Ibid., 253.

12. Most of the carriage manufacturers suffered the same fate as the buggy whip makers. Studebaker and Durant were notable exceptions.

13. Joshua Davidson, "Durant, William Crapo," Generations of GM History, GM Heritage Center, December 15, 2007. Durant's pension was $10,000 a year. According to the folks at dollartimes.com, that was equivalent to 108,000 in 2014 dollars in 1947, and 169,000 in 2014 dollars in 1936, when the pension started.

14. Alfred P. Sloan Jr., *My Years with General Motors* (New York: Currency/Doubleday, 1990), 30.

15. Ibid., 140.

16. Ibid., 53.

17. Ibid., 429.

18. Amazingly, two-thirds of the $12 billion of military equipment GM manufactured during the war had never been produced by the company before.

19. Though GM did not delegate any responsibility to its factory laborers, a fact that concerned Drucker deeply.

20. Peter F. Drucker, *Concept of the Corporation* (New Brunswick, NJ: Transaction, 2008), 63–64.

21. Ibid., 65. In *Concept of the Corporation*, Drucker concluded—optimistically and very incorrectly—that the objective policy required to preserve GM's decentralization and open discourse was its accounting system and focus on divisional return on capital. His idea was that GM's financial controls alone would allow rational decision making to prevail. GM's younger generation of managers agreed with this point. After Sloan retired, GM began to view its policies and structure as a science with unbending rules, and installed accountants, rather than operators, to run the business.

22. Sloan's book also had a ghostwriter—John McDonald from *Fortune* magazine.

23. Wright, *On a Clear Day You Can See General Motors*, 12.

24. Ibid., 7.

25. DeLorean later lamented that the episode probably did more to damage GM than help it, as the engineering committee significantly ramped up its oversight of the divisions in response to the subterfuge.

26. Wright, *On a Clear Day You Can See General Motors*, 27.

27. Amanda Bennett, "GM Picks Roger B. Smith to Guide Auto Firm Through Critical Decade," *Wall Street Journal*, September 10, 1980.

28. Lee, *Call Me Roger*, 96, and Levin, *Irreconcilable Differences*, 126.

29. Mike Tharp, "US and Japan Agree on Ceilings for Car Shipments Through 1983," *New York Times*, May 1, 1981.

30. GM had always been too insular, so Smith increasingly looked outside the company for new ideas. He based the organizational restructuring on input from McKinsey, and he entered into several joint ventures, including one with a Japanese robot maker.

31. Lee, *Call Me Roger*, 154.

32. Ibid., 144.

33. Levin, *Irreconcilable Differences*, 205–6.

34. Ross Perot, speech to the GM board, November 4, 1985.

35. Lee, *Call Me Roger*, 18.

36. In his 1985 speech to the GM board, Perot quoted a Honda executive reacting to one of GM's newest plants, "GM Saturn—$5 billion investment; 400,000 to 500,000 cars a year; 6,000 Saturn employees. That's what I read in the newspapers. At Honda, we have invested $600 million, will make 300,000 cars with only 3,000 workers. I must be missing something." The other examples are from Perot's speech to the GM board on November 4, 1985, quoting James Harbour.

37. Drucker, *Concept of the Corporation*, 298.

38. Lee, *Call Me Roger*, 26

39. "403: NUMMI," *This American Life* radio program, aired March 26, 2010, Chicago Public Media.

40. Michael Moore, *Roger and Me* (Burbank, CA: Warner Home Video, 2003), DVD, minute 69.

41. Jeffrey Liker, an engineering professor at the University of Michigan at Ann Arbor: "This kind of very flexible, self-contained approach is exactly what Toyota did in the early days of the Toyota Production System." Alan Ohnsman, "Tesla Motors Cuts Factory Cost to Try to Generate Profit," Bloomberg Business, April 12, 2012.

42. "NUMMI," *This American Life*.

43. Maryann Keller, *Rude Awakening: The Rise, Fall, and Struggle for Recovery of General Motors* (New York: Morrow, 1989), 131, and James Womack, Daniel T. Jones, and Daniel Roos, *The Machine That Changed the World* (New York: Free Press, 1990), 82–84.

44. Ross Perot, speech to the GM board, November 4, 1985.

45. Ibid.

46. Levin, *Irreconcilable Differences*, 251.

47. Lee, *Call Me Roger*, 27.

48. Levin, *Irreconcilable Differences*, 261.

49. Ibid., 28.

50. Ibid., 323.

51. Lee, *Call Me Roger*, 124.

52. Ibid., 207. Perot's relationship with GM also took a turn for the worse when Perot would not let GM auditors into EDS. Perot's deal with GM specifically entitled EDS to its own auditors, but GM wanted to double-check EDS's cost-plus billings. Perot

finally relented, but only under severe pressure.

53. Levin, *Irreconcilable Differences*, 311.
54. Lee, *Call Me Roger*, 198.
55. Joseph B. White, "Low Orbit," *Wall Street Journal*, May 24, 1991.
56. This is actually an interesting question to ponder. If his intention had been to embarrass GM all along, why actually sign the deal? It seems like the move was either a calculated attempt by Perot to spin the buyout in his favor, or he genuinely had misgivings. I tend to believe that (1) Perot genuinely didn't think GM would go through with the deal, and that (2) once it all happened, he really was hoping that GM's board or the shareholders would scuttle it. It's also worth pointing out that GM refused to let Perot publicize the deal before they executed it.
57. Keller, *Rude Awakening*, 189–90.
58. Lee, *Call Me Roger*, 253.
59. Ibid., 258.
60. Robert A. G. Monks and Nell Minow, *Case Studies: Corporations in Crisis*, dated June 30, 2011, http://higheredbcs.wiley.com/legacy/college/monks/0470972599/supp/casestudies.pdf, 29; Robert A. G. Monks and Nell Minow, *Power and Accountability: Restoring the Balance of Power Between Corporation, Owners and Society* (New York: HarperCollins, 1992), 186.
61. Jacob M. Schlesinger and Paul Ingrassia, "GM's Outside Directors Are Ending Their Passive Role," *Wall Street Journal*, August 17, 1988.
62. Ibid.
63. Monks and Minow, *Power and Accountability*, 183.
64. Luis A. Aguilar, "Institutional Investors: Power and Responsibility," speech, Georgia State University, Atlanta, April 19, 2013.
65. Sloan lived until he was ninety; most of the other GM owner-capitalists were much older than him.
66. The government argued that DuPont's minority ownership violated antitrust laws by restricting trade in automotive fabrics and finishes, which the company supplied to GM. DuPont's representatives resigned from the GM board, and the company distributed its GM shares to DuPont shareholders.
67. Peter Drucker, *The Unseen Revolution: How Pension Fund Socialism Came to America* (Oxford: Butterworth-Heinemann, 1976), 7–10.
68. Ibid.
69. The high-performance rear engine coupled with its swing-axle suspension made the rear spin out during high speed turns.
70. This was Bucky Knudsen, who ran Pontiac and then Chevrolet for GM. He was also the son of William Knudsen, a former GM president who was tabbed by Roosevelt to lead the production of war materials.
71. Rather than mind its own troubled affairs, the company exacerbated its problems by hiring detectives who spied on Nader and spread rumors that he was homosexual.
72. Alex Taylor III, Andrew Erdman, Justin Martin, and Tricia Welsh, "U.S. Cars Come Back," *Fortune*, November 16, 1992. GM's product failures also had large repercussions because of the company's use of "badge engineering" to get maximum use out of new designs. GM began rebadging its cars in the early 1970s by making Pontiac, Oldsmobile, and Buick models out of the Chevrolet Nova. While this reduced

GM's production, development, and engineering costs, it gutted the creativity of the automotive divisions. None of the standardization resulted in meaningful improvements in quality. GM cars were as crappy as ever, and now they all looked the same.

73. Ricki Fulman, "Shareholder Activism: Pension Funds Led Corporate Governance Revolution: Not Just for Gadflys Anymore, Investor Activism Gets Results," *Pensions and Investments*, February 9, 1998.

74. Robert A. G. Monks and Nell Minow, *Corporate Goverance*, 5th ed. (Hoboken, NJ: Wiley, 2011), 208.

75. HBS California PERS (A), Case 9-291-045, August 17, 2000. Permission to use quotation granted by Harvard Business Publishing.

76. Doron P. Levin, "GM Executives to Explain Perot Buyout to Institutional Investors and Analysts," *Wall Street Journal*, December 15, 1986.

6: KARLA SCHERER VERSUS R. P. SCHERER: A KINGDOM IN A CAPSULE

1. Karla Scherer, "Corporate Power, the Old Boys' Network, and Women in the Boardroom," speech, University of Windsor, Windsor, Ontario, September 12, 1997.

2. Ibid.

3. Greer Williams, "He Did It with Capsules," *Saturday Evening Post*, April 9, 1949, 29.

4. See Icahn's Theory of Reverse Darwinism.

5. Ibid.

6. *Remington: The Science and Practice of Pharmacy*, edited by University of the Sciences in Philadelphia, 21st ed. (Philadelphia: LWW, 2005), 923.

7. Williams, "He Did It with Capsules."

8. Ibid.

9. Ibid.

10. "R. P. Scherer Historical Outline," R. P. Scherer press release, 1983.

11. Ibid.

12. Philip R. Pankiewicz, *American Scissors and Shears: An Antique and Vintage Collectors' Guide* (Boca Raton, FL: Universal-Publishers, 2013), 150.

13. "Historical Outline" press release.

14. John Goff, "A Woman Scorns," *Corporate Finance*, November 1989. "But there was a lack of direction coming from the corporate headquarters."

15. "Historical Outline" press release.

16. Robert Jr. had one success, Storz Instruments, which he sold to American Cyanamid for over $100 million. He continued wheeling and dealing through a public company called Scherer Healthcare, which generated mediocre returns over its lifetime.

17. "Historical Outline" press release.

18. R. P. Scherer dealbook, prepared by Goldman Sachs, circa 1988, 81–82.

19. Ibid., 48–50.

20. R. P. Scherer 1985 Annual Report discloses that the company bought Lorvic/Scientific Associates in 1985 for $5,075,000 (661,578 shares plus cash). The 1988 Annual Report discloses that the company bought Southern Optical in 1987 for $9,627,000

(660,059 shares at $13 plus cash). R. P. Scherer stock was ultimately bought by Shearson Lehman Hutton for $31.75.

21. R. P. Scherer 1992 Annual Report.
22. R. P. Scherer 1986 Annual Report.
23. "Paco Status Report," R. P. Scherer company memo, February 2, 1989.
24. Karla Scherer, interview with the author, August 26, 2013.
25. Michigan let Karla take classes year-round to accelerate her degree.
26. Karla notes that after her mother died in 1980, she and her sister got divorced, her younger brother got married, and she never saw her older brother, Robert Jr., again.
27. Scherer interview.
28. Ibid.
29. "R. P. Scherer Corp. Stock Prices," January 1979 through May 1988.
30. Scherer interview.
31. R. P. Scherer Proxy Statement, July 15, 1988.
32. Scherer, "Corporate Power" speech.
33. Scherer interview.
34. Scherer, "Corporate Power" speech.
35. R. P. Scherer 1988 Proxy Statement.
36. Scherer, "Corporate Power" speech.
37. R. P. Scherer 1988 Proxy Statement; Scherer interview.
38. R. P. Scherer 1988 Proxy Statement.
39. Ibid.
40. Scherer interview.
41. R. P. Scherer Board Minutes, June 8, 1988.
42. R. P. Scherer Proxy Letter, August 4, 1988.
43. Morrow and Company, "R. P. Scherer Corporation—Combined Classes," shareholder analysis, 1988.
44. "Scherer Management Yields Shareholder Names on Eve of Trial; Brother of Major Owner Claims of Major Harassment of Sister," Casey Communications Management press release, July 7, 1988.
45. James Janega, "Theodore Souris, 76: Michigan Court Justice and 'Exemplary' Lawyer," obituary, *Chicago Tribune*, June 22, 2002.
46. In a later letter, Fink and Mack refer to Karla's plan to sell the company as a "scheme."
47. Morrow, "Combined Classes" shareholder analysis.
48. Technically, Richardson was chairman and CEO of Manufacturers National Corporation, the parent company of the bank. His official title of the Manufacturers National Bank subsidiary was chairman.
49. William M. Saxton and Philip J. Kessler from Butzel, Long, Gust, Klein & Van Zile, brief in support of motion to remove Manufacturers National Bank as trustee, August 10, 1988.
50. Ibid.
51. "Schedule 14D9," R. P. Scherer, May 5, 1989.
52. See Robert A. G. Monks and Nell Minow, *Corporate Governance*, 5th ed. (Hoboken, NJ: Wiley, 2011), 252: "They are the middlemen (and a few middlewomen) who provide balance and mediate the conflicts of interest between a small group of key

managers based in corporate headquarters and a vast group of shareholders spread all over the world."

53. See Jonathan Macy, *Corporate Governance: Promises Kept, Promises Broken* (Princeton, NJ: Princeton University Press, 2011), 51: "Perhaps the most basic principle of corporate law in the United States is that corporations are controlled by boards of directors, rather than shareholders. . . . Specifically, under U.S. law, corporations are managed by or under the direction of boards of directors, making the directors literally the governors of the corporation."

54. This is Karla's memory of what Peter said about a friend who was ultimately appointed to the R. P. Scherer board.

55. Arthur Levitt, *Take on the Street* (New York: Pantheon Books, 2002), 201.

56. Monks and Minow, *Corporate Governance*, 257.

57. Macey, *Corporate Governance*, 64.

58. James Madison, Federalist 10, again per Macey, *Corporate Governance*.

59. Warren E. Buffett, "2002 Chairman's Letter," Berkshire Hathaway, February 21, 2003.

60. Jim Jelter, "Coca Cola Executive Pay Plan Stirs David Winters' Wrath," *WSJ Marketwatch*, March 24, 2014.

61. Form 8-K, Securities & Exchange Commission, April 23, 2014.

62. Carl C. Icahn, "Why Buffett Is Wrong on Coke," *Barron's*, May 3, 2014.

63. Warren E. Buffett, 2014 Berkshire Hathaway shareholders meeting, May 3, 2014.

64. George W. Bush, "Remarks on Signing the Sarbanes-Oxley Act of 2002," July 30, 2002, *Public Papers of the Presidents of the United States: George W. Bush, Book II: Presidential Documents—July 1 to December 31, 2002* (Washington, D.C.: U.S. Government Printing Office, 2002), 1319–21.

65. Macey, *Corporate Governance*, 81.

66. Alex Erdeljan, interview with the author, July 21, 2014.

67. All of these figures come from R. P. Scherer annual reports between 1984 and 1999.

68. Erdeljan interview.

7: DANIEL LOEB AND HEDGE FUND ACTIVISM: THE SHAME GAME

1. Or, as his lawyers succinctly put it, the filing "shall not be construed to be an admission by the Reporting Persons that a material change has occurred in the facts set forth in this Schedule 13D or that such amendment is required under Rule 13d-2 of the Securities Exchange Act of 1934, as amended." Ron Burkle, "The Yucaipa Companies," 13d Morgans Hotels, amendment 10, September 3, 2013.

2. Ibid.

3. Robert A. G. Monks and Nell Minow, *Corporate Governance*, 5th ed. (Hoboken, NJ: Wiley, 2011), 220.

4. Jack D. Schwager, *Market Wizards: Interviews with Top Traders* (New York: HarperBusiness, 1989), 117.

5. Warren Buffett, "Our Performance in 1963," letter to partners, January 18, 1964: "Our willingness and financial ability to assume a controlling position gives us two-way stretch on many purchases in our group of generals." Warren Buffett, "Our Performance in 1964," letter to partners, January 18, 1965: "Many times in this

category we have the desirable 'two strings to our bow' situation where we should either achieve appreciation of market prices from external factors or from the acquisition of a controlling position in a business at a bargain price. While the former happens in the overwhelming majority of cases, the latter represents an insurance policy most investment operations don't have."

6. Letter from Robert L. Chapman to Mr. Lawrence W. Leighton, Securities and Exchange Commission Schedule 13D, May 18, 1999.

7. Letter from Robert L. Chapman to Riscorp/Mr. Walter L. Revell, Securities and Exchange Commission Schedule 13D, October 28, 1999.

8. Letter from Robert L. Chapman to ACPT/J. Michael Wilson, Securities and Exchange Commission Schedule 13D, March 30, 2000. Chapman uses such crazy words, I don't know if "underserved" is a typo or not.

9. Deepak Gopinath, "Hedge Fund Rabble-Rouser," *Bloomberg Markets*, October 2005.

10. "Around the World with Robert Chapman," interview by Emma Trincal, January 5, 2006, http://www.thestreet.com/print/story/10260146.html.

11. Gopinath, "Rabble-Rouser."

12. The "buyside" refers to the investment management business while the "sellside" refers to the broker-dealer business.

13. Gopinath, "Rabble-Rouser."

14. Jefferies pleaded guilty to two felony charges in 1987 and resigned from his company.

15. "DBL Liquidating Trust Payouts to Creditors Exceed Expectations . . . Trust Aims to Complete Activities in One Year," Business Wire, April 26, 1995, http://www.thefreelibrary.com/DBL+LIQUIDATING+TRUST+PAYOUTS+TO+CREDITORS+EXCEED+EXPECTATIONS+. . . . . .-a016863686.

16. "Liquidation of Drexel Is Ending on a High Note," *Los Angeles Times*, March 28, 1996.

17. Katherine Burton, *Hedge Hunters: After the Credit Crisis, How Hedge Fund Masters Survived* (New York: Bloomberg Press, 2010), 195.

18. Robert E. Wright and Richard Scylla, "Corporate Governance and Stockholder/Stakeholder Activism in the United States, 1790–1860: New Data and Perspectives," in *Origins of Shareholder Advocacy*, edited by Jonathan G. S. Koppell (New York: Palgrave Macmillan, 2010), 244.

19. Connie Bruck, *The Predators' Ball: The Inside Story of Drexel Burnham and the Rise of the Junk Bond Raiders* (New York: Penguin, 1989), 315.

20. Gopinath, "Rabble-Rouser."

21. William Thorndike, *The Outsiders: Eight Unconventional CEOs and Their Radically Rational Blueprint for Success* (Boston: Harvard Business Review Press, 2012), has an entire chapter on Stiritz.

22. Dan Loeb letter to William Stiritz, Agribrands, September 8, 2000.

23. Agribrands definitive proxy statement March 19, 2001.

24. Daniel Loeb letter to James Dearlove chairman and CEO of Penn Virginia, December 11, 2002.

25. Letter from Daniel Loeb to John W. Collins, chairman and CEO of InterCept, Securities and Exchange Commission Schedule 13D, May 27, 2004.

26. Letter from Daniel Loeb to John W. Collins, chairman and CEO of InterCept, Securities and Exchange Commission Schedule 13D, June 24, 2004.

27. Gopinath, "Rabble-Rouser."
28. Star Gas is a publicly traded master limited partnership, so "shares" are really "units," but I'm going to stick to "shares" and "stock" for simplicity's sake.
29. Star Gas Partners, third-quarter 2004 earnings conference call, July 29, 2004.
30. Star Gas Partners third-quarter 2003 earnings conference call, August 6, 2003.
31. All these figures are from Star Gas Partners SEC filings.
32. I'm using EBITDA minus capital expenditures, as Star Gas amortizes its acquired customer lists. Sevin's best year was $93 million of EBITDA minus capex. In 2014, SGU did $99 million of EBITDA minus capex.
33. Full disclosure, I own SGU shares, as does the fund I manage.
34. R. Kelly, "Ignition (Remix)."
35. Randall Smith, "Some Big Public Pension Funds Are Behaving Like Activist Investors," *New York Times*, DealBook, November 28, 2013.
36. Steve Fishman, "Get Richest Quickest," *New York*, November 22, 2004.
37. Max Olson, "The Restaurant Investor," Max Capital Corporation/Futureblind .com, November 25, 2009.
38. Greg Wright, "Friendly Ice Cream Cool to Overtures from Dissident Biglari," Dow Jones Newswires, March 8, 2007.
39. Olson, "The Restaurant Investor."
40. Biglari Holdings Form 4 filing, January 15, 2015.
41. The rights price was $250 per share and the closing price on the day of the announcement was $432.
42. Jeff Swiatek, "Steak 'n Shake-up Looming? Investor Launches Effort to Oust Parent Firm's CEO Biglari," *Indianapolis Star*, January 18, 2015.
43. Letter from Sardar Biglari to Friendly's Shareholders, Securities and Exchange Commission Schedule 13D, March 6, 2007.
44. Jonathan Maze, "Biglari Holdings Co-Owns a Few Jets," *Restaurant Finance Monitor*, September 17, 2014. http://registry.faa.gov/aircraftinquiry/Name_Results .aspx?Nametxt=BIGLARI&sort_option=1&PageNo=1.

8: BKF CAPITAL: THE CORROSION OF CONFORMITY

1. Katrina Brooker, "How Do You Like Bill Ackman Now?" *Bloomberg Markets*, February 2015.
2. Pershing Square Capital Management LP, Securities and Exchange Commission Schedule 13F, November 14, 2014. The 13F excludes foreign positions, unlisted companies, debt securities, and short positions.
3. These figures are from the presentation "Think Big," Pershing Square Capital Management LP, May 16, 2012.
4. I could swear I heard Ackman make this analogy himself, but I can't remember when or where.
5. Svea Herbst-Bayliss and Katya Wachtel, "Hedge Fund Manager Ackman Says Mistakes Made in JC Penney Turnaround," Reuters, April 5, 2013.
6. Brooker, "Bill Ackman."
7. For an example see Lucian A. Bebchuk, Alon Brav, and Wei Jiang, "The Long-Term Effects of Hedge Fund Activism," which tackles both operating performance and

stock performance in the five years following an activist 13D filing. http://www
.columbia.edu/~wj2006/HF_LTEffects.pdf.

8. Jonathan R. Laing, "Hold 'Em Forever: How Baker Fentress Invented Long-Term
Investing," *Barron's*, December 31, 1990.

9. Baker, Fentress & Company, 1995 Annual Report, February 27, 1996.

10. "[O]ne of the reasons that Baker Fentress is going to be very helpful to us is that
through their public portfolio, the portfolio that we manage, we can help us attract
other investment managers to our firm. We can give them funds to run for Baker Fentress immediately, so it really helps us feed managers in the business, so it's a pretty
big plus." Jessica Bibliowicz, "CEO Interview," *Wall Street Transcript*, March 1, 1998.

11. John Levin's long-only accounts only generated about 0.5% of assets in net fees. His
son's hedge fund charged double that plus a 20% cut of investment profits.

12. BKF Capital Group Inc. SEC filings show 80% growth from year-end 1998 to year-
end 1999.

13. John A. Levin, phone interview by the author, January 28, 2015.

14. Ibid.

15. From the company's proxy statement, and Warren Buffett's Securities and Exchange Commission Schedule 13G, August 3, 1999.

16. The stock was written up three years in a row on ValueInvestorsClub, and of
course Buffett's ownership had attracted attention.

17. Levin, author interview.

18. Gabelli Asset Management Inc., Securities and Exchange Commission Schedule
13D, July 3, 2001.

19. James McKee, General Counsel of GAMCO, letter to Norris Nissim, General
Counsel of BKF Capital Group Inc., filed as exhibit to Securities and Exchange
Commission Schedule 13D, September 19, 2003.

20. Phillip Goldstein, Opportunity Partners LP, letter to Norris Nissim, General
Counsel of BKF Capital Group Inc., filed as exhibit to Securities and Exchange
Commission Schedule 13D, November 17, 2003.

21. Warren Lichtenstein, SL Full Value Committee, letter to Owen Farren, President
and CEO, SL Industries Inc., filed as exhibit to Securities and Exchange Commission Schedule 14A, February 16, 2001.

22. Yahoo! Finance, includes dividends.

23. BKF Capital Group Inc. Proxy Statement, and Walter Lichtenstein letter to Board
of Directors, BKF Capital Group Inc., filed as exhibit to Securities and Exchange
Commission Schedule 14A, December 16, 2004.

24. Ibid.

25. BKF Capital Group Inc. Proxy Statement, filed as exhibit to Securities and Exchange Commission Schedule 14A, May 18, 2005.

26. BKF Capital Group Inc. Proxy Filing, filed as exhibit to Securities and Exchange
Commission Schedule 14A, May 26, 2005.

27. Ibid.

28. Ibid.

29. BKF Capital Group Inc. Proxy Filing, and Warren Lichtenstein open letter to
shareholders, filed as exhibit to Securities and Exchange Commission Schedule
14A, May 24, 2005.

30. Joe Nocera, "No Victors, Few Spoils in This Proxy Fight," *New York Times*, July 22, 2006: "Mr. Cannell, the hedge fund manager in San Francisco, wrote a series of flamboyant, incendiary letters that deeply offended the BKF board and Mr. Levin, accusing the company in one letter of having 'a culture of greed and self-dealing.'"

31. "Manna from Hedging," *Institutional Investor*, June 1, 2003.

32. J. Carlo Cannell, "Investor Insight: Carlo Cannell," interview, *Value Investor Insight*, March 31, 2006.

33. Ibid.

34. Value Investing Congress, 2009, in Pasadena, California.

35. "Carlo Cannell Announces He Is Stepping Down as Manager of Cannell Family of Hedge Funds," Business Wire, February 27, 2004.

36. Cannell Capital LLC, Securities and Exchange Commission Schedule 13G, February 14, 2005, and Securities and Exchange Commission Schedule 13D, June 1, 2005.

37. Carlo Cannell, interview by the author, January 27, 2015.

38. Ibid.

39. William H. Janeway, *Doing Capitalism in the Innovation Economy: Markets, Speculation and the State* (Cambridge: Cambridge University Press), 26.

40. Elizabeth Peek, "Farewell, Peter Cannell," *New York Sun*, May 3, 2005.

41. Ibid.

42. Joseph B. Werner, "Money Manager Interview," *Wall Street Transcript*, October 6, 1997.

43. Townsend Hoopes and Douglas Brinkley, *Driven Patriot: The Life and Times of James Forrestal* (Annapolis, MD: Naval Institute Press), 62.

44. Dividend announcement was April 6, 2005, according to BKF Capital Group Inc. Securities and Exchange Commission Exhibit 99.1, April 6, 2005.

45. Steel Partners, Proxy and Letter to Shareholders, filed as exhibit to Securities and Exchange Commission Schedule 14A, June 9, 2005.

46. Dated May 26, May 18, and June 8, 2005.

47. John Levin, letter to Institutional Shareholder Services, BKF Capital Group Inc. Proxy Filing, Securities and Exchange Commission Schedule 14A, June 17, 2005.

48. BKF Capital Group Inc., Proxy Filing, filed as exhibit to Securities and Exchange Commission Schedule 14A, June 23, 2005, and Steel Partners, Press Release, filed as exhibit to Securities and Exchange Commission Schedule 14A, June 23, 2005.

49. All this information comes from BKF Capital Group Inc. SEC filings.

50. Yahoo! Finance.

51. BKF Capital Group Inc. annual proxy statements.

52. "Lack of Accountability" was the section heading in the May 16 letter to shareholders from Warren Lichtenstein, in BKF proxy filing May 16.

53. BKF Capital Group Inc. Securities and Exchange Commission Schedule 8K, April 22, 2005, and SEC Exhibit 10.1, April 19, 2005.

54. The first hedge fund I worked for sold itself to a large bank in 2002, and the subsequent 50/50 fee split was an utter failure that resulted in a massive exodus of talent.

55. Steel Partners, BKF Proxy Filing, Securities and Exchange Commission Schedule 14A, December 16, 2004.

56. Levin, author interview.

57. Cannell, author interview.

58. Nocera, "No Victors."

59. Levin, author interview.
60. Ibid.
61. Cannell, author interview.
62. Levin, author interview.

CONCLUSION

1. Ben McGrath, "13D, " *New Yorker*, August 7, 2006.
2. Michael Lewis, "The Man Who Crashed the World: Joe Cassano and AIG," *Vanity Fair*, August 2009.
3. Lynn Stout, *The Shareholder Value Myth* (San Francisco: Berrett-Koehler, 2012), 23.
4. Public company shares bestow certain contractual rights to holders, including the right to vote for directors and the right to a fractional interest in the proceeds from a liquidation of the assets. Shareholders can also propose nonbinding resolutions and sue the directors and management for failure to perform their duties. Other than the shareholders' right to sell their shares, that's really about it.
5. Many legal scholars cite *Dodge v. Ford Motor* in arguing that the law does require directors to maximize profits for shareholders. Also, see Leo E. Strine Jr., "Our Continuing Struggle with the Idea That For-Profit Corporations Seek Profit," *Wake Forest Law Review* 47 (2012): 135–72.
6. Shareholder Rights Project at Harvard Law School, http://srp.law.harvard.edu /companies-entering-into-agreements.shtml.
7. Herbert Allen, "Conflict Cola," *Wall Street Journal*, April 15, 2004.
8. Warren Buffett, letter to Bill and Melinda Gates, June 26, 2006.

Index

Page numbers in italics denote text from the original letters found in the appendix.

About the Author

JEFF GRAMM runs a hedge fund and has served on several public company boards of directors. He is an adjunct professor at Columbia Business School, where he teaches value investing. Jeff lives in Brooklyn, New York, with his wife and two children.